SEWING
Outdoor
Gear

SEWING
Outdoor
Gear

Easy Techniques for
Outerwear That Works

Rochelle Harper

The Taunton Press

To my daughters, Madeleine and Karina, and their "constructivist" class-mates: May they gain a new vision of this tangible and interactive world by using sewing and other fine crafts as a fun and easy way to learn:

- *quality of design*
- *math*
- *color and textural relationships*
- *pride in workmanship*
- *recycling*
- *problem solving, and much more*

 **The Taunton Press**
Inspiration for hands-on living™

The Taunton Press, Inc., 63 South Main Street, P.O. Box 5506, Newtown, CT 06470-5506
e-mail: tp@taunton.com

Distributed by Publishers Group West

INTERIOR DESIGN: Gloria Melfi
LAYOUT: Suzie Yannes
ILLUSTRATOR: Ron Carboni
PHOTOGRAPHY: Jack Deutsch, Scott Phillips

LIBRARY OF CONGRESS CATALOGING-IN-PUBLICATION DATA
Harper, Rochelle.
    Sewing outdoor gear : easy techniques for outerwear that works / Rochelle Harper.
        p. cm.
    ISBN 1-56158-283-2
    1. Coats. 2. Sport clothes. I. Title.

TT530 .H37 2001
646.4'5--dc21   2001027028

Printed in the United States of America
10 9 8 7 6 5 4 3 2 1

Acknowledgments

Thank you to The Taunton Press: Cherilyn DeVries who provided me with a much better road map and encouragement, Jolynn Gower and Sarah Coe for holding up under the scope of this volume, Chris Timmons and Roxy (Laura) White for being cheerleaders and providing diversion, and copy editor Daphne Hougham.

My thanks to all the sportswear-related companies that have provided information or samples: Schoeller Textiles—especially Lynn Belmont for obtaining excellent quality slides; Columbia Sportswear through Pat Golebieski; REI for information and the loan of the Alpine Lakes parka; RCT (Rose City Textiles) through LuAnn Rukke (a friend who also deserves my heartfelt personal thanks!); 3M Corporation for information and photos; North Face—Meg Perkins for customer support and warranty information; W. L. Gore for providing sealing tape in the late '80s that resulted in the seam-sealing method shown in this book; Susan Chamberlin and DuPont Insulations; and Lois Green and Albany International.

Special thanks to the sewing-related companies and associations that have contributed to this book: Quest Outfitters for product donations at a moment's notice; Professional Association of Custom Clothiers (PACC) for professional support and terrific friendships; thanks to Pat Hagen for loaning her wonderful parka; Pati Palmer for personal support and the Palmer/Pletsch International School of Sewing; Fabric Depot in Portland for donating classroom space; Viking/Husqvarna, Barbara Wright, and Sue Hausmann for providing sewing machine feet and a fantastic serger; and Linda at

Bernina Sewing in Corvallis, Oregon—thanks for the sewing machine feet and tips on using them!

I am grateful to the following individuals who donated their custom-made garments for photographs in this book: Penny Schwynn, who has provided so much besides her clients' garments; thanks, Priscillo, for giving up your union suit; May Chang, a terrific client, friend, and dentist!—thanks for loaning your jacket; Diane Saiget-Cantor for providing her jacket; and Will and the girls, who waited patiently through winter for their new coats.

I owe personal thanks to so many. To name but a few: Glenn Brown (patent attorney and friend) for willingly answering product-related questions; my students, from whom I learn so much; the Creative Science and Bridger School community for being a supportive family and the teachers there from whom I have learned so much about the way our minds absorb information; and to Jackie Thompson, who so kindly provided me with a monitor when mine bit the dust.

Ever and always my thanks to the Mt. Tabor Moms: Deb, Joyce, May, Kelly, and Wendy, for being my chosen sisters and wonderful friends.

Thanks to the Harper/Howes and Lemke/Endicott families for their enthusiasm for this project. To my children, Maddie and Karina, I am so lucky to be with you! You are such appreciative and interested people. Thank you so much for sharing your "mom time" with my projects and writing. To Will, thank you for being a great dad, for the financial support allowing me to be flexible with my time and to enjoy our children, and for so many other reasons.

Contents

Introduction

Since the development of nylon in the late '30s and all the way up to NASA's use of thermal management technologies in the late '90s, outerwear has been transformed from oiled animal-hide parkas and waxed cotton rainwear to waterproof, breathable, laminated microfiber nylon parkas, with microfiber thermal interlinings and high-wicking polymer mesh liners. The benefit of these new technologies is that we can play and work harder and longer in any kind of weather and still be comfortable.

But now that home sewers can buy these fabrics, the fabric is only the beginning of the outerwear story. By layering garments and making simple adaptations to a piece or a pattern, you can construct high-performance outerwear for your specific activities and measurements. In this book my expertise will help you look past catalog jargon, claims, and brand names to discover what outerwear you really need. From essential pieces to customized pockets, this book is designed to aid you in finding and making gear that's specifically suited to your body and your outdoor activities.

I have sewn since the age of 10, and I started sewing custom outerwear about 16 years ago when I made a pair of insulated maternity ski bibs for a friend who taught cross-country skiing. Then, while working at just about the only business in the United States that provided outerwear fabrics through a retail outlet, I went from being a clerk to being the manager of the retail and mail-order divisions, as well as a fabric buyer and a patternmaker for outerwear. This experience gave me a unique background for providing materials and troubleshooting for clients from Nike, Columbia Sportswear, Duffel, and other manufacturers in the Portland area who needed small quantities of fabrics and notions for product development.

During that period, I designed many patterns that are still in use and developed many of the techniques presented in this book, such as applying seam-sealing tape with an iron and a Teflon presser sheet, and cutting nylon appliqués with a hot tool. Later, while designing and selling children's hats, I started making and using fleece cord.

The first part of the book is a crash course on the basics of outerwear. In the first two chapters we'll:

- explore ways to build an outerwear wardrobe that provides both comfort and economy through layering

- look at technical fabric types and treatments and how they work together in layering to move beyond the confusion of trademark names into more manageable categories

■ discuss what to look for when selecting a pattern, and examine alterations that might be worth considering

The remainder of the book will encourage you to design (or redesign) your own outerwear with easy techniques and approaches for simplifying the construction process, such as:

■ updating a garment with some quick and easy redesigning

■ helping you stock a "toolbox" of techniques for custom outerwear, look for design adaptations, and show practical clothing parts for designing-as-you-go

■ using pockets and flaps in easy ways to get the functional design features you want in a garment

People often turn to custom-made clothing strictly for the purpose of getting a well-fitting garment that is flexible and functional. To achieve that goal, I include:

■ specifics on altering for fit and flexibility to give you even more opportunity for maximizing the wearability of your outerwear

■ basic tools and techniques for sewing and maintaining a wide variety of outerwear fabrics as related to seams, seam sealing, repair ideas, notions, and hardware that is most commonly used in outerwear

To the average person, the prospect of sewing an outerwear wardrobe may seem daunting, but it's easy when taken one step at a time. Success with a simple fleece vest can soon lead to a customized parka!

As a young person, I never imagined that my creative path would lead me into sewing, much less outerwear sewing. I was lucky to begin riding this wave of fabric and technological developments when and where I did. Outerwear has provided stimulation for my insatiable curiosity in its scope and provided broad potential as a creative outlet. I hope you find the same rewards and satisfaction.

Chapter 1

The Essential Outerwear Wardrobe

When you're out in the elements, what's on the very outside isn't all that matters. For downhill skiing in the Colorado Rockies on a clear December day, one of many combinations might be an insulated one-piece suit worn over stretch-fleece long underwear. For hikes in the North Cascades, a comfy set of thermal long underwear layered beneath a fleece layer and a waterproof and breathable (w/p/b) shell jacket would be the ticket. To battle the chilling winds on the streets of Chicago, a down car coat with a fleece hat and gloves is perfect, and it still looks great for a meeting downtown. For an afternoon of spring sailing off Cape Cod, a waterproof jacket, pants, and hat stowed in the hold would be an appropriate safeguard against a sud–den storm.

Outerwear comes in almost limitless shapes and sizes to handle every variation in temperature, climate condition, use, and personal taste. The new generation of outerwear fabrics has expanded the possibilities immensely. There is some very serious, very pricey, highly engineered technical outerwear available that seems to have landed from some otherworldly place. At the other end of the spectrum is outerwear that only seems to serve fashion trends, using minimally effective fabrics that do little more than cover the layer beneath. This wide

Stay comfortable while running errands on a cool fall day with a fleece jacket. This one is trimmed with a woven print cotton and fleece cord used as a closure.

When you are considering sewing with this new generation of fabrics, the terms "technical fabrics" and "technical outerwear" can be intimidating. It is important to note from the beginning that the technical aspect of a fabric has to do with how the fabric has been designed to function. Coatings, fiber textures, and finishes are technical features that contribute to how well the fabric functions for a particular use, and are already in the fabric before you start sewing.

"Technical outerwear" refers to clothing that is highly functional for what may be a very simple garment. Individual garments have specific design features and are made with specific technical fabrics that enhance their functions. Most of these features, in and of themselves, are not difficult to make, especially when looked at as separate elements (as we do in this book).

range of outerwear also includes a lot of inexpensive pieces made by mass merchandisers. They often copy successful garment lines by producing poorly assembled versions made from less-expensive fabrics of lesser quality.

I prefer a holistic approach to outerwear. I don't assume that I'm limited to what I can buy off the rack. If a product is well made, fits properly, and has the right features at a price I can afford, I feel justified in buying it. If I have an idea for something I need or want that seems unavailable within my financial resources, I find out what I need to know to make it myself and then do it. If I have something that can be repaired or restyled to give it a longer life, that is still another option. Finding out what you need to know is what this book is about.

Layering: Dressing Perfectly for the Outdoors

Layering is the best antidote to unknown and changeable weather. It allows us to control our comfort level outdoors by being able to quickly adjust to the current conditions. A thick, lofted parka provides quick warmth when going from the front door to the car but, depending on the temperature and the activity (like snowshoeing or hiking), wearing that same parka can become an endless process of unzipping it, taking it off, stowing it, getting it out and on again, over and over. Even a low-aerobic activity like shopping can involve similar costume changes.

Layering doesn't always eliminate the need to remove or add clothing, but it may cut down on it. By wearing a few technically efficient layers that move perspiration away from the body, prevent precipitation from getting inside the layers, and maintain a comfortable temperature, you can often be comfortable in conditions that vary by as much as 20° without adding or losing a layer.

"Moisture management" and thermal retention can be accomplished using a three-layer combination that works together: the shell, the insulating or thermal layer, and the wicking layer. The shell layer repels moisture and cuts the wind, the thermal layer provides warmth, and the wicking layer moves perspiration away from the body. Sometimes one fabric may provide two of these functions: Long underwear made of fleece both wicks and provides thermal protection, and Polartec® Windbloc® fabric fleece provides shell and thermal layers together.

With effective layering, each piece can function independently while also support-

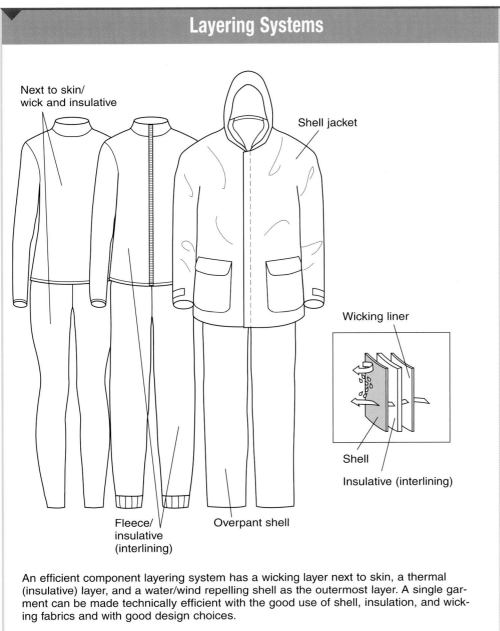

Layering Systems

Next to skin/
wick and insulative

Shell jacket

Wicking liner

Shell

Insulative (interlining)

Fleece/
insulative
(interlining)

Overpant shell

An efficient component layering system has a wicking layer next to skin, a thermal (insulative) layer, and a water/wind repelling shell as the outermost layer. A single garment can be made technically efficient with the good use of shell, insulation, and wicking fabrics and with good design choices.

ing the work of the others. Interior moisture can be controlled with next-to-skin technical fabrics that pull interior moisture out, but the thermal and shell layers have to be able to continue the process of moving the moisture out or condensation will form, moisture will be trapped, and the garment will be wet on the inside.

A layering system for a winter environment might include a fingertip-length, lightly insulated or uninsulated hooded parka made from a wind-resistant fabric,

Chimney Effect

This term defines the natural flow of air through a garment when fresh, cool air enters a waterproof garment through the bottom or cuffs and forces warm air and vapor out through the collar or hood. To achieve the chimney effect, some space for air movement is allowed at the hem and cuff area**s** and at the collar for air to escape.

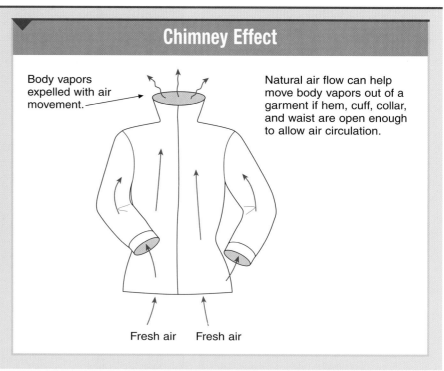

Chimney Effect

Body vapors expelled with air movement.

Natural air flow can help move body vapors out of a garment if hem, cuff, collar, and waist are open enough to allow air circulation.

Fresh air   Fresh air

and overpants made from the same type of fabric. If this jacket had a water-repellent surface, it also could be worn without a thermal layer. The thermal layer would be a high-loft or down jacket that could be worn under or zipped into the parka. The wicking layer would be a stretch-fleece turtleneck and leggings. A nice addition to this combination would be a fleece vest that could substitute for the insulated jacket in warmer temperatures.

For a temperate, rainy environment, a similar style of shell (hooded, below hip length), using a w/p/b fabric with underarm vents, a fleece vest for extra warmth when needed, stretch-fleece leggings, and a high-wicking knit mock turtleneck would be excellent.

Dressing for the rainy urban street might begin with a loose swing coat from a single layer of a very breathable microfiber; then go on to add a hip-length asymmetrical fleece vest over a microfleece top, and a long, synthetic stretch skirt.

> **TIP**
>
> To evaluate your outerwear needs, start by considering your climate, activity level, and personal style. Then make a chart of your activities, the climate for each, the outerwear you have, and what you need.

Practical Considerations: Buy It or Make It?

Once you know which pieces your outerwear wardrobe needs in order to function at its best for you, your first impulse may be to start canvassing stores and catalogs (and sales!) for the right items. That may be a great option for you, especially if you live near quality stores and don't want to sew. But it's not the only option. If you use your sewing machine, you may be able to save money and get exactly what you want by making it yourself. Don't be intimidated by what you see in catalogs. Many outerwear and layering garments don't require a lot of complicated construction, fancy stitching, or impossible-to-find fabrics.

The Intimidation Factor

The most important thing about deciding to sew something yourself is to choose not to be afraid. Even the experienced sewers in many of my classes need a lecture on courage. What's the worst that could happen while you're sewing? An accidental cut right in the front of a parka? Create a patch pocket or appliqué to cover it! Your topstitching looks uneven? Test changes in tension and needle types on a sample first. Worried about sizing? Fit the pattern with pins on one side of the body before sewing.

It is amazing how many people talk themselves out of trying something because of unnecessary fears. The key for novice sewers is to select a pattern that matches

A very practical jacket to make and to wear is this simple combination of shell and fleece fabrics. Custom features (zip-out sleeves and reversibility) were added to this jacket while planning the design.

Ready-Mades and the Newest Technology

If you want the first crack at the newest technology in fabrics and hardware, then buying ready-made is going to give you about a six-month's lead over items you'd make yourself. There are some patented materials that take a while to arrive in fabric stores. To avoid patent infringement, an effort is made by the patent holder to prevent the product from being sold under the name brand as a garment manufacturer's excess materials, though the materials often end up being sold without the brand name and with an implied comment from the seller as to its true identity.

Basic Equipment for Sewing Outerwear

There are a lot of options these days for sewing aids, including useful machine feet, needles for specific uses, and many seam-finishing products. You may find uses for some of your own tools that you've never tried!

Thread

- Good quality all-polyester thread with long staple fibers can be used in every aspect of outerwear sewing.

- All-polyester cone serger thread should be confined to the loopers because it isn't strong enough as a seaming thread.

- Woolly nylon serger thread can be used for seaming, even as an upper thread and in the bobbin of a regular sewing machine. You might have to use a needle threader to get the fluffy fiber through the needle hole.

- Decorative threads should be compatible in content to the fabric: synthetic threads on synthetic fabrics.

Cutting and Pinning Equipment

- Sharp scissors—a must for cutting synthetics. I use dressmaker shears, pelican (or appliqué) scissors for trimming seams, and a pair of small, sharp, pointed scissors for clipping corners and thread ends.

- Rotary cutter and mat, especially for cutting bindings and fleece cord.

- An 18-in. graded ruler for cutting bindings and fleece.

- Small diameter sharp pins. (I prefer glass heads.)

Sewing Aids

Here are a few common items that I have truly found useful:

- Water-soluble stabilizer for free-motion stitching and difficult-to-stitch fabrics. It will wash out but can easily be wiped off with a damp cloth. Extra scraps can be dissolved into a squirt bottle for a liquid stabilizer.

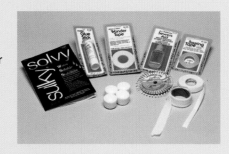

- Wonder Tape, Solvy KK2000 temporary spray adhesive, a fabric glue stick, and basting tape for quick holds while working without pinning.

- Sewers Aid helps thread to glide through the machine more easily, causing fewer tension problems, especially with specialty threads.

- Narrow roll of bias fusible knit interfacing to stabilize narrow areas such as zipper openings and hems. Or cut strips yourself from wide interfacing by the yard.

Sewing Machine

- A regular straight-stitch sewing machine will work with all of these fabrics to one degree or another, but add a zigzag function and you can really go to town.

- Home sergers or overlocks are useful for finishing fraying edges and sewing stretch fabrics easily while maintaining the maximum amount of stretch.

- A dry iron and Teflon presser sheet or "slipper" for adhering seam-sealing tape with the iron.

Presser Feet

Here is a list of a variety of machine feet.

- Zigzag foot—for all-purpose sewing, wide opening for adjusting needle positions; and for double-needle hemming.

- Reverse feed foot (reverse feed zigzag)—for stitches that move forward and backward.

Machine feet that will enhance basic outer-wear sewing from left to right: reverse feed zigzag (slot to side of foot), walking foot or dual feed (for Viking and Bernina machines), zipper foot (B), edgestitching (B) and edge-joining foot (V), roller foot (B and V), edgestitching foot (V), Teflon foot and adhesive-backed Teflon pieces for other feet (V), darning foot (B and V).

- Overlock foot—for narrow stretch seams on lightweight knits.

- Zipper foot—for stitching around snaps and grommets, attaching zippers, piping.

- Blindstitch foot—for blind hemming on knits and left-position edgestitching.

- Jeans foot—for straight-stitch sewing through thick layers.

- Darning, quilting, or free-motion guide foot—for free-motion stitching and quilting.

- Edgestitch or edge/joining foot—for edgestitching, topstitching to finish binding or other trims, attaching fleece cord to cut edges, butting two edges together.

- Bulky overlock foot—one option for sewing on fleece cord and twisted cord. (See chapter 5 for other options.)

- Three-groove pintuck foot—for sewing fleece cording, making mock ribbing on fleece.

- Rolling foot—for sewing difficult fabrics, such as laminates, that grip the foot.

- Walking or dual-feed presser foot—for sewing any fabric that has difficulty feeding.

A Teflon surface makes it easier for a foot to slide over difficult fabrics, and many sewing machine companies offer feet with Teflon on the bottom. Adhesive-backed Teflon can also be purchased separately and applied to the bottom of any of the presser feet except the walking foot.

Sewing Machine Needles

When it comes to correcting a poor stitching line or skipped stitches, the needle is one of the first things to check. A new needle and a correctly threaded machine can sometimes make all the difference.

- Microtex and sharps in sizes 8/60 to 14/90 are for light- to medium-weight fabrics such as microfiber taffetas, ripstops, Taslan and Supplex.

- Denim or jeans needles in sizes 10/70 to 18/110 for medium- to heavy-weight shell fabrics and especially for coated and laminated fabrics and multilayer stitching.

- Topstitch or Metallica needles for top-stitching shell fabrics with a larger diameter thread or specialty thread. Both have larger eyes (the Metallica also has a thread groove).

- Universal and stretch needles in sizes 11/75 to 12/80 for heavy knits, piles, and fleeces.

- Lighter weight knits found in next-to-skin layers use universal or stretch needles as well, but in smaller sizes, depending on fabric weight.

- Double (and triple) needles, available in a universal, denim, or stretch. Stretch double needles, 4.0 or wider, are excellent for hemming all types of knits and fleece and making mock ribbing. The denim double needle may be useful for topstitching on wovens in some cases, but the back looks like a zigzag so I wouldn't use it on edges where both sides may show.

Marking Tools

With any of the these marking methods, make sure to use products made so that the marks will come out, leaving no trace. This may require a test on a sample of the fabric.

- Marking pens and pencils.

- Chalk wheels, tailor's chalk, and wax markers.

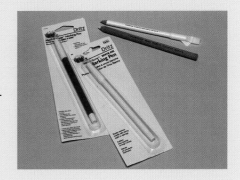

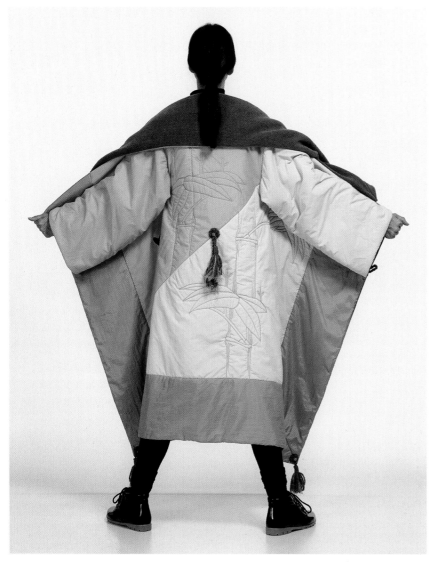

With a handmade coat you have the opportunity not only to have it fit perfectly, but to have it become an extension of your personality. You select the fabric color and texture, the length, the cut, and the detailing. Making a garment yourself allows you to wear your signature color or just one that everyone else isn't.

T I P

If you are just returning to sewing, you may be surprised at how easy it is to sew with some of the tools and techniques developed in recent years. They produce quick results that are better looking than most ready-to-wear.

Technical Fabrics: A Guided Tour

When planning for the most effective outerwear wardrobe, it's important to understand the wide variety of possible uses for what are often termed "technical fabrics." Technology has helped create an almost dizzying array of fabrics, and with new technologies being developed every year, along with discoveries in fibers and finishing treatments, the consumer can sometimes be overwhelmed.

Fabrics and insulations are designed to meet a variety of conditions: shell fabrics that counteract wet weather and/or block the wind, insulative materials for maintaining body temperature in a variety of temperatures, and next-to-skin fabrics (also called wicking fabrics) that move perspiration away from the skin to keep the wearer drier during a heavy workout. There are also a lot of terrific ways to use these same fabrics within the context of fashion and handcrafted art-to-wear.

their skill level. Making a wicking-layer turtleneck may involve only a few straight seams and ribbing at the neck. A parka, on the other hand, requires much more planning for fit, functional features like pockets and a hood, and other techniques. It's amazing to see how quickly your skills increase with each new project.

T I P

You may want to contact one of the outerwear fabric retailers listed in Resources on p. 182 to order swatches of the fabrics mentioned in this book. The cost is small compared with the convenience of handling and really looking at the fabrics, and often can be deducted from an order placed later.

The Tradeoff between Water-Repellent and Waterproof

There is often misunderstanding when referring to a waterproof or water-repellent shell. One would think that if you had a choice between them, the obvious choice would be waterproof. Before you choose, ask yourself what is more important to you: moving perspiration away from your skin or preventing precipitation from getting to your skin.

A waterproof shell will definitely keep the rain out, but its tight weave or coating will also trap sweat next to your body. It's a good choice if you sail or are in the rain but not working hard. A water-repellent shell is a better choice for runners and cross-country skiers. It has a looser weave, which provides protection from the wind but allows perspiration to more easily pass to the outside of the fabric. Just remember that the more waterproof, the less breathable.

Keep in mind that even the term waterproof is not an absolute. Most of these fabrics will leak at some point of pressure, depending on the thickness of the membrane or coating, the adhesion, and the exterior fabric.

Shell Fabrics

To plan and sew the most effective outerwear garments, it's important to understand the broad range of shell fabrics available and the limitations and advantages of different fabrics and treatments. Most important, you should know what to expect from a particular fabric. How a shell fabric performs depends on the type of fiber, its size, the weave and surface density, and added treatments and coatings.

Fibers Today, the fibers that are generally used for shell fabrics are water-repellent synthetics made with organic polymers. They have a natural ability to repel moisture because they can't absorb it. However, synthetic fabrics can allow moisture to pass between the fibers (and, as you will see with wicking fabrics, can be encouraged to do just that) so the density of the fabric and additional treatments and coatings are factors in water repellency. Two particular fibers are used for the vast majority of shell fabrics: nylon and polyester. Luckily, they can be manipulated through different extrusion and milling processes to create a wide variety of weights and textures.

Nylon is the most commonly used fiber for a naturally water-repellent fabric. Some of the varieties in different weights include lightweight ripstops, high thread-count taffetas, texturized (air-blown) nylon in two- and three-ply yarns, Supplex fabrics that have an appearance and texture similar to cotton, and nylon canvas and oxford in 200-denier weight and up. By manipulating the finishing process of the fabric, nylon can have a great variety of surface effects, like crinkled, embossed, and ciré (an ironing process that causes the fabric to have a satin-like finish). You may recognize trademark

Various types of nylons (left to right): woven pattern microfiber, Supplex, crinkle-textured nylon, 1,000-denier brushed Cordura, cross-weave (iridescent) twill, Taslan, 70-denier ripstop.

Various types of polyesters (left to right): taffeta blend with reflective print, microfiber sueded twill, microfiber woven plaid.

Microfibers in a variety of textures. Clockwise from bottom: sage-green sueded twill, red three-ply Supplex, woven plaid, woven stripe, cross-weave seersuckers, yellow Supplex.

names like Antron, Taslan, Supplex, Cordura, and Tactel from the nylon family.

Polyester has become an important fiber in outerwear for reasons that include its durability and drapability as well as its ability to be water-repellent in so many forms. Though not as water-repellent as nylon, polyester accepts printing and water-repellent treatments more easily than nylon, and is quieter than nylon in comparable fabrics. Polyester is available in many of the same forms as nylon (taffetas, ripstop, canvas, etc.) and in a few forms you rarely see in nylon, such as fleece and pile. A smooth polyester yarn makes a great water-resistant shell, while fluffier yarns are more likely to be used in insulating fabrics. Polyester fabric names you might find are Microsilk, Climatec, Celtech, or Peachskin.

Microfibers are extruded synthetic fibers that are so small it might take a hundred fibers to make a yarn. These yarns are woven into a fabric that has thousands of fibers to the inch. With microscopic fibers from nylon, polyester, and other synthetics, mills can weave fabrics with extremely high surface density, toughness, and water repellency. The advantage is that you get very good water repellency (although not as good as a coated fabric), but with much better breathability than a coated fabric. Keep in mind that there are some versions of microfiber fabrics that are coated and thus have decreased breathability.

Other synthetic fibers are used in blended shell fabrics. New variations of acrylic have shown it to be much more versatile and usable than it has been. Past acrylics looked limp after wearing; pilling was often a problem; and when woven densely, it was very hot and didn't breathe well. Now, when used

Cotton and cotton-blend shell fabrics (left to right): printed Tri-blend (poly/cotton/nylon), Superblend, 10-oz. cotton canvas.

in blends or with texture variation in the fibers, it can result in very attractive and usable fabrics for both shell and next-to-skin fabrics. Olefin, polypropylene, and Dacron (a subset of polyester) are fibers used often in next-to-skin layers and insulation, but are also found in shell fabrics when blended with other fibers. Kevlar, a type of nylon used in bulletproof vests, has been increasingly used blended for making strong, abrasion-resistant fabrics for shells.

Cotton is an interesting exception to the technological leanings of shell fabrics. The fiber is very absorbent but very breathable, and when woven tightly, it can be a sufficient windbreak. For a number of years cotton has been blended with synthetic fibers to boost breathability and create a softer texture—a softer hand. This blending offered the appearance of a natural-fiber fabric with the advantages of polyester's strength and body, cotton's breathability, and nylon's water repellency. The main drawback to these types of cotton-blend fabrics is maintenance. Surface-applied treatments need to be maintained to achieve anything more than light water repellency after laundering.

When cotton is treated with oil and/or wax, you might recognize it as the fabric used in the traditional Australian drover's coat or outback coat (made by Driz-a-bone). According to product information, it is waterproof and breathable, but oil- and wax-impregnated fabrics require much more maintenance than other shell fabrics. The water-repellent applications need to be reapplied annually.

Heavy cotton canvas or duck has become more popular recently as a favored fabric for barn coats such as the Carhartt coat, or simple oversize jacket that, as a shell, can be worn in many types of weather (other than prolonged wet periods). Cotton canvas is rugged and becomes more comfortable after breaking in. It has some of the best qualities of an old pair of jeans, including its ability to conform to the body at flex points and its natural breathability. If paired with a polyester fleece zip-in lining, its usefulness in a variety of temperatures will increase much more (see the top left photo on p. 115, a barn coat with fleece lining).

There are several ways in which knits are incorporated into outerwear. In shell layers they usually need additional bonding to vapor and/or wind barriers to be able to keep moisture and windchill out. Fleece and pile fabrics are most often knit, and are sometimes designed specifically as shell

A selection of laminated and stretch fabrics (left to right): purple nylon/Lycra with polyamide flocked backing, Darlexx print (waterproof and breathable—w/p/b—membrane with wicking liner), red stretch nylon crepe with urethane coating, black Power mesh (used for stirrups, not laminated), dark purple Polartec® AquaShell™, green Darlexx solid with white tricot backing, and black Exoskin Thermal.

Denier, Weave, and Surface Density

The denier of the fiber (or filament), the number of plies to the yarn, the surface density, the tensile strength, and the weave of the fabric are some of the many variables in outerwear fabric.

The denier of the fiber refers to the size of the fiber or the yarn (fibers twisted together to form a strand for weaving). The lower the denier number, the finer the fiber or yarn; the higher the number, the heavier/thicker the fiber. Most fabrics used in garment shells will be made from fibers under 200 denier in weight. The smaller yarn size produces greater surface density when woven and results in better water repellency. Patches made of 1,000-denier or higher fabrics are used in high-wear areas (like elbows, knees, and ankles) for greater durability. When shopping for patch or rugged fabric, you'll often find denier listed, especially for the heavier weight fabrics. On the other end of the denier scale, fibers that are so small as to be measured in microns are sometimes referred to as microdenier, but the specific denier number isn't usually listed. The term microfiber refers to a microdenier fiber.

The weave of a fabric gives it texture, and in shell fabrics it enhances the fabric's technical and fashion qualities. A dense weave will allow the fabric to shed water and block wind more effectively, which is the purpose of most shell fabrics. These high-count weaves are excellent for outer shells, and low-count weaves work well as linings because there is more open area to allow vapor to pass through. For variations on the usual shell fabric texture, look into twill, crepe, satin, and dobby weaves.

Multiple microdenier fibers go into one ply of yarn in this densely woven fabric.

layers. They can be bonded with mesh, another fleece, or microfleece to create fabrics such as Polartec® Windbloc® fabric, or with nylon/Lycra tricot to produce a fabric like Polartec® Aqua Shell™, both from Malden Mills.

There are many variations of tricot knits that are used for stretch outerwear fabrics. Usually they are laminated or coated and then bonded to another stretch fabric or backing to repel moisture and block the wind while retaining only some of the fabric's original stretch. The bonding of a coating or additional layer of fabric hinders the natural stretch in the fabric, so these garments need to be sized near to the actual measurements of the body. When left unbonded, superstretch Lycra fabrics are sometimes used for form-fitting "skins," especially designed for downhill ski racing (using a stretch thermal layer underneath), ice skating, and other sports in which wind resistance and flexibility are factors.

Coatings, laminates, and surface treatments

While a fabric can be water- and wind-resistant on its own, it often needs help to become a powerful weapon against wet weather and driving winds. Laminates, coatings, and surface treatments give shell fabrics the extra edge they need to protect the person underneath the fabric. If a fabric is truly waterproof and breathable, it is likely that it has a coating or laminate of some type.

One of the first waterproof treatments for fabric was rubber, which eventually cracked and peeled over time in its early forms. Urethane and polyurethanes are more commonly used now as completely waterproof coatings. Better compounds in these plastics have resulted in more flexible and longer-wearing products, though they may still crack and peel after prolonged use and exposure. Elastomers are another option now being used for effective waterproof coatings. Patagonia's SealCoat is an example of this and appears to be very flexible and long wearing.

Waterproof nonbreathable coatings are successful in some ways, but they are simply inadequate for activities that require a lot of movement, especially when used in a wide variety of temperatures and for aerobic sports that generate a lot of body moisture. Precipitation is prevented from entering the

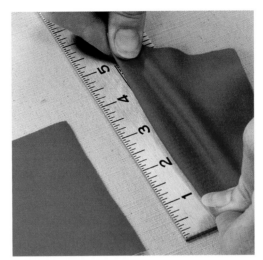

Bonded knits have limited and stiff stretch. This example shows a 4-in. section of fabric that only stretches to 5 in. (a 25 percent stretch). For comfortable fit and good circulation, the fabric should not be forced to stretch to its maximum.

A woven twill, nylon/wool/Lycra stretch ski-pant fabric from Schoeller has become a classic over the last several years. It can be made into a very slim-looking pant with flexibility and comfort.

garment but perspiration is prevented from escaping and cooling the body. For high activity levels, uncoated fabrics or fabrics with a w/p/b membrane have the big advantage of being able to expel body vapor.

In 1976 the W.L. Gore Company introduced a revolutionary fabric. The company

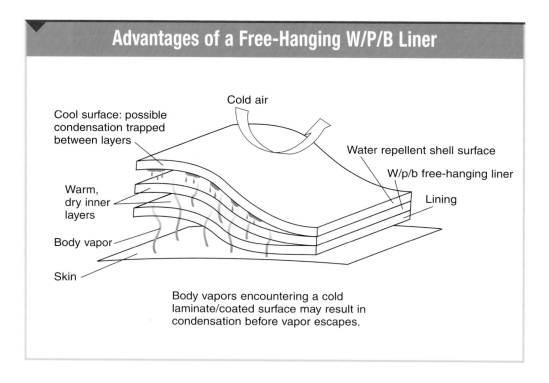

Advantages of a Free-Hanging W/P/B Liner

Cold air

Cool surface: possible condensation trapped between layers

Water repellent shell surface

W/p/b free-hanging liner

Warm, dry inner layers

Lining

Body vapor

Skin

Body vapors encountering a cold laminate/coated surface may result in condensation before vapor escapes.

had been looking for commercial applications for PTFE (polytetraflouroethylene), also known as Teflon, and the development of the first waterproof and breathable laminate was one of the results. Gore-Tex® and clone w/p/b treatments—ceramics, urethanes, and polyurethanes—all work on essentially the same principle. They have a surface containing pores that allow vapor (water molecules) to escape to the outside of the garment, yet water droplets outside the garment can't get in.

Gore-Tex® fabric is essentially any fabric (usually a water-repellent shell fabric) with a Gore (Teflon) monolithic membrane laminated on the back of the fabric. Other brands may also use laminated membranes or, like Entrant, apply a liquid coating to the back of the fabric. Some product names you may be familiar with besides Gore-Tex® are Celtech, Ultrex, Avalanch, Omni-tech, and Darlexx, a stretch fabric.

The density of the fabric, coatings, and laminations that make a fabric more waterproof also make it less breathable by degrees. One student of mine used a waterproof/breathable fabric for a parka and wanted to make sure it would keep the moisture out, so she lined it with the same fabric. She couldn't understand why she was still getting wet, until I explained that she was getting wet from the inside because the capacity for the fabric to breathe was greatly reduced by using two layers.

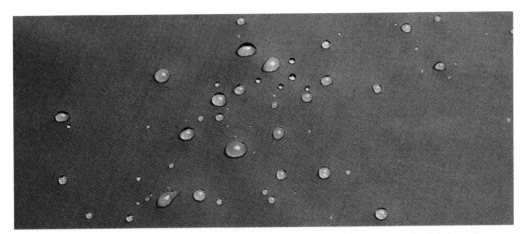

Water-repellent surface treatments are evident when water droplets bead up on the fabric surface and roll off. If the water soaks into the fibers, the surface treatment should be reapplied. (Photo by Sloan Howard; courtesy *Threads* magazine, © The Taunton Press, Inc.)

Surface treatments to increase water repellency on shell fabrics are routinely used in the fabric finishing process. A durable water-repellent finish is referred to as a dwr. This is a liquid spray or fabric bath that coats the surface of the fibers to help repel moisture and oils, and also increases durability. The visible evidence of a surface treatment is in the way that water beads up on the surface of the fabric. Scotchgard, Zepel, Teflon, Patagonia's H2No and Durapel are examples of surface treatments. These finishes are quite effective until the garment has been washed a few times, then they gradually diminish. Many manufacturers recommend reapplication of a dwr and will specifically recommend treatments designed for technical shell fabrics. Nikwax, Tectron, Amway, and Scotchgard all manufacture dwrs for reapplication.

Coated and laminated fabrics require seam sealing to prevent moisture leaking through needle holes in the seams of a waterproof garment. Needles and pins that puncture the fabric will leave permanent

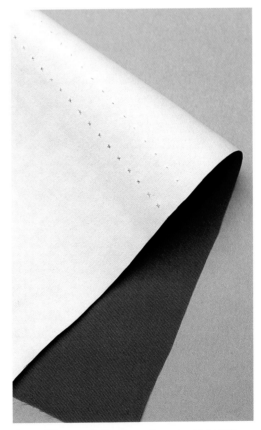

Assembling a w/p/b garment produces needle holes that must be filled or sealed to prevent leakage.

General Recommended Uses of Shell Fabrics

This chart offers information for suggested fabrics for various activities. Fabric selection should consider weather, temperature, and activity level in determining appropriate uses. Garment design, as well, may effect these general use guidelines. Be aware that a fabric, treatment, or process (such as a waterproof/breathable treatment) developed for use by garment manufacturers may appear with only a slight variation in the actual product under several different names. A compelling trademark name is chosen to increase marketability, allowing the manufacturer to market its features without promoting a would-be competitor with essentially the same product.

Fabric Types	Walking	Running	Cycling	Climbing/ Backpacking	Ski/Nordic	Ski/Alpine	Mountaineering	Motorcycling
160 x 90 nylon taffeta	X	X	X	X		X as parka insulated shell		
Two-ply textured nylon[1]	X	X	X	X	X	X as parka shell		
Three-ply textured nylon[1]	X	X	X	X	X	X as parka shell	X as parka shell	
Woven microfiber[2]	X	X	X	X	X	X as parka shell	X as parka shell	windbreak
Urethane-coated taffeta (waterproof)			X vented					X
Urethane-coated 400-denier nylon						X as panels	X as panels	X
Urethane-coated 1,000-denier nylon[3]						X as panels	X as panels	X
Lightweight (70-denier) two-layer w/p/b laminates/coatings[4]	X	X	X	X vented	X	X	X as parka shell	
Medium-weight two-layer w/p/b laminates/coatings[4]	X		X vented		X	X	X as parka shell	X
Heavyweight (300-denier) two-layer w/p/b laminates/coatings[4]			X vented			X	X	X
Lightweight stretch laminates/coatings[5]	X	X	X vented	X	X	X		
Stretch fleece laminates[5]					X	X	X	X
Three-layer w/p/b laminate on medium-weight shell[6]	X				X	X	X	X

Name brands might include:
[1] Supplex
[2] Versatech, Savina DP, Microsuede, Super Microft
[3] Cordura
[4] w/p/b laminates/coatings: Celtech, Aquaguard, Ultrex, Entrant, Xalt, Gore-Tex®
[5] stretch laminates/coatings: Polartec® Aqua Shell™ and Aquafleece, Aerologic, Darlexx, Vapex, Exoskin
[6] three-layer w/p/b: Gore-Tex®, Sympatex

holes. Even though the thread of the seam occupies the holes, the holes will allow moisture to seep into the garment. The seamline and any other stitching or pinholes should be sealed with either a seam-sealing liquid or tape (see the sealing process in chapter 4).

Insulating Materials

Insulators are often the silent ally within a warm coat. Especially for cold climates, some amount of insulation is sewn into coats, which saves you from having to put on two or three pieces for warmth every time you head out the door.

Insulators like wool and down have been around for centuries, but the new technical ones are able to provide maximum warmth with minimum thickness. In the old days the warmer you wanted to be, the heavier your coat was. Today's insulators provide a high degree of warmth without weighing you down, which is essential for active workers and athletes who need both maximum mobility and warmth.

A major advantage to technical insulators is that they absorb much less moisture (less than 1 percent by weight of water while wet). If you've ever worn wet down, you know it doesn't keep you warm, which can be dangerous.

Insulation, whether it's in your coat or your house, works on one or both of two principles: trapped air and reflected heat. In the first group are insulators that trap warm air molecules to the surface of a fiber. Down, fleece, and technical battings like Thinsulate have tiny fibers with miles of surface to allow air molecules to hold in warmth. Generally, the higher the loft, the more heat is trapped. Reflected thermal insulators bounce heat back to the source, so heat doesn't just move away from a warm body.

Air insulators Adding an air-insulating barrier can be accomplished with a layering piece like a fleece shirt or jacket, or as an attached lining or interlining of a wind/water-resistant shell, like a Thermolite Plus–filled parka. Pairing air insulators with a wind-resistant shell is important for the most effective thermal protection. To keep warm air trapped, it mustn't be allowed an easy avenue of escape. That brings us back to the benefits of layering to avoid overheating!

Fleece and pile are insulative, while allowing body vapor to pass through easily. They can be used in several different weights and treatments for a variety of results. For light insulation (as well as wicking ability), a semifitted mock turtleneck from microfleece or single-faced Lycra fleece under a shell can be a complete layering system for a temperate climate. For colder weather, heavy fleece or pile used as a jacket or vest lining or as a separate layer under a w/p/b parka can provide excellent insulative qualities (see the CLO values in the chart on p. 22). Pile fabrics especially have the capacity for a very high loft, providing more thermal protection. The thermal value will vary with the type and density of the fiber used.

Wind can make wearing fleece on its own a problem. Some varieties of fleece and pile are produced with a wind-blocking layer that is bonded between two single-sided fleece layers, but when using fleece and pile with no wind block, a shell layer is necessary for complete thermal protection in wind.

Most fleeces and piles are knits, so they have some flexibility. With spandex or Lycra added, they have even better stretch and recovery. This makes them excellent choices for a thermal layer in very active or sports-oriented uses. When bonded with other stretch layers, it can be made into a single-layer garment that has shell, thermal, and wicking functions all in one.

Consider This

Leftover bits and pieces are valuable for making coordinating hats, gloves, and headbands. The microfleece gloves fit easily inside the shell gloves to provide layering for your hands. The shaped glove pattern is from Controlled Exposure.

Suggested Insulations for Various Garments and Activities

As with shell fabrics, insulations come in a wide array of weights and thicknesses, and even as fabrics, such as fleece and pile. Here are some more commonly found insulations or fabrics to help you compare warmth and what they might be used for. Keep in mind that individuals have their own distinctive thermostats and may need to be regulated up or down from what is on this chart.

Insulations	Oz. per sq. yd.	CLO units	Thickness (in.)	Quilted (Q) (in.) or Edge-stabilized (ES)	Climbing/ Backpacking (low elevation)	Hunting/ Fishing	Ski/Nordic	Ski/Alpine (high elevation)	Children's Wear	Sleeping Bags	Coat Liner (removable)
Thinsulate CDS 40	1.3	0.7	0.1	ES	P/M	P/O	S/P	P	—	Liner	X
Thinsulate CDS 100	3.1	1.3	0.3	ES	P/J/VM	P/J	J/V/M	P	P/M	—	X
Thinsulate CDS 150	4.6	1.9	0.4	ES	J/V/M	P/J	J/V/M	P/J/V	P/J/V/O/M	—	X
Thinsulate CDS 200	6.2	2.5	0.55	ES	J	J/V	—	P/J/M	J/V/O/M	—	—
Thinsulate CS 250	8.3	3.1	0.7	Q 6-8	J	J/V	—	J	—	—	—
Thinsulate UDS 200	6.2	3.0	0.8	Q 6-8	J	J/V	—	P/J/M	—	—	—
Thinsulate THL 2	2.8	2.5	0.8	Q 6-8	J	J/V	J/V	P/J	P/J/V/O	X	—
Thermolite micro 100-weight	3	1.78	0.42	ES up to 24-in. panel	P/V/M	P/J/V	P/J/V	P/O	P/J/V/O	—	X
Thermolite micro 150-weight	4.4	2.67	0.63	ES up to 24-in. panel	P/J/V/M	P/J/V	J/M	P/J/V/M	P/J/V	—	X
Primaloft One (100 gr/sqm)	3.0	2.16	0.5	Q 10-12	J/VM	J/V	—	J/V	J/V/O	X	X
Primaloft One (133 gr/sqm)	4.0	2.88	0.7	Q 10-12	VM	J/V	—	J/V/M	V	X	—
Primaloft One (200 gr/sqm)	6.0	4.32	1	Q 10-12	V/M	V/J	—	V/M	—	X	—
Polarguard	10.0	5.2	1.5	Q 6-8	V	V	—	J/V	J/V/O	X	—
Hollofil 120	ca. 3.3	1.76	0.78	Q 6-8	V/M	V/M	—	J/V/M	J/V/M	X	—
Hollofil II 150	ca. 4.5	2.3	0.84	Q 6-8	V	—	V	J/V	X	—	—
Quallofil 150	ca. 4.5	2.3	1.0	Q 6-8	V/M	V/M	—	J/V/M	J/V/M	X	—
550 fill goose down	7.0	4.8	1.1	Q 6-8 (baffles)	V	V	—	V	V	X	—
Polartec® 100	ca. 6	ca. 1	Varies	—	Next to skin	Next to skin	Next to skin	Next to skin	Next to skin	Liner	X
Polartec® 200	ca. 8	ca. 1.2	Varies	—	J/V	J/V	J/V/M	J/V/M	J/V/M	—	X
Polartec® 300	ca.10.9	ca. 1.4	Varies	—	J/V	J/V	J/V/M	J/V/M	J/V/M	—	X
Glenpile 880	ca. 5.35	ca. 1.2	Varies	—	J/V	J/V	J/V/M	J/V/M	J/V/M	Liner	X
Glenpile 1280	ca. 9.5	ca. 1.3	Varies	—	V	J/V	—	J/V/M	J/V/M	—	—

Key:
ca. = about, approximately
CLO = units of relative warmth
J = jacket
M = mittens and hats
O = one-piece suits
P = pants
S = shell
V = vest

Whether a technical insulator or a quilted filling, insulations that come by the yard are often referred to as bat or batting. They may also be referred to as fill and in pattern directions as interlining and inner lining. There is a tremendous variety of thicknesses and quality for a multitude of purposes, which is why it's important to identify just how much warmth you really want.

Thinsulate, from 3M, is a flat bat known for its use as a thin insulation and has proven itself to be one of the best of its kind. It boasts patented microfibers 10 times smaller than a human hair, so that more fibers in less space create more surface area on which boundary air layers can form. You'll find Thinsulate in different thicknesses and forms for use in outerwear, footwear, gloves, and sleeping bags.

DuPont's Thermolite is a similar microfiber product line of insulations in varying weights and lofts.

High-loft soft insulations offer increased thermal values (see the Glossary on p. 180) and a different design aesthetic than flat insulations. They have a similar look to down without the worry of losing effectiveness when wet. Quallofil, Dac II (Hollofil II), Primaloft, Polarguard, Thermolite Plus, Thinsulate Ultra, and Thinsulate Lite Loft (bats that are a combination of flat and high loft) are examples of these technical high-

A small portion of the fleece and pile fabrics available. From left to right, top to bottom: Polartec® Windbloc® fabric fleece, pile print, sherpa pile print, Boundary, Polartec® 200 print, twisted fleece cord (see p. 112). Microfleece cut for binding, border cut from 200-weight print, Polartec® 200S (Powerstretch), microfleece.

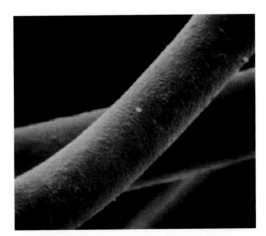

The microdenier fibers used in Thinsulate are similar in size to down fibers on which air molecules can be trapped. In contrast to down, these microfibers will maintain loft when wet and therefore keep you warmer. (Photo courtesy 3M Corp.)

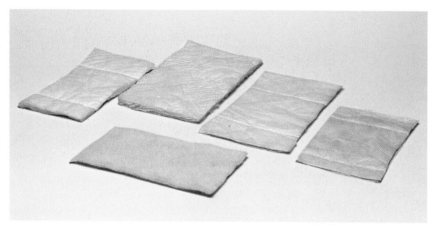

Trapped air insulations are available in a variety of thickness and for a variety of purposes. Thinsulate (top row) has a scrim. Three of these examples have prequilted lines. From left, they are 150-weight, 200-weight, 100-weight, and 40-weight. In front is a sample of 100-weight Thermolite.

loft battings. The materials' increased compressibility is also the result of a looser fiber structure. With the loftier fiber insulations it is very important to have some type of binder, scrim, or glazing on at least one side of the material to prevent it from bearding through the shell fabric and falling apart while you work with it.

Technical battings that come with a scrim (sometimes referred to as remay) on either side and prequilted "stitching lines" holding it together are easier to handle when sewing. The scrim prevents the microfibers from bearding through the attached fabric and the quilting prevents the insulation from shifting, allowing larger pattern pieces to be cut without additional quilting. If your insu-

> ## TIP
>
> For more thermal efficiency, use a lighter weight insulation in sleeves and pants than in the body of a jacket. The thicker insulation on the torso provides warm blood for circulation, while the thinner insulation on the arms and legs gives better flexibility and limb rotation.

lation doesn't have a scrim, place a thin, inexpensive nonwoven, nonfusible interfacing between the insulation and the outer shell when stitching it in place to prevent bearding. If your shell fabric has a membrane or coating, it is usually unnecessary to use a scrim.

It is very difficult to beat the natural appeal of goose down—lightweight, highly compressible, and wonderfully warm. Though new technical high-loft insulators try to copy these qualities, they have found down hard to beat. The main limitation of down is that it flattens and loses its insulating power when wet. By adding a shell layer of a w/p/b fabric, down's disadvantage becomes less of an issue.

Down quality is measured in fill power. The higher the fill power, the better the quality of the down as well as the better its insulating power (550 fill is a good standard). Mixes of down and feathers are available but are not nearly as good for outerwear. How much down you need varies with how warm the garment needs to be and the quality of down being used.

When using down, it is important that it is surrounded by downproof fabric because down's errant quills with their minute barbs can grab hold of the fabric fibers and work their way through. Downproof fabrics are tightly woven with a very high thread count, and come in nylon and other synthetics for water-repellent applications. Look for new insulation products soon that combine synthetic fibers and down!

Phase change and reflective insulators New temperature-regulating fibers and fabrics (such as products with Thermasorb, Comfortemp, and Outlasts!) are making their way into the home market. They trap heat at the cellular level in a "phase change capsule" so it can then be released back to the body when needed. They are referred to as active insulators (keeping the body cooled or warmed), in comparison with passive insulators, which insulate by trapping air. The capsules are made for a variety of uses for cold and hot weather. The capsules are small enough to be added, during the manufacturing of the fiber, in a coating or treatment for fabric or as a thin foam layer laminated to a tricot backing that is used like a batting or lining.

Thermal R and Insul-Bright are thin insulations with a Mylar-type membrane that creates a thermal barrier to reflect heat back toward the body. Microscopic holes penetrate the membrane and allow body vapor to pass through. These days, this fabric is used less in garments and more in window shades.

Other thermal and insulative alternatives
Wool has been used for warmth for many millennia. It has a lovely hand and can be shaped, using steam and heat. It can also retain warmth when wet but only to a point, and it's a low point. As with down, wool makes an effective insulative layer when protected from moisture while also allowed to breathe. One important consideration is that it can cause allergic reactions and itching for many people, in which case a fleece garment would be a better choice. It is also extremely heavy when wet, and requires far more care than fleece to prevent shrinkage. Wool is being blended with synthetics to produce pile and other next-to-skin fabrics for outerwear layering, which makes it more useful for a broader range of applications.

There are many times when technical fibers are either overkill for a project or

Comfortemp foam insulations use phase change technology to trap and release excess body heat. This technology is referred to as active insulation.

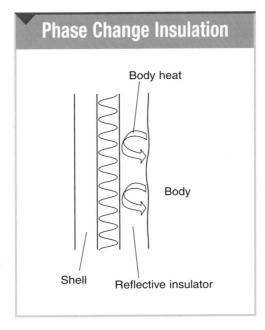

Phase Change Insulation

Body heat

Body

Shell   Reflective insulator

unavailable. Perhaps you are making a casual jacket that features quilting techniques. You would probably prefer the texture, hand, and ease of quilting that needlepunch or cotton bats offer. Needlepunch is a flat poly batting that has been used for many years in skiwear and comes in a few

Other insulation options, left to right: glazed 4-oz. quilt batting, 5.2-oz needlepunch, needlepunched Thermal R, (back) prequilted red high-count nylon with Dac II batting and nylon liner, (front) 4-oz. needlepunch, stretch needlepunch.

Wicking mesh fabrics can be found in a wide variety of knitted and woven forms, from very open to an almost closed weave. It might be referred to as mesh, mini-mesh, open mesh, and a variety of other terms. Mesh can be stable or flexible, even superstretchy as a Lycra blend. Because of the open spaces in the mesh, it allows more moisture to escape as vapor rather than having to be transported as solid moisture.

weights—4.2-oz. and 5-oz. weights are common for jackets. These are not as thermally efficient as the flat battings featured above. Flat poly/cotton and cotton battings designed for quilting can produce really nice results when using natural fiber outer fabrics. Follow the manufacturer's directions for use.

Neoprene is an excellent choice for wet conditions such as rafting, scuba diving, surfing, and fishing. It comes in various thicknesses, which are measured in millimeters (mm) and with a knit surface on one or both sides.

Neoprene can be a real challenge to use for a home sewer because it may require specialized techniques and equipment, such as a Teflon-coated needle and a rolling presser foot. Consider Aqua Fleece or Exoskin as an easier sewing alternative.

Next-to-Skin or Wicking Fabrics

Although the technical fibers in shell and insulative fabrics are new, the whole concept of wicking, as well as the fibers and treatments, is even newer.

Wool, silk, cotton, and other natural fibers absorb rather than just wick, and take a long time to dry because water molecules bond to the protein molecules of the fiber. The new wicking fabrics do not absorb but instead pull moisture to the outside along the synthetic fiber strands. These fabrics dry three to four times faster than cotton. There is an array of underwear for many activity levels that is so lightweight, warm, and dry that it's easy to forget that it's being worn. Brand names to help recognize this group of fabrics include CoolMax (a hydrophobic four-channel polymer fiber), Thermax (a crimped hollow-core fiber), Hydrofil, Polypropylene, Qwick, Dryline, Polartec® Power Dry®, and Wickaway.

Wicking fabrics come in a variety of weights and styles. Left to right, top to bottom: red Wickaway jersey, Bipolar mesh, waffle weave, open mesh liner, shiny pique Wickaway with Lycra, light-weight jersey.

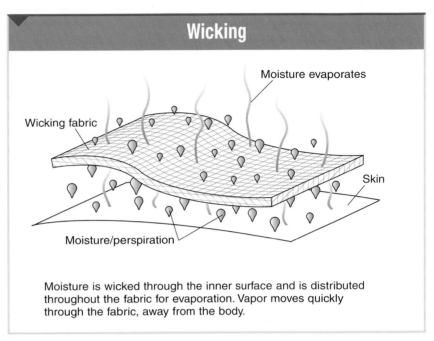

Wicking

Wicking fabric

Moisture evaporates

Skin

Moisture/perspiration

Moisture is wicked through the inner surface and is distributed throughout the fabric for evaporation. Vapor moves quickly through the fabric, away from the body.

Forms of wicking fabrics Early next-to-skin fibers were made into fabrics for long underwear, but now they can be found as linings in multilayered garments, single layers in running or aerobic gear, and from light- to heavyweight layering components. Wicking fabrics are also being bonded to other fabrics. Wicking linings can be found bonded to insulations, waterproof/breathable fabrics, or a w/p/b membrane only.

Taffeta fabrics made from wicking fibers can also be very efficient for linings. Taffeta is solid and slick so that a garment with a taffeta lining slides on and off easily over other layers.

A tightly knitted tricot is similarly used next to the skin and is available in various degrees of stretch for different purposes. It can be used as a lining when it has limited stretch. When used in heavier weights with Lycra, it makes excellent tights and running and other aerobic gear that can be used for

next-to-skin layers under thermal and shell layers. Other knit forms commonly used include pointelle, piqués, and jerseys.

Fleeces are a natural form for wicking and are perfect for thermal underwear and component layering. They come in a variety of weights for many temperatures and uses. Malden's Polartec® Power Dry®, Polartec® Power Stretch, microfleeces, and Lycra fleeces are examples of wicking fleece fabrics.

When you make your own clothing, you are a small manufacturer. Don't underestimate your power. The more you know about these fabrics, the better your results. Once you know what these fabrics will do, you can apply many of your existing sewing tools to sewing outerwear and produce excellent results!

TIP

A disadvantage to using some small-yarned mesh fabrics as linings is that they snag on rings, fingernails, and any other poky object that the fabric comes in contact with. Fortunately, when used as a lining, it is less obvious.

Chapter 2

Considering Design for Pattern Selection and Alteration

There's almost nothing more annoying than dreaming of a piece of clothing you really need, spending hours looking for it, laying out a lot of money, and then being disappointed in it. Unfortunately, this can happen fairly easily if you don't realize that it is the functional details that make a garment your best friend or nemesis.

A waterproof and breathable (w/p/b) jacket designed without front flaps to cover the zipper will let water leak through to your skin. Thermal fleece leggings that are too tight will cut off circulation and make you vulnerable to frostbite. A jacket with pockets that don't easily zip closed with a gloved hand can be aggravating.

The purpose of this chapter is to discover which design features are important for various outerwear purposes (the level and type of activity) and weather conditions, and to help you select patterns that incorporate the best features. We give general guidelines in pattern design, focusing on maintaining water repellency, providing flexibility and freedom of movement, general ease of use for pockets, hoods, and zippers, and more. Even if you're planning to buy outerwear, the information in this chapter can help you find a garment that has all of the features you need.

Beneficial Features in Outerwear Patterns

While no garment is perfect, you can pick one that's nearly perfect for you. This section can help you avoid many design problems, but only you know what works best for yourself. Think seriously about how you'll use a piece of outerwear and the demands you'll place on it. Recall what details you've loved or hated on outerwear you've owned and use that as a guide, too.

Seam, Vent, and Flap Placement

Water repellency, breathability, and moisture control can be affected by the placement of these details. Water may be directed, just like the function of gutters on a house, moving it to where it can flow off easily from the garment.

Seams Proper seam location is essential to making a garment water repellent. The seam profile (the slight fold made by seam allowances and topstitching lines) creates a trough that can funnel water down the garment through the needle holes or hold it in place if the seam runs horizontally. Water will have a harder time collecting on the jacket and seeping through if there aren't exposed seams on the top of the shoulder or the yoke areas. It is true that seam sealing

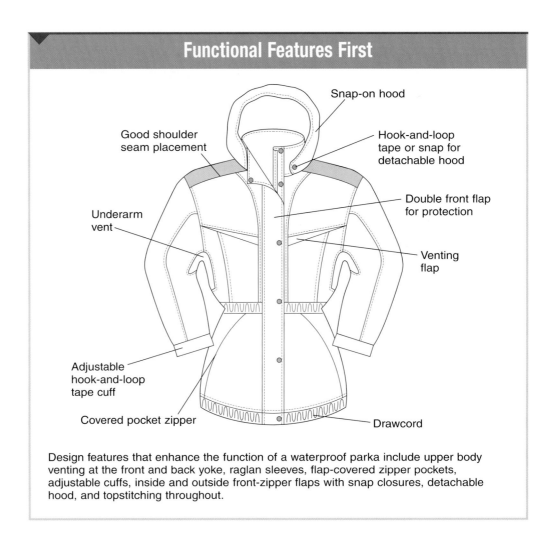

Functional Features First

Good shoulder
seam placement

Snap-on hood

Hook-and-loop
tape or snap for
detachable hood

Double front flap
for protection

Underarm
vent

Venting
flap

Adjustable
hook-and-loop
tape cuff

Covered pocket zipper

Drawcord

Design features that enhance the function of a waterproof parka include upper body venting at the front and back yoke, raglan sleeves, flap-covered zipper pockets, adjustable cuffs, inside and outside front-zipper flaps with snap closures, detachable hood, and topstitching throughout.

can stop most leaking, but a better defense is to have a raglan, saddle, or drop shoulder, and an over-the-shoulder yoke.

Vents Designing vents into a waterproof garment increases air movement and breathability. A vent in a waterproof or w/p/b garment is a flap of shell fabric over an underlayer of open-weave mesh or a thinner weave fabric. Sometimes there is no underlayer at all and the shell flap is spot-stitched or zippered to allow air circulation while still retaining the shape of the garment. The most common areas for large vents are the upper front and upper

back because hot, moist air will rise to the upper torso where it can then escape through the vent.

Many active outerwear garments benefit from a more isolated vent under the arm, casually referred to as a "pit zip." By adding a small mesh vent as a gusset, with a thin zipper for closing when needed, many outerwear garments are given a far greater comfort range. If the garment is for extremely foul weather or a greater variation of temperature is desired, a pit zip or open mesh vent should have single or double flaps over it with a hook-and-loop tape or snap closure (see p. 162).

Flaps Zipper and pocket flaps block moisture and channel it away from openings in the garment. For optimum performance, pocket flaps should be placed at an angle or close to vertical (rather than horizontal) to direct moisture away more effectively, guiding it down to the bottom of the flap where it can drip off.

Wet-weather gear should have flaps covering all openings. Center-front jacket zippers, side-leg zippers, and pocket openings with zippers are susceptible to moisture penetration. One outside flap will protect against normal precipitation, but a front-opening zipper with both an outside and inside flap will provide complete protection. The inside flap serves as a gutter (it is sometimes called a gutter flap) for water that makes it past the zipper. It is also effective to have two overlapping exterior zipper flaps. The edge of the underneath flap can be edgestitched down to create a trough for an even more effective gutter. A short, shaped inside flap with fleece backing can provide protection from the front zipper.

Topstitching around the exposed edge of a flap will help it stay flat against the surface of the garment. Snaps or hook-and-loop tape will keep the flaps in place during windy weather.

Pattern Features for Flexibility

The challenge in fitting outerwear is that the human body bends in so many different ways. The back can increase in width by a few inches when reaching and flexing forward. Arms rotate at the shoulder in wide arcs. The hip joint, a curving spine, and folded knees and elbows are all areas of motion that can be accommodated better by design considerations and/or adaptations to active outerwear clothing.

A pit vent with an inseam zipper and outer flap with a hook-and-loop tape closure. The extra row of loop tape allows the flap to be folded out of the way so it won't catch on things.

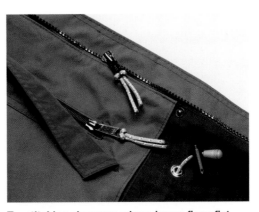

Topstitching sharpens edges, keeps flaps flat against a garment, and can emphasize design line by using a contrast color.

TIP

Closures can become a very creative part of the garment and need not look typical to be functional. Hot-cut nylon pieces (see p. 97) and snaps can make the closures much more interesting.

When fitting active outerwear, it is very helpful to do a few stretches. If the garment is for streetwear, your main consideration for fit might be whether there is easy rotation in the arms and across the back of the shoulders, and whether it will fit over other layers. Besides fitting over multiple layers, sport-specific or active outerwear may also require that you do deep knee squats, tucking, long stride movements, or whatever movement mimics the activities the garment

How to See a Pattern's True Features

When looking at a pattern book, does it become confusing when three photos showing the same garment look completely different? I have found it much easier to understand the basic design of a garment pattern by looking only at the line drawing. I can quickly tell whether the pattern is useful for my purposes because I get a clear understanding of the location of seamlines.

A line drawing is usually shown in the catalog, on the outside of the pattern envelope, and in even more detail on the pattern instruction sheet. This can be a valuable tool when enlarged on a photocopier. Use it for planning changes or additions to the pattern.

Unfortunately, many of the alternative pattern sources listed in Resources on p. 182 do not show line drawings of specialty outerwear patterns in their catalogs or Web sites, but you can call or e-mail, and their customer service representatives will usually provide a much more detailed description of the pattern than you require, as well as give suggestions on how the pattern goes together.

Reading the pattern description provided on the envelope will also clear up what type of fabric the pattern is intended for, whether design features shown are functional or only decorative, the type of ease allowed in the pattern, and other information.

What does it really look like? Evaluating a pattern's design is easier when a simple line drawing is provided on the pattern envelope. After buying a pattern, an enlarged version of the line drawing is useful for showing your own design changes.

will be used for. Some sports require an aerodynamic, close-fitting stretch garment, but it should still allow for easy movement without cutting off blood circulation, especially at the joints.

Back Greater freedom of movement for the upper body is available from patterns that have a generous cut across the back shoulder, bellows or pleats at the center or side back, and extra ease at the back of the sleeve cap.

Sleeve The success of active outerwear depends on the sleeve because of the rotation and movement of the arm and shoulder. For a skin suit (made from a spandex/Lycra blend), a well-designed raglan sleeve

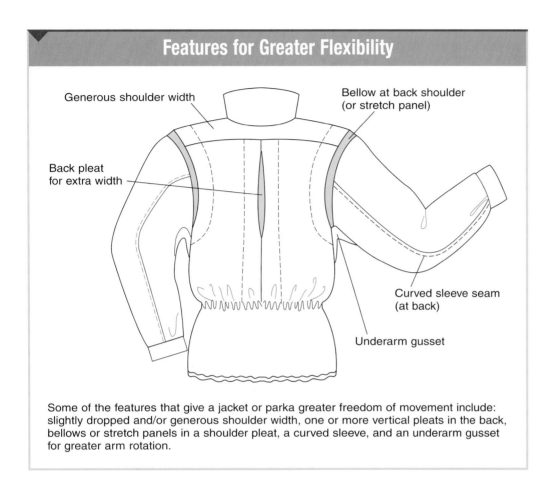

Features for Greater Flexibility

Generous shoulder width

Bellow at back shoulder (or stretch panel)

Back pleat for extra width

Curved sleeve seam (at back)

Underarm gusset

Some of the features that give a jacket or parka greater freedom of movement include: slightly dropped and/or generous shoulder width, one or more vertical pleats in the back, bellows or stretch panels in a shoulder pleat, a curved sleeve, and an underarm gusset for greater arm rotation.

provides good flexibility for activities that require reaching forward, like cross-country skiing or downhill racing. A jacket made from a stable fabric (rather than stretch) needs to have more ease and shape added for the same flexibility.

Though they are less common, jacket or parka patterns designed with a shaped or curved sleeve allow for the natural curve of the arm and lots of arm movement, and are very comfortable. This type of sleeve design can usually be identified by a seam at the back (intersecting with the armscye—armhole—at the back pattern notch) rather than under the arm, where it would intersect with the side seam.

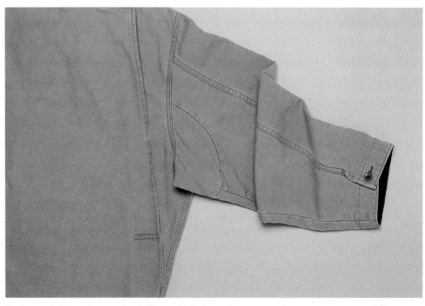

A shaped sleeve has extra fullness built into the pattern for greater arm mobility.

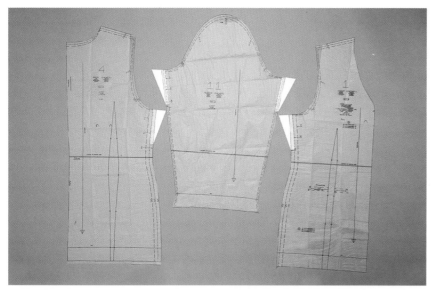

An underarm gusset adds good rotation to a straight sleeve and jacket body. A gusset can be incorporated as part of the pattern piece for the same results. A pattern that has been designed with gusset shaping will look like the outside lines of the sleeve and body pieces shown. Lines indicating a straight sleeve have less arm flexibility.

> **TIP**
>
> Fabrics that have a coating or membrane have little capacity to gather or drape (fall into folds). When using them, avoid patterns that have gathers, ruffles, or extra easing in a seam. For stiffer fabrics, I suggest using a dropped shoulder; it has a flatter sleeve cap, so there is less ease built into the sleeve pattern.

To get the advantage of a shaped sleeve, extra ease is added at the elbow, allowing for better freedom of movement as well as better fit. When the sleeve fits appropriately, you don't need as much ease in the body. (See p. 132 for changing a straight sleeve pattern to a curved sleeve.)

Underarm While the shaped sleeve accommodates the curve of the arm and a back-and-forth motion, a sewn-in or cut-on gusset provides for arm rotation. A separate gusset can be made strictly for movement or, when made from mesh as mentioned

above, can provide ventilation at the same time (see p. 134 for gusset alteration). A cut-on gusset incorporated into the pattern piece can be identified by the curve at the underarm edge of the sleeve and by the extra curve immediately under the armscye on the body of a jacket/top. A straight sleeve and body, which is not cut for rotation, will have less fullness at the underarm area.

Sleeve cuff For the best fit and adjustability, select a pattern with a cuff that has a hook-and-loop tape tab adjustment, so it can be readjusted, and an elastic section for more comfortable fit. It is important to make the cuff large enough to fit over a gloved hand. (See pattern alteration on p. 137.) If you don't require the detail of this type of cuff, consider adding a small tab to a simple sleeve edge, with a snap or hook-and-loop closure for better fit.

Hem edge The length of a shell garment is important for function. For serious rainwear, a finished hem length that covers the seat is more functional than a waist-length jacket unless rain pants are being worn as well. When making a hip- or thigh-length parka, a drawstring and casing at the hem edge allows the wearer to cinch it in or loosen it, depending on weather or the need for flexibility. A stretch drawcord will keep the hem edge flexible even when cinched up.

A pattern that has an optional fold-down extension at the hem offers extra protection for the seat when needed, and a snow/

> **TIP**
>
> A two-way front zipper is an easy way to add flexibility at the hem because the lower pull can be unzipped for increasing stride.

Powder Skirt, Snow Skirt, or Waist Gaiter

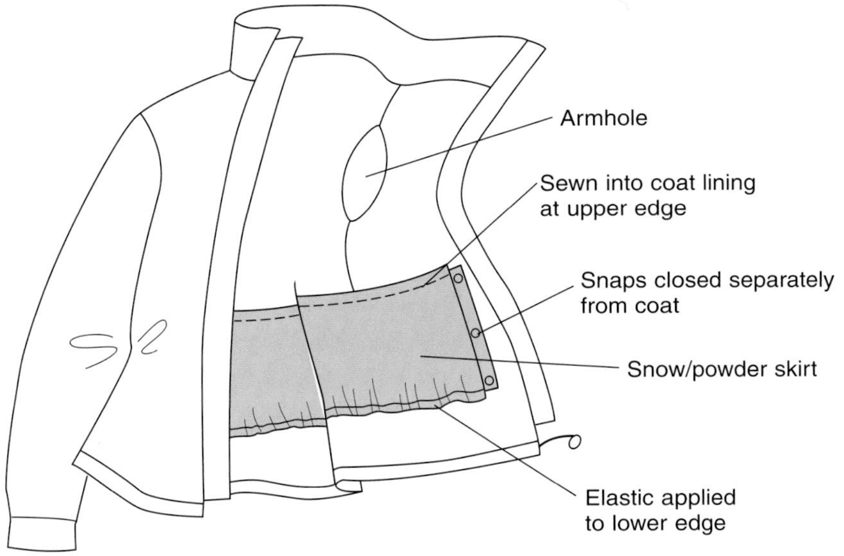

Armhole

Sewn into coat lining
at upper edge

Snaps closed separately
from coat

Snow/powder skirt

Elastic applied
to lower edge

A powder skirt attached to the lining of a parka or shell protects against snow or wind driving up the inside of a jacket. This gaiter is a straight piece of fabric with a finished elastic bottom and three snap front tabs. The piece is only attached to the lining at the top edge.

powder skirt will prevent a parka full of powdery snow when skiing becomes a contact sport.

A curved or shaped hem on a jacket or shirt, where the hem is long in back and short in front, provides good coverage of the lower back and seat but prevents unwanted bulk at the front, allowing the flexibility needed for certain sports. (See the photo at left on p. 36.) This hem shape is especially useful in activewear that needs to be close fitting, because it streamlines the front or the hip joint, covers the extended curved back, and curves under the seat. A light stretch elastic in a narrow casing can encourage a curved hem to stay curved under. A less extreme curve is attractive for many nonsport shells.

TIP

Gripper elastic in a snow cuff or gaiter adds extra reinforcement to keep it over the boot.

A pattern for a downhill ski pant that fits over the boot should have a snow cuff. (See the top right photo on p. 36.) If it is a close-fitting stretch ski pant, then the hem edge should fit very snugly over the boot and the inside of the hem should be finished with heavy gripper elastic. Measure the circumference of the boot and compare it to the pattern at the hemline (and consider the stretch of the fabric) to avoid making the pant too small. Ski pant hem edges should

A snow cuff attached to the lining a few inches up from the hem and hemmed with gripper elastic helps keep the pant firmly over the boot and prevents snow from coming inside.

Cycling is a sport that benefits from a shaped hem. The shaping at the back hem helps cover the body more thoroughly while riding, and the front is shaped higher to prevent bunching and chafing.

be shaped lower in the back than the front to eliminate bunching in the front while providing coverage in the back.

Flexing points The stable shell fabric and the flat insulation used in making insulated ski pants have little or no give in them. The pants either have to be made loose, with a lot of extra ease, sometimes causing the pants to be too bulky, or made with strategically placed stretch panels for a trimmer profile. Stretch panels may be a full-length panel or show up in areas of a garment that are subject to stress because of constant flexing: the back shoulder at the armscye, the lower back, or the side leg at the hip. Stretch panels are most commonly included in patterns for insulated ski pants, bibs, and one-piece suits.

The fabric for a stretch insert needs to give but be firm enough to match the weight of the surrounding fabric. A heavy gauge nylon knit in one or two layers with stretch insulation (Lycra fleece can be used with the stretch going around the body) should suffice. With other new stretch technical fabrics (such as stretch waterproof/breathables), you may be able to find a stretch fabric that is bonded with an insulation already, like Malden Mills' Polartec® Aqua Shell™.

Keep in mind that these bonded fabrics are often limited in their ability to stretch and may not provide the flexibility needed to complement the stable areas of the garment. Test the amount and direction of the stretch of the fabric and make sure the pattern placement correctly follows the direction of stretch availability.

Design Considerations for Stretch-Garment Patterns

Design features discussed in the previous section often apply to stretch garments as well, but there are additional considerations that apply specifically to choosing patterns (and garments) for use with moderate-stretch knit, superstretch, or woven stretch fabrics.

When buying garments made from knits, usually next-to-skin layers, look for a fit that will not restrict or bind. The most strategic areas are at major joints: knees, front hip, elbows, shoulders, as well as feet. If the garment is too tight or folds of the fabric get wadded up in a joint and restrict blood flow, frostbite can be the result.

A skin suit for snow-sport racing events requires a much tighter fit than for the next-to-skin layers discussed above. Anatomic shaping can provide a good fit at the joints to allow proper blood circulation, especially when designing for efficient aerodynamics

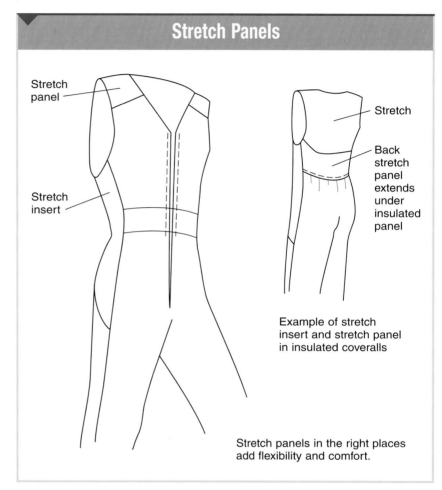

Stretch Panels

Stretch panel

Stretch insert

Stretch

Back stretch panel extends under insulated panel

Example of stretch insert and stretch panel in insulated coveralls

Stretch panels in the right places add flexibility and comfort.

Unisex Garment Patterns

Patterns designed as unisex garments often don't fit women well because they are generally designed for men's proportions. For many women, crotch length and/or depth is a continual problem. A sign of a too-short crotch length is that the crotch seam rides up. A too-long crotch length feels as if the crotch is halfway to your knees—there is a constant desire to pull up your pants, or there is a lot of extra fabric at the waist. Fortunately, these problems can be solved with relatively easy alterations, so there is no need to settle for something that simply doesn't fit. Refer to more about this on p. 54.

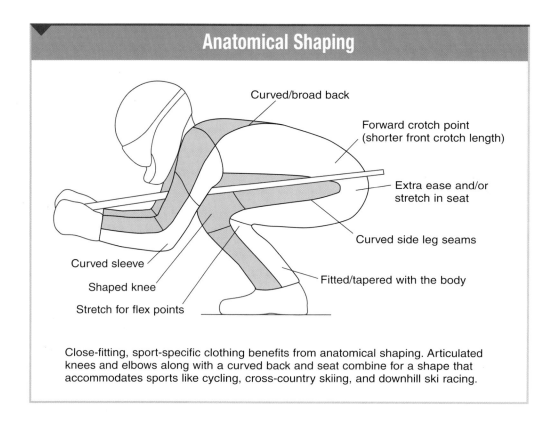

Anatomical Shaping

Curved/broad back

Forward crotch point
(shorter front crotch length)

Extra ease and/or
stretch in seat

Curved side leg seams

Fitted/tapered with the body

Curved sleeve

Shaped knee

Stretch for flex points

Close-fitting, sport-specific clothing benefits from anatomical shaping. Articulated knees and elbows along with a curved back and seat combine for a shape that accommodates sports like cycling, cross-country skiing, and downhill ski racing.

(see below). Because there is not a lot of warmth in these suits anyway, a separate thermal/shell layer should be available when not racing.

Moderate-stretch knits, in general, are forgiving, resulting in a greater range of fit for the size. Sizes will usually be listed as small, medium, large, and so forth and are often unisex. Superstretch garments are also forgiving in fit, but are often made quite snug for specific sport uses, so it is important to pay attention to crotch length/depth measurements. Fabrics with a limited stretch (bonded/coated) also need extra attention to fit.

Checking Pattern and Fabric for Degree of Stretch

When selecting a pattern that requires stretch fabric, it is important to match the degree of stretch in the fabric to the amount

of ease provided in the pattern. A pattern sized for 100 percent stretch needs a super-stretchy fabric with spandex (Lycra) because the pattern is smaller than the body (this is known as negative ease). A pattern designed for moderate-stretch fabrics has added ease for the size but not as much as a pattern that is designed for fabric with no stretch. (See more information on fitting stretch and ease amounts in the chart on p. 58.)

Anatomical Shaping

Superstretch garments, such as a downhill ski racing suit, can be made like an aerobic bodysuit or can be shaped more to the curve of the body in a "tucked" position (anatomical shaping.) A straight bodysuit pattern can be found at many of the widely distributed pattern companies. An anatomically shaped pattern is rare, but there are a few ways to adapt a pattern for your own use. When you consider that manufactured bodysuits cost hundreds of dollars, you can see how making a pattern can pay off, especially if you have a growing child involved in winter sports.

Forward Crotch Point

A feature to look for or adapt in a stretch bodysuit is a forward crotch point (see p. 62). Its purpose is to shorten the front crotch length and lengthen the back crotch length for an appropriate fit when the body is in a curved or tucked position. The outside of a pattern envelope may not tell you whether the pattern is shaped this way, so you may have to take the pattern pieces out of the packaging to examine them. See the example in the top illustration on p. 63 to see how the pattern pieces will look if they have a forward crotch point.

Pattern Considerations for Component Layering

As we mentioned earlier, the features above help make garments more functional and comfortable. There are also design features relevant to particular outdoor sports and activities that should be considered.

In this section we will show garment profiles for component layering that are suited to a range of activity levels and types. Designing for city street-oriented outerwear may have a greater range of design elements available than cross-country skiing, but both styles of dressing can be made more effective by layering.

Streetwear and Couture

Generally, couture and/or street-oriented clothing has more room for design flamboyancy than active sportswear because it does not have to meet fit and flexibility require-

Washed silk shantung interfaced and lined with a single layer of microfleece is an elegant and lightweight combination for cool, dry days or summer nights.

ments. On the other hand, technical outerwear has been incorporated into streetwear because of its comfort and effectiveness.

In the past few years some very creative designer outerwear patterns have been available to the home-sewing market. Issey Miyake, for instance, has created outerwear patterns that easily lend themselves to the

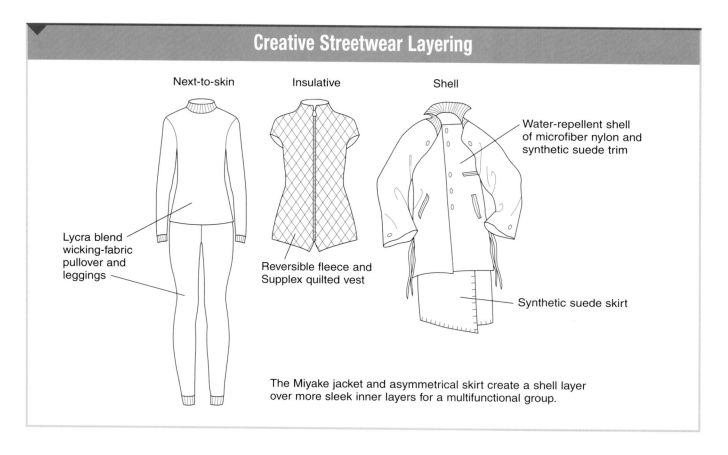

Creative Streetwear Layering

Next-to-skin

Insulative

Shell

Water-repellent shell of microfiber nylon and synthetic suede trim

Lycra blend wicking-fabric pullover and leggings

Reversible fleece and Supplex quilted vest

Synthetic suede skirt

The Miyake jacket and asymmetrical skirt create a shell layer over more sleek inner layers for a multifunctional group.

interesting textures and varied drape of the new outerwear fabrics. Other pattern companies and designers have followed suit with more coat and jacket patterns for a greater selection than has been seen before in the United States.

Above is an example of how this particular Issey Miyake design creates a nice shell layer with a high collar for protection of the back of the neck. The button-on yoke adds the benefit of venting, making it possible to use the pattern with a more substantial fabric (w/p/b-laminated/coated). The shaping of the body has a softer profile than many more "industrial" looks in women's outerwear.

By using a midweight fleece quilted with three-ply Supplex nylon for the vest, a reversible layer of warmth is added that can

also be worn easily without the coat. A synthetic suede wrapped skirt gives lower body protection from wind and rain.

As an inner layer, technical wicking fabrics provide a sophisticated look with performance. The combination of Lycra blends for close fit and comfort, with the simple pullover top and leggings would be suitable for the fashion avenues in any major city.

Outerwear for a High Activity Level

Active outerwear design, especially, needs to consider wicking (breathability/moisture transport) and flexibility of movement. The layering system represented on the facing page can be used for cross-country skiing, running, and cycling (with a few design variations) by varying the number of thermal layers. In addition to these, there are

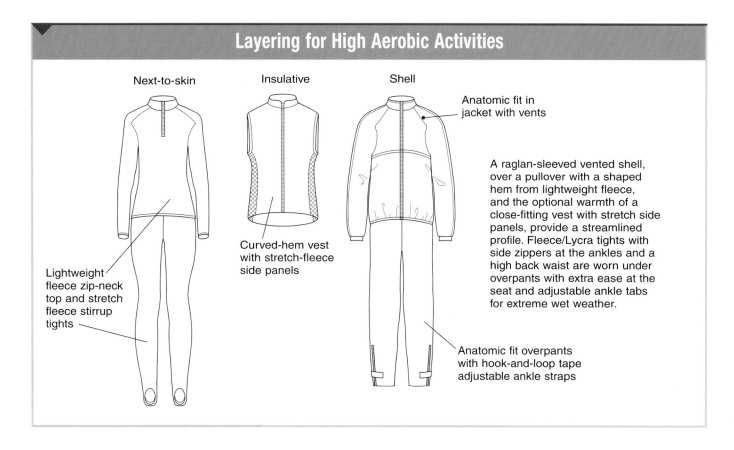

Layering for High Aerobic Activities

Next-to-skin

Insulative

Shell

Anatomic fit in jacket with vents

A raglan-sleeved vented shell, over a pullover with a shaped hem from lightweight fleece, and the optional warmth of a close-fitting vest with stretch side panels, provide a streamlined profile. Fleece/Lycra tights with side zippers at the ankles and a high back waist are worn under overpants with extra ease at the seat and adjustable ankle tabs for extreme wet weather.

Curved-hem vest with stretch-fleece side panels

Lightweight fleece zip-neck top and stretch fleece stirrup tights

Anatomic fit overpants with hook-and-loop tape adjustable ankle straps

many other activities that can use a similar combination with only slightly varied design and thermal layers.

Shell/jacket Because you may encounter a wide variety of temperatures and activity levels, it's important that an active outerwear shell have either excellent venting and/or a very breathable shell fabric. The outer shell for a component layering system is sometimes removed during especially heavy exertion and/or warmer temperatures, and when made as a single, compact shell layer, it can be stowed easily. If the garment's main function is to be used in especially cold temperatures, a lightweight fleece lining or insulation (40-weight Thinsulate, for example) may be added.

For the best freedom of movement, minimize pockets on the front of the shell. As mentioned before, a curved hemline will help prevent interference in stride. A back pocket or pouch can be used for lightweight storage.

The type of collar chosen for a shell (or for underlayers) will vary from one activity to another. While cycling or cross-country skiing, a high collar gets in the way, but a 2-in. or 3-in. high, close-fitting collar made from a heavy stretch fabric or lined with lightweight fleece can prevent excessive chill on a sweaty neck.

Thermal layer Even when the conditions are at their best, it is still a good idea to take along an extra insulating layer. A thin, close-fitting insulated vest does the trick and can

Linings

Linings are an important part of a coat, but manufacturers tend to skimp on them, which can lead to all sorts of problems. For lining the body of a jacket, I've found that a slick, firm, slightly open mesh fabric allows for vapor transmission, slides over other fabrics easily, and resists most snags from rings and fingers.

A combination of mesh in the upper body and more durable lining fabrics in the sleeve and lower body adds durability and allows ventilation where it is needed. A high-count taffeta or similar densely woven synthetic used in the sleeve and lower body as well as the facing area near a center-front zipper will add life to the lining, an area that often needs repair in the life of a parka or shell.

Consider This

Hand stirrups keep those sleeves in place and, with Lycra fleece, add warmth, too. With a back sleeve seam, make the sleeves 6 in. to 8 in. longer than the wrist, cut a thumb opening, and shape the stirrup after the back sleeve seam is sewn. A stirrup can be added to the hem of an existing sleeve by using a strip of stretch fabric to cut and shape until the desired fit is achieved. An over-locked edge is sufficient for finishing.

Long johns with a "whiz zip" for quick pit stops, this stretch fleece, one-piece suit can be worn under most types of layering systems and provide warmth as well as wick moisture. Custom designed and sewn by Penny Schwynn.

easily be stowed in a light pack. The close fit is suggested to prevent excess fabric chafing under the arm, especially for an activity like cross-country skiing where swinging your arms can cause irritation. A pattern with a side underarm panel would be a good choice for adding an insulated stretch panel to provide better fit and comfort.

Next-to-skin layer The next-to-skin layer for high-level activity is often a single layer that can, at times, serve as a thermal layer and in some instances also be exposed to the elements. Lycra, in conjunction with wicking fibers and bonded layers, gives such good protection and fit that other layers are sometimes unnecessary. I have a favorite pair of black stretch pants made from Polartec® Aqua Shell™ fleece that are used for running, cross-country skiing, and other multipurpose winter wear.

Aerobic-wear patterns and other sport-specific patterns for full-body stretch suits with a zipper added at the center front are very useful for next-to-skin layers for cross-country skiing, downhill skiing, and a wide variety of other activities. The same type of pattern is also good for an all-in-one layering system for cross-country skiing and even water sports, when used with technical bonded-stretch fabrics as seen in the left photo on p. 16. Stirrup tights paired with a zip-neck mock turtleneck are my usual choice for women, though, because a full body suit makes a trip to the outhouse mighty chilly. For men, a two-way separat-

A short zipper at the side ankle makes it easier to put on or remove tights.

ing zipper at the center front of a one piece suit can be an alternative to a fly opening.

Next-to-skin layers for cycling are similar in style to two-piece cross-country skiwear, but jacket and top patterns with a lower back hem will provide better coverage. Cycling shorts and tights should be higher at the back waist (longer back crotch length) for the same reason.

Overpants Overpants for active outerwear should have the same back waist shaping (high with longer back crotch) but more ease in the seat and stride because they are usually made from a more stable fabric than the next-to-skin layer. A narrow lower leg for a more efficient stride can be accomplished with a zipper at the lower leg (in back or at the side) and a hook-and-loop tape tab for drawing in the extra ease at the ankle. Reinforced (double layer) panels at the seat, knees, and inside ankle area are an option to consider for especially foul weather and/or high wear areas.

Multifunction overpants with a base layer of stretch fleece and overlay panels of woven microfiber and Taslan. The inseam area provides stretch fit, and reflective strips and tabs are added for safety. Custom-designed for a very tall cyclist by Penny Schwynn.

Hats and gloves A comfortable hat or hood is a necessary item for many of these layering combinations, as are gloves and/or mitts. With skiing, a fleece hat or headband will wick, breathe, and insulate and so stay comfortable. Fleece gloves are flexible, high wicking, and allow for better control of poling. A pattern that has side panels in the fingers and anatomical shaping is available for an excellent fit (see Resources on p. 182). A w/p/b overmitt or glove should be easily retrievable for wet/cold conditions.

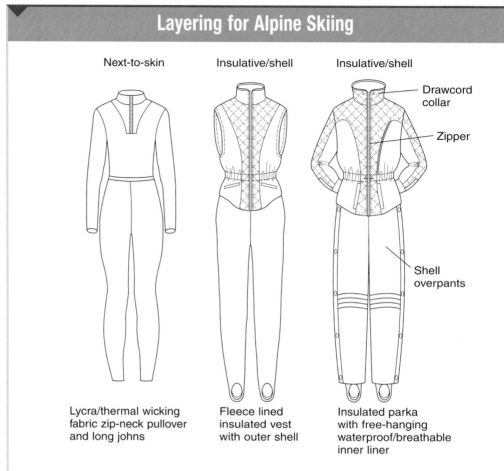

Layering for Alpine Skiing

Next-to-skin

Insulative/shell

Insulative/shell

Drawcord collar

Zipper

Shell overpants

Lycra/thermal wicking fabric zip-neck pullover and long johns

Fleece lined insulated vest with outer shell

Insulated parka with free-hanging waterproof/breathable inner liner

The lightly insulated parka has a high drawstring collar, zip-on hood, and fold-up inner collar with a double set of flaps down the center front. The sleeve has a wrist zipper with inside gussets and adjustable hook-and-loop tape tabs. The semifitted thermal-layer vest has a 2-in. collar with storage pockets. The fitted stretch ski pants are made from waterproof/breathable stretch fabric and an optional shell overpants for extreme weather.

Alpine and Arctic Outerwear

There is a huge range of styles available for cold and snowy conditions. For alpine skiing, snowboarding, or snowmobiling, our layering focuses on patterns that allow for more insulation, have highly flexible pattern elements, and include details to prevent snow from getting in through the collar, jacket bottom, and pants legs. Though vapor transmission is still important, the key factors are insulation and protection.

Beneficial features on these types of patterns are: extra ease in the pattern to accommodate inner layers or insulation, articulated or shaped elbows and knees, side-leg zippers, powder skirt or snow cuffs, easy-opening large pockets for storing extra gear and gloves, generous pocket and zipper flaps, and a zip-on or snap-on hood.

Shell/parka When putting together a component layering system for alpine sports, begin by determining what type of outer shell will go over all layers. An uninsulated shell, insulated parka, or one-piece shell suit each requires a different combination of layers to accommodate a variety of temperatures and conditions.

T I P

What's the difference between a parka and a jacket? For this book, the term "parka" refers to an insulated jacket, "jacket" to a single layer.

Long jackets or parkas with a drawstring at the bottom and waist are useful for keeping snow out and can be adjusted to allow air to flow up through the garment as well as adding extra covering for your seat on an icy chairlift. Shorter parkas (with the hemline about hip level) with a drawstring and/or elastic waist are usually less bulky, and when layered well with stretch ski pants and a well-fitting overpant, they can be very comfortable and attractive.

One-piece shell A one-piece shell pattern should have the same types of features that a jacket shell has for fit and function. As a single unit, top to bottom, it seals out snow, preventing it from getting up your back, down your pants, and with snow cuffs at the bottom of the leg, from coming up your leg. Pit zips and additional venting allow for a greater range of temperature. By adding your choice of pockets, a snap-on hood, D-ring tabs and other personalized features, you can stay away from the ski lodge all day unless you need a restroom break, which, for women, means completely undressing when wearing an all-in-one garment.

One-Piece Shell

Double front flaps with gutter

Shaped sleeve

Underarm vent

Adjustable cuff

Covered zipper pockets

Shaped knees

Ski guards

Elastic ankle

A w/p/b one-piece shell offers many variables for inner layers and a lot of protection from the elements.

Body length adjustments are critical in a one-piece garment, so the pattern should have lengthen/shorten lines for easy alteration (see pp. 61 and 64). When using a nonstretch fabric for a one-piece suit, 2 in. of ease for blousing (length) should be added to the body measurement above the waist and 1½ in. of ease added for crotch depth measurement (see the right photo on p. 112).

Vests can offer varying degrees of thermal protection. The down vest on the left provides maximum warmth in very cold but dry conditions. Fleece, in the middle, adds warmth in a single layer or under other layers. The Rono vest at right is made of polyester microfiber, terrific for cutting the wind and repelling moisture in high activity.

Thermal layer A vest can be a very useful thermal layering component when made with one of the technical insulations or down. A lofty vest will add bulk, so plan for how it will be used. If it doubles as an outer-layer option, it will need a water-repellent or w/p/b shell attached (especially for down) and possibly a tall collar that is loose enough to cover the chin. The outermost shell layer that is worn with a lofty vest should have enough ease to accommodate the thickness of the vest.

A vest using a light nylon face fabric with a fleece or pile lining would also provide excellent warmth to the torso without adding a lot of bulk. For the easiest layering, choose or design a vest pattern that is more fitted, with a shaped hem and a short collar that fits close to the neck.

A long-sleeved pullover or zip-front jacket design in fleece or pile adds easy warmth and another option for layering. This type of garment often becomes a favorite for spring and fall as a light jacket. There are many excellent pattern options for a long-sleeved thermal or transitional layer. This type of garment adapts well and helps make the transition from one set of conditions to another. Some that I have especially enjoyed look very atypical, have asymmetrical openings, use natural fibers as the outer fabric, and have unusual closures.

When choosing a pattern, imagine how it might be used when adjusting layers under cold and wet conditions. A jacket with a front-separating zipper is easier and faster to remove than an anorak-style shell that you have to pull over your head. A slim, more fitted pattern, such as one with princess seams (side front seams) will allow for better shaping. Narrow, fitted sleeves are better for inner layer garments, as long as you don't sacrifice arm mobility.

If you are worried about fleece layers catching instead of sliding easily into a shell layer, use a fine denier ripstop nylon as a shell for the fleece, making it a light two-layer jacket. The ripstop will allow the two layers to slide easily, one inside the other, without severely limiting the breathability of the fleece garment. It also adds some wind-break for when it's worn alone.

Classic stretch ski pants, in the boot or over the boot, are very comfortable and flattering for most wearers. The firm stretch of the fabric helps the style look great on plus sizes.

Snowpants, bibs, and stretch ski pants

For layering your lower half, options include stretch ski pants or bibs, insulated ski pants or bibs, shell-only or insulated overpants, as well as one-piece units that include attached pants.

A pattern for a close-fitting, flexible garment should take advantage of the new technical stretch fabrics or the older but still great looking wool/nylon/Lycra blend fabrics that have been traditionally used in ski pants. A stretch ski-pant pattern should be specifically fitted to accommodate the limited stretch of these types of fabrics. If the pattern doesn't say what type of stretch is required, take out the pattern and flat pattern measure it to see for yourself. Often, the stretch-pant pattern pieces will appear shorter and wider than most pant patterns because the fabric stretches vertically over the body.

Stretch ski-pant fabric should be cut so that the most stretch is in the length (verti-

In-the-boot stretch ski bibs over a lightweight wicking mock turtleneck and leggings are the basis for this layering system. Extra details on an inside fleece layer and a parka create continuity to this unique combination.

cal on the body). The waistband should be firmly stabilized with a nonstretch interfacing to prevent the pants from becoming hip huggers, or have a bib or shoulder straps to keep them up. For most adolescent boys (and even some adult males) who have no hips to keep the waist up, bibs are a better choice for stretch pants.

Pattern options to look for are a stirrup in-the-boot finish or an over-the-boot finish that has a hidden inner stirrup. A good pattern will have a separate stirrup pattern

A loose-fitting w/p/b overpant with articulated (pleated) knees and snow cuffs, heavy-denier knee seat, and ankle guard.

piece that can be made with power mesh (the superstretchy Lycra mesh fabric also used in "body shapers"). This provides a less bulky fit inside the ski boot and also anchors the garment to the bottom of the foot, allowing it to stretch over the body.

The pattern for the looser fitting overpant shown above has many terrific features for alpine sport pants. It has articulated knees and snow cuffs, and can be made from a waterproof/breathable fabric and used as a shell-only layer over stretch ski pants, or insulated for more extreme conditions. The waterproof, heavy-denier knee and seat areas and the inner ankle guard give extra protection at the most abused areas, and full side-leg zips allow for easy on and off as weather conditions change.

Wicking layer An inner wicking layer for skiing can be made in many comfortable

fabrics, but the designs for these types of garments vary only slightly. Generally, a trim or close-fitting long-sleeved top and pull-on leggings or pants will fit the bill.

For a top, I prefer a zip-neck mock or regular turtleneck pattern, using a soft dress zipper at the neck. This combination provides neck warmth but also quickly releases excess heat when unzipped. More traditional long underwear designs are often used for lighter-weight wicking knit fabrics. Underarm gussets of a lightweight wicking stretch mesh increase breathability as well as flexibility and can be easily added to a standard sleeve design (see p. 134).

Most standard legging or tights patterns will be too small for the limited stretch in Lycra fleece fabrics, but should work for flat knits with Lycra content (check the amount of stretch on the pattern envelope). A gusset at the crotch is a nice feature that will increase comfort in the stride because it increases the back crotch length. You may not want to use the stretch mesh in this gusset, however, unless the leggings will always be kept as an inside layer.

With stretch fabrics used in the wicking layer, always check to see what the fabric requirements for your pattern are and use fabric accordingly. I have found that Stretch & Sew and Kwik-Sew patterns provide a lot of information about amount and direction of stretch and about altering for fit, and have a good selection of sportswear and next-to-skin types of patterns.

Layering all-in-one garments An efficient garment that has all layers in one piece needs to have some of the same considerations as individual components of a layering system. Effective venting is a must in all conditions, as are plenty of pockets, inside and out. Other essential elements are flaps

One Piece—All Layers

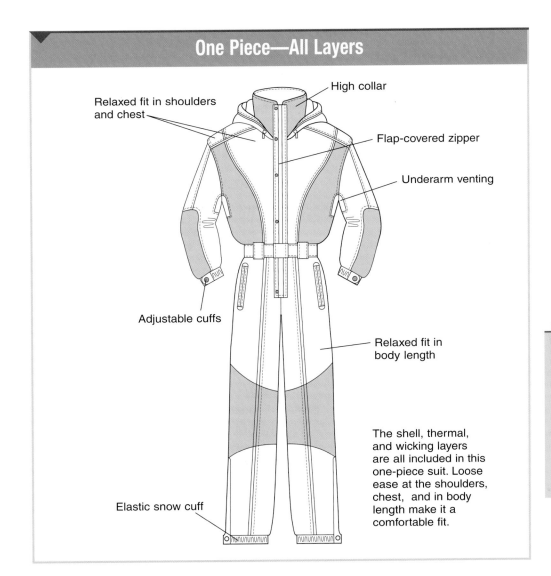

Relaxed fit in shoulders and chest

High collar

Flap-covered zipper

Underarm venting

Adjustable cuffs

Relaxed fit in body length

Elastic snow cuff

The shell, thermal, and wicking layers are all included in this one-piece suit. Loose ease at the shoulders, chest, and in body length make it a comfortable fit.

TIP

When available, a prequilted insulation and lining fabric can simplify and speed up assembling an insulated garment. But don't sacrifice quality of materials for quickness!

to prevent cold and wet spots at the front zipper and an attached or optional hood. As mentioned above, look for a pattern with the features and design lines that you want most, then plan on adding the missing design elements.

When you have shell, thermal, and wicking layers all in one garment, your pattern should be sized to accommodate the loft of the insulating layer. Pattern pieces for the shell should be larger than those for the lining to make room for the loft of the insulation. Depending on the style of the garment,

the insulation may be attached to the shell pieces, the lining pieces, or in the case of fleece, may actually be the lining.

If the shell fabric requires seam sealing, insulation should be attached to the lining pieces, not the shell. This also limits cold spots caused by the compressed insulation at seamlines.

Patterns should offer cuff and ankle protection, like elastic and/or hook-and-loop adjustable tabs at the cuffs, to seal areas where snow and cold air can get in. Elasticized snow cuffs that extend over the

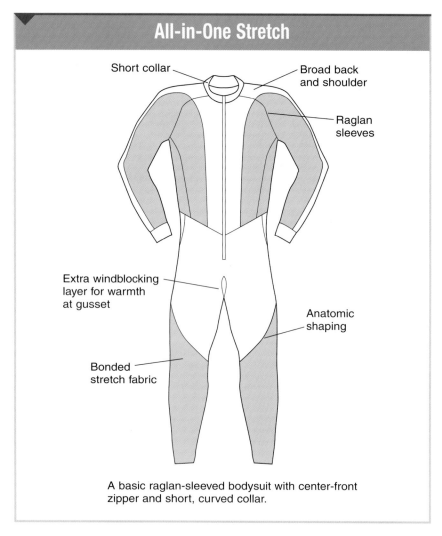

All-in-One Stretch

Short collar

Broad back and shoulder

Raglan sleeves

Extra windblocking layer for warmth at gusset

Anatomic shaping

Bonded stretch fabric

A basic raglan-sleeved bodysuit with center-front zipper and short, curved collar.

purposes you should probably have an additional next-to-skin layer even if this layer is a wicking fabric.

Stretch all-in-one layering combination
Some technical bonded-stretch fabrics have been composed so that they perform the function of all three of the layers we have discussed: water repellency, thermal retention, and wicking. Downhill skiing, diving, luging, rafting, and other sports have adopted these fabrics for close-fitting, streamlined, thermally comfortable, technically efficient gear.

Patterns for these fabrics will be form-fitting and should indicate the approximate amount of stretch required. It is very important to test the stretch of the fabric (see p. 59). You will almost always have to make adjustments to the pattern so as to best use the stretch. These bonded stretch fabrics will only allow comfortable use of a small percentage of stretch and the adjusted pattern will often be very close to the actual body measurements. (See the chart on p. 58 for ease amounts.)

For downhill ski racing, patterns may have a short crotch length in front, a longer one in back and a broad back shoulder measurement so as to match the body shape of the tuck position of the racer. See the adjustment for a forward crotch point on p. 62.

Flexible body-suit patterns often have a raglan-sleeve construction, a short, single-layer collar, and long center-front zipper. Specific variations may be desired for certain sports but the example shown at left is a general style useful for many sports.

Finding Patterns
Finding specialty patterns can be a treasure hunt at best. Some mainstream pattern

boots or an elastic casing at the ankle is an important addition for a ski suit. A high collar with a drawstring at the top edge that covers the chin and mouth and a soft inner collar for protecting the neck are good features (see the illustrations on pp. 100 and 105).

The lining pattern pieces should be simple, with maybe a few pockets for storage. A lightweight wicking taffeta or a closed mesh with shell fabric facings will provide excellent breathability and firm edges for a lining in an insulated one-piece suit. For practical companies offer a few nice outerwear patterns or ones that can be adapted. As mentioned earlier, some very creative and fashionable outerwear patterns are showing up in *Vogue* as well as other major pattern companies. This is especially true with the popularity of fleece and pile fabrics.

With the large companies, look for outerwear patterns as the fall pattern books arrive because they discontinue all but the hottest sellers for the spring and summer issues. Burda, Kwik-Sew and Stretch & Sew are a few companies, in particular, that continually offer outerwear and sportswear patterns with some very useful features. Look to the specialty outerwear fabric retailers for the best selection and the more technically designed garments.

We have listed retailers in Resources on p. 182 that specialize in outerwear and sewing-related products and provide some type of mail-order service. Some of these specialty businesses carry small pattern company products well worth noting: Storm Mountain Designs, Controlled Exposure, DK Sports, Green Pepper, Sew-Go, The Rainshed, and Jean Hardy (equine specific). These pattern companies often develop when people involved in a particular activity want a better or less expensive product than they can purchase. As a result of their efforts, patterns designed by fellow outdoor enthusiasts are available with the details that they have found useful.

In summary, the choice of your patterns has a lot to do with your personal taste and specific requirements. As your own designer, take the time to plan what you want so there is much more likelihood that you will actually get it.

Examples of pattern companies that have a good selection of outerwear designs: outerwear specific brands include Storm Mountain and DK Sports and the more commonly found Stretch & Sew, Burda, and Kwik-Sew.

Mail-order catalogs are an excellent source for outerwear fabrics, patterns, and notions. They often include sewing techniques and tips. See Resources on p. 182 for a listing of names.

Making It Fit: Basics for Measuring Yourself and Your Pattern

Over the years the general public has come to expect less and less in how their clothing fits. Manufacturers have intentionally designed clothing to be loose fitting so their clothes would fit more people by using the simplest patterns. In spite of this trend, most people want clothes that fit well, and when they find something that does, it becomes a favorite.

I had a client, a former professional basketball player, who is 7 ft. tall and mostly legs, which put his waist at my shoulder level. He had shopped around the world but had never been able to buy a pair of ski pants that were long enough. You can imagine how happy he was not to have to wear warm-ups for skiing anymore! Sometimes altering a ready-made purchase will give you the results you want, but in this case, it was easier to start from scratch than try to integrate added length into the simple design he was looking for.

For my tall client the stretch ski-pant pattern I used obviously had to be lengthened, as he needed a 45-in. inseam. Even for someone of average height, a purchased pattern may have fitting issues—just as found in ready-made garments—and need to be altered. By measuring a couple of areas of the body before selecting the pattern size, you are much closer to a good fit and fewer pattern changes.

Matching Your Size to a Pattern Size

When choosing a pattern size for the upper body, the bust/chest measurement is the most important. For women, if a "high bust/upper chest" size is listed, use it instead of the regular bust measurement because that is affected largely by cup size and is often not a good indicator of general size. Some pattern companies are only now adding the upper chest measurement to their size guides. A pants pattern should be selected based on the hip/seat measurement. If the pattern is a one-piece suit that covers both upper and lower body measurements, I prefer to select the pattern size based on the bust/chest and then alter the pattern hip width if necessary.

If a pattern is grouped in general sizes (small, medium, large), there should be a measurement guide to determine what falls within each range. Take extra care to flat-pattern measure (measuring the pattern within the seam allowances to determine total circumference) when using a unisex pattern that uses general sizes. When trying to fit everyone, as in ready-to-wear, sometimes patterns fit no one! So measure first and select the appropriate cutting line.

Unisex Patterns and "She's Using His" Pattern

Knit fabrics can be very forgiving, so patterns for stretch fabrics are often unisex. Designs that have little shape, such as a very straight, loose parka, may also use unisex sizing. A pattern may indicate that it is designed for both genders, but as with any pattern, it's important to check the fit, especially in certain areas.

These areas can usually be altered so that the garment fits you well even with a pattern design that is only available in sizing for the opposite sex. There are specific differences in body shapes between men and women commonly found in a few areas. Sometimes the pattern offers men's and women's cutting lines in these areas, but I think it's worth measuring anyway. You may be lucky and not have to make an alteration. These are the areas that are suggested to check the fit:

■ Men's arm lengths are usually longer for a similar body size.

■ Men's cuff size (circumference) is usually larger.

■ Neck size is usually larger on a man.

■ Biceps, thigh, and calf measurements are usually larger on a man of similar body size. These are especially important to check for very athletic men and women when making close-fitting garments, even when using stretch fabrics.

■ Crotch length and depth are usually shorter on a man than a woman.

■ More difference in width from waist to hip in women, more curves to accommodate.

■ Men often have wider shoulders.

Aside from fit, consider how a garment closes. Traditionally, a man's jacket closes left over right and a woman's closes right over left. If you prefer this traditional closing, be sure to adjust that if necessary. A fly can also be right or left opening (right for men, left for women) so note the direction you want it to go and check the pattern.

Measurements for a Pattern's Fit and Ease Allowance

Garment ease is the excess room that allows for comfortable fit and movement. The design of a garment may add to or take away from the needed ease. Some patterns will note "loose-fitting," which has more ease than "close-fitting," which would have very little ease.

Factors Affecting Ease

The amount of ease needed depends on the fabric used, the design of the garment, the thickness of the insulation and underlayers, the personal taste of the wearer, and the relative size of the wearer. With these variables, ease is specific to the garment, pattern, and person. Because of design and fabric, a very loose-fitting swing coat made of a woven fabric may have 30 in. to 40 in. of ease at the bust. A loose-fitting outer shell may have an extra 20 in. to 30 in. at the chest/bust to allow for fitting over layers and still provide freedom of movement. A high-lofted insulated garment needs greater ease to accommodate the extra bulk of the insulation. At the other extreme, a Lycra garment worn next to the skin may be smaller than the body measurement. Because of the fabric's stretch, no ease is added and it may even have negative ease—where the garment is smaller than the body.

My 7-ft.-tall client could have relatively more ease added to his ski pants than another client who might measure in at 4 ft. 11 in. Ski pants have an average ease for crotch depth at $1\frac{5}{8}$ in. A very tall person might be more comfortable with 2 in. of crotch depth and a shorter person with $1\frac{1}{4}$ in.

My clients have proven to me that personal taste in fit is very important. I've had to take in what I thought was an unreasonable amount on ski pants before the client felt that they fit perfectly. It's surprising that they could still bend over in their pants much less ski in them! And as mentioned before, very loose fitting is another personal preference.

Where to Measure

Important areas of body-to-pattern comparison for adding or subtracting ease are: chest/bust, waist, and hip/seat. Other measurements for comparison that require less added ease but need to be appropriately fitted are neck circumference; center-back neck to waist; center-back neck to the desired finished length of the garment or hem; center-back neck to wrist with bent elbow (or shoulder plus sleeve measurement); crotch depth and length; inseam, and waist to length of garment. (See the illustration on p. 57.)

This shirt pattern from Sewing Workshop is described on the pattern envelope as an "oversized shirt/jacket." It fits easily over another shirt or top. Shown here in microfleece, it provides some warmth with easy comfort, much like a sweater.

Do Something Unpredictable!

This wrap skirt and jacket made from Aqua Fleece was amazingly simple and fast! It has the ease of sewing and comfort of fleece and the look of leather, and it can be made very close fitting because of its stretch. And, if you must, it can also be used for skin dive suits, kayaking, and other water gear.

Though it is important to add ease for flexibility in some areas, too much ease can be detrimental to good fit. An appropriate fit at the shoulders and neck keeps the garment hanging correctly on the body. If an armscye is too low and loose on the body, the bottom of the jacket rises by several inches when the arm is raised. (See the photo on p. 116.)

When fitting yourself, you probably know which areas to check that might need to be adjusted. When checking someone else for fit, a visual assessment may show obvious areas that may not fit the "average" pattern. A round stomach or seat may require lengthening a center-front measurement or a back crotch-length measurement. For some very muscular individuals, especially with close-fitting garments, important comparisons to make are at the upper arm, upper thigh, and calf measurements.

Certain equipment or activities may require additional measurements. The circumference of the ankle area of ski or snowboard boots is important for sizing the width of the pant leg and snow cuff. The pant leg should have a finished width of at least a few inches larger than the boot unless the garment has Lycra/spandex stretch.

It's easy to remember and understand the need for ease in the width of a garment, but also remember that small amounts of ease added to length measurements accommodate bending, contributing greatly to ease of movement and flexibility. Blousing in the upper part of a waisted jacket or one-piece suit, the extra length in the sleeve above a cuff (also called blousing), and ease in the crotch depth are examples of areas where length ease is important.

The chart on p. 58 is for general ease requirements for various outerwear applications depending on whether the garment is

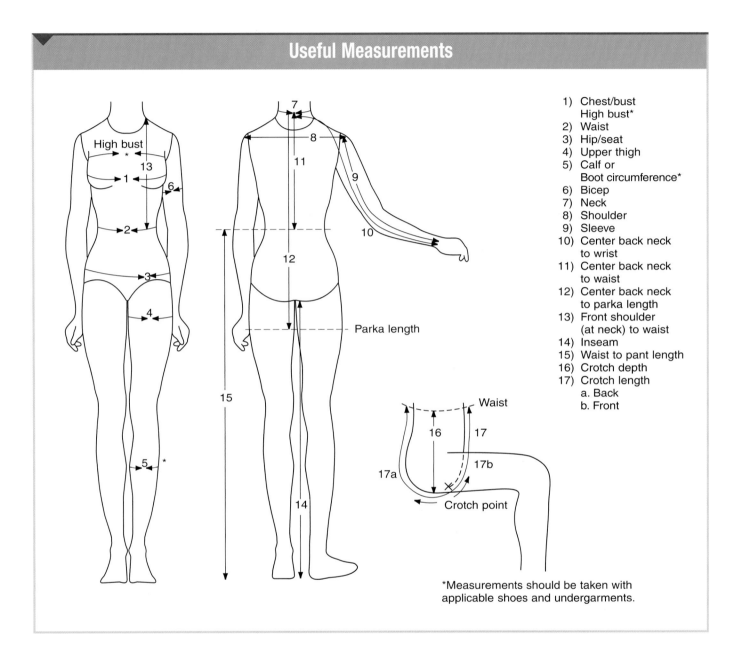

1) Chest/bust
   High bust*
2) Waist
3) Hip/seat
4) Upper thigh
5) Calf or
   Boot circumference*
6) Bicep
7) Neck
8) Shoulder
9) Sleeve
10) Center back neck
    to wrist
11) Center back neck
    to waist
12) Center back neck
    to parka length
13) Front shoulder
    (at neck) to waist
14) Inseam
15) Waist to pant length
16) Crotch depth
17) Crotch length
    a. Back
    b. Front

*Measurements should be taken with
applicable shoes and undergarments.

an outer shell, midlayer, or next-to-skin using stable fabric or easy stretch (Lycra). Obviously, this is only a general reference. A large cape or poncho will have a larger number than shown here. A very stretchy spandex skin suit will be much further into the negative numbers than listed here. The range of ease amounts is also proportional for a person's size. Adequate ease for a small person is more likely to be found in the lower numbers of a listed range, while a larger person would need the greater number.

Note that the 75 percent stretch column indicates ease for bonded stretch fabrics that have a much stiffer stretch. If you are working with an easy stretch fabric with good

Ease Amount to Be Added to Body Measurement

	Insulated garment (in.)	Single layer outer shell (in.)	Insulating/ mid layer (in.)	Next-to-skin layer (in.)	75% (moderate) stretch (in.)	100% stretch (in.)
Bust/chest (1*)	15 – 30	15 – 30	12 – 20	4 – 8	-½ – 0	-3 – -5
Waist for semifitted jacket (waist for pants – 0) (2)	8 – 12	8 – 12	7 – 11	4 – 8	-½ – 0	-3 – -5
Hip/seat in jacket or top (3)	15 – 30	15 – 30	12 – 20	4 – 8	-½ – 0 (for body suit)	-3 – -5 (for body suit)
Hip/seat in pants (3)	8 – 15	8 – 15	8 – 12	4 – 8	-½ – 0	-3 – -5
Upper thigh (4)	3 – 4½	3 – 4½	2½ – 4	2 – 3	-½ – 0	-1¾ – -2½
Calf (5)	3 – 4½	3 – 4½	2½ – 4	2 – 3	-½ – 0	-1¾ – -2
Bicep (6)	3 – 4½	3 – 4½	2½ – 4	2 – 3	-½ – 0	-1¾ – -2
Neck (7)	3 – 5	3 – 5	3 – 4	½ - 2	-¾ – 0	-¾ – 0
Shoulder (for drop shoulder, use neck to wrist) (8)	¼	0	0	0	0	-¾ – 0
Sleeve (add 1 in. – 3 in. more for blousing above cuff) (9)	½ – 1	½ – ¾	½ – 1	0	0	0
Back neck to wrist (with bent elbow) (10)	½ – 1	½ – ¾	½ – 1	0	0	-½
Back neck to waist (ease for blousing) (11)	1½ – 3	1½ – 3	1½ – 2½	1 – 2	not often used	0
Back neck to length (parka length ease for blousing) (12)	2½ – 4½	2½ – 4	1½ – 4	1 – 2	not often used	0
Inseam, no cuff (14)	½ – 1	½	½	½	-2 with stirrup, 0 without	-3 – -4 with stirrup, 0 without
Inseam with elastic ankle cuff (14)	1½ – 2	1½ – 2	1 – 2	1 – 1½	not often used	—
Waist to length, no cuff (15)	½ – 1	½ – 1	½ – 1	½	-2 with stirrup, 0 without	-3 – -4 with stirrup, 0 without
Waist to length, elastic ankle cuff (15)	1½ – 2	1½ – 2	1½ – 2	1 – 1½	not often used	—
Crotch depth (16)	1¼ – 2	1¼ – 2	1¼ – 2	1¼ – 2	-¾ with stirrup, ½ without	-1 – -1½ with stirrup, 0 without

Numbers correspond to the illustrations on pp. 57 and 64.

memory, take out even more ease (subtract inches equals negative ease) as indicated in the 100 percent stretch column.

Calculating a Pattern's Ease

To compare body measurement to the flat-pattern measurement, measure the pattern at the corresponding location for each measurement and mark the pattern pieces with the totals for future reference. If the pattern piece is only one half of the garment (as in a back piece cut on the fold), double the amount to get the total measurement for that piece. Do not include areas or pattern pieces that don't add to the width or length of the finished garment, such as facings, hems, seam allowances, pockets, and overlapping edges. A pleat or bellow adds ease but may not necessarily be part of the width; consider it bonus ease to the total measurement.

Testing the Percentage of Stretch

To determine how much stretch can be used in the fit of a garment, grip a 4-in.section of crossgrain fabric and stretch it next to a ruler to see how far the fabric stretches easily. Avoid stretching it on a cut or selvage edge of the fabric. If it doubles in length, it has 100 percent stretch available, as the black nylon/Lycra in the right photo indicates. The pink is a bonded nylon Lycra, which does not stretch easily and then only an inch more than its original length. With such a stiff stretch, this fabric should be fit with very little (if any) ease subtracted from the body measurement.

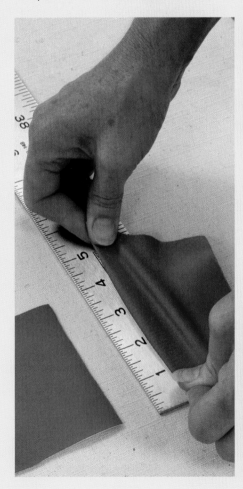

Keep the pattern measurement totals on a simple diagram. They can provide a quick reference while making alterations, and when stored with the pattern, they will be useful when using the pattern again.

Figuring Ease Amounts

This is an example of how to figure the amount of ease a pattern allows by comparing measurements.

	Pattern measure-ment (in.)	Less	Body measure-ment (in.)	Equals	Ease (in.)
Bust/chest:	49	-	38	=	11
Waist:	38	-	30	=	8
Hip/seat:	56	-	42	=	14

Next to the flat pattern measurements, write the body measurements for a comparison to find available ease. The pattern measurements are probably greater than the body measurements, and the difference is the amount of ease that is available. At this point, evaluate whether the ease is adequate for your needs. If it is, terrific! If it isn't, decide on the best course for adding (or subtracting) what is needed.

A simple way to determine what kind of ease you want in a garment is to find a similar ready-made (or previously made) garment that fits as you wish the new garment to fit (a lot can be accomplished in a dressing room during a five-minute span). Measure the garment at the key points (see "Useful Measurements" on p. 57) and use those measurements as a guide for your pattern.

Order of Pattern Alterations for Fit

The order in which to make adjustments is important to avoid backtracking and reworking an area already adjusted. First, alter measurements that will affect the width

Order for Pattern Adjustments

Here is the order in which adjustments should be made to a parka pattern:

1. Neck-to-waist length

2. Total length

3. Width around body at torso, waist, and hip (the pattern should have been purchased to match the bust/chest)

4. Shoulder

5. Sleeve length

6. Other width adjustments

The order of adjustments to pants:

1. Crotch depth, then crotch length (the crotch point adjustment affects the crotch length, see "Altering a Pattern's Crotch Length or Point") on p. 62

2. Total length

3. Waist adjustment

4. Straps/bib upper body

5. Other width adjustments

and then the length of the garment. For example the adjustment made for the crotch depth or length will affect the total length measurement, whether shorter or longer, so it should be made first. A back neck-to-waist alteration will also affect the total length of a jacket so it should be made before the back neck to total length adjustment is made.

Some design elements, such as pocket locations and color blocking, may interfere with size alterations and can be removed before altering and added back to the pattern later. Pocket markings are easy to duplicate and move. To adjust a pattern with color-blocked panels, overlap and tape the pattern pieces together after matching the seamlines. When the size adjustments have been completed, redraw the seamlines (making a new pattern piece if necessary) and add seam allowances to the new edge.

Fit adjustments should be made before adding design elements such as pockets, bellows, and flaps. Placement lines can be redrawn after size alterations have been made. Minor pattern adjustments may sometimes be taken care of at a seam or hemline. Larger sizing adjustments benefit from the slash-and-spread technique shown at right.

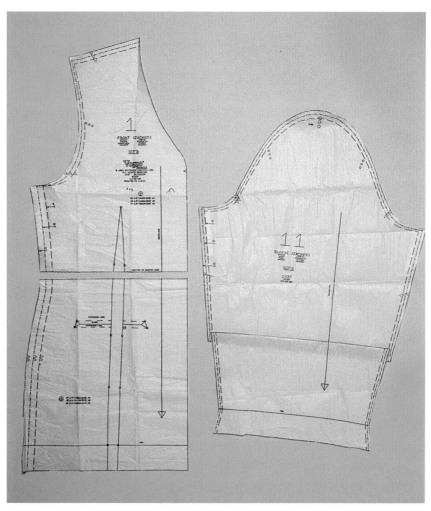

To lengthen a pattern, slash and spread as in the front pattern piece. To shorten a pattern, slash and overlap or fold out the extra as in the sleeve pattern.

> **TIP**
>
> Always double-check the amount of change and use the flat-pattern measure method while altering so you can catch errors.

Common Length Adjustments

After measuring the body and adding ease amounts as needed, alterations can be made to a pattern fairly quickly, using the order above and the slash-and-spread method shown in the photo above. Length adjustments are made by adjusting the pattern pieces in areas that are free of shaping and detailed design. (See p. 64.)

A length alteration should be made evenly front to back, on all connecting pattern pieces. If the sitting crotch depth needs an extra 1 in., it should be added both to front and back at the lengthen/shorten line. Even if the front and back crotch length need adjusting, that should be done separately, after the crotch depth is adjusted.

Altering a Pattern's Crotch Length or Point

Cycling, climbing, and skiing are examples of sports that use a longer stride and greater range of motion, creating a need for pants that move easily but aren't overly loose.

A forward crotch point (the intersection of the inseam and crotch seam) and longer back crotch seam length increases the flexibility of the leg, allowing more room for the leg to be extended forward and up. In everyday slacks the crotch point is best if positioned just out of sight when viewed from the front, but many pattern companies position them farther back, so this pattern alteration (in a less extreme forward position) can be useful for all your pants patterns.

To move the crotch point on a pattern not designed with this stride shaping, determine where the new point will be on the front pattern piece. For high stride or leg extension, position the crotch point just at or just below the front crotch curve. Use a ruler or dressmaker's curve to draw a new inseam line from the crotch point to the existing seam line above the knee. Cut the pattern on the new seam line, and move the wedge of pattern to the back pattern piece, overlapping the original inseam stitching lines. The seamline of the new back-to-front crotch curve should be smooth. If it isn't, use a dressmakers curve to smooth it out. Add seam allowances along the cut edge of the new seamline.

For even more flexibility in bringing the leg forward, extra back crotch length can be added at the top of the center back at the crotch seam and at the crotch depth shorten/lengthen line. If your pattern does not include this adjustment line, it can be drawn horizontally through the front and back pant pattern pieces midway between the lowest point of the crotch and the waist as shown in line 16 of the pant illustration on p. 64.

Above, we noted that additions and subtractions should be applied equally to the front and back pieces. This is an opportunity to break that rule. An uneven change can be made at these two points as long as the length of the matching seamline (in this case the side seam) stays the same. In the illustration, the wedge-shaped addition doesn't effect the side seamline. The amount you can add in one or both of these two places will vary with the size of the pattern. In an average adult size, 1 in. to 1½ in. at the lengthen/shorten line and 1½ in. to 2 in. at the top of the center back would be a maximum amount when both alterations are used.

When altering a pattern for better stride in superstretch pants, the crotch point can be moved to the point where the curve of the crotch ends at the front. The front crotch seam can be removed so that the center front is placed on a fold instead. This alteration is good for climbing tights. A well-shaped and placed gusset is another alternative for flexible climbing tights/pants.

Lowering Crotch Depth

An alteration I use a great deal that hasn't specifically been described in the rest of book (except as a gusset) is lowering the crotch depth. A too-short crotch measurement can be very uncomfortable and many women have this problem when buying ready-to-wear. When working with a ready-made lined garment, you will need first to open up the lining, which is usually attached at the zipper or hem.

Place one leg inside the other so that the crotch seam is continuous. Mark the new crotch length. If there is a zipper that extends low into the crotch seam, the new seamline has to make a smooth transition from that point. The new seam should be reshaped so it is only lower at the curve and *not* wider (front to back). It is critical to keep the transition smooth between the old and new seams. Keep the two layers together, pin, and stitch at the new seamline. The excess seam allowance must be cut away before there is any noticeable difference in fit. Be sure to finish the cut edges to prevent fraying or seam-seal if necessary.

Pattern Alteration for Additional Stride Ease

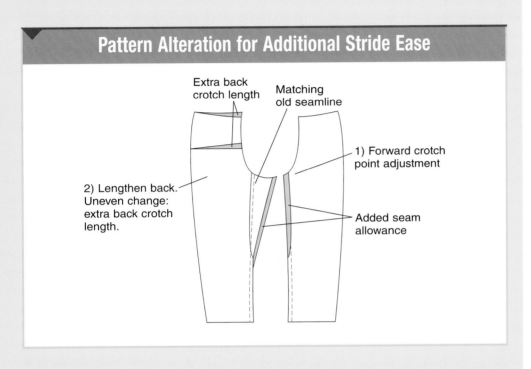

Extra back crotch length

Matching old seamline

1) Forward crotch point adjustment

2) Lengthen back. Uneven change: extra back crotch length.

Added seam allowance

Redrawing and Stitching the Crotch Curve

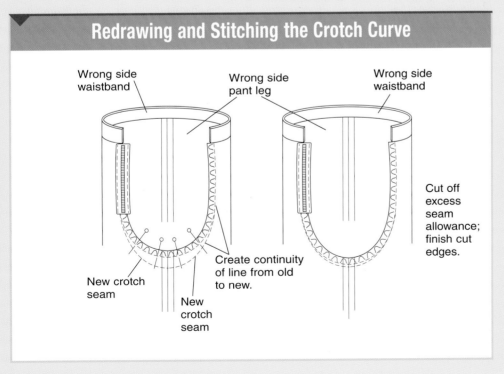

Wrong side waistband

Wrong side pant leg

Wrong side waistband

Cut off excess seam allowance; finish cut edges.

Create continuity of line from old to new.

New crotch seam

New crotch seam

Altering length

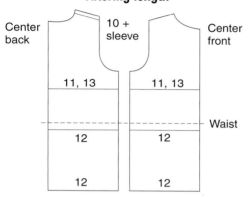

Center back

10 + sleeve

Center front

11, 13 | 11, 13

Waist

12 | 12

12 | 12

Length change should match at side seams.

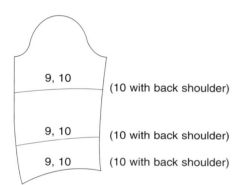

9, 10 (10 with back shoulder)

9, 10 (10 with back shoulder)

9, 10 (10 with back shoulder)

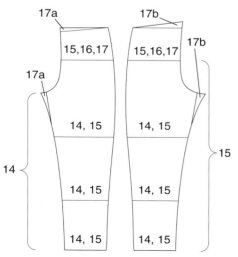

17a | 17b

15,16,17 | 15,16,17 17b

17a

14, 15 | 14, 15

14

14, 15 | 14, 15 15

14, 15 | 14, 15

Length change should match at side seams.

Altering width

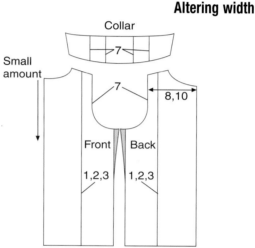

Collar

7

Small amount

7

8,10

Front | Back

1,2,3 | 1,2,3

Cut pattern to spread (make wider) or overlap (make smaller).

Small amounts

Sleeve

1, 2, 3

Must match side seam.

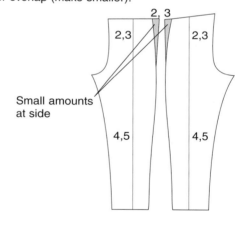

2, 3

2,3 | 2,3

Small amounts at side

4,5 | 4,5

Note: The numbers correspond to the measurements on the illustration on p. 57.

Simple Width Adjustment

The simplest way to adjust a pattern affecting the width of the body is to add or take out at the seamlines. Add or subtract evenly at front and back along the side seams, dividing the total change by four. A 1-in. adjustment on the front and back pieces at the side seamline will result in a 4-in. change. When subtracting width, keep the adjustment below the armscye to retain the sleeve shaping. When adding width using this method, the same amount must be added to the underarm as shown. The wedge-shaped additions to the sleeve can add extra flexibility for shell layers, as a gusset might. If small amounts of width are needed in the bust/chest, a gusset (see p. 136) may sometimes add all that is needed without a pattern alteration.

If your pattern needs major size adjustments, try the slash-and-spread method in which you cut apart a pattern piece and adjust the new pieces to match your measurements. (See the photo on p. 61.) Significant changes beyond these involve pattern drafting techniques that are better found in the many excellent books on this subject. When learning to fit clothing, select one method that seems the most understandable to you and stick with it. If you try to incorporate too many different fitting techniques, it can become confusing.

Finalizing Pattern Pieces for Layering

After you have made size alterations to the pattern, compare the shape of the garment with the other layers to be worn with it. A little fine-tuning of length and shape can make a garment that is more easily layered.

Slash-and-Spread Method

Keep shoulder even with highest neck edge*

width 1 (and 2 or 3)

Cutting line

length 12

Front

New cutting line

Extra width and length at side seam (add width to under sleeve)*

Uneven change, with width added to upper body and little change to lower body. Move armsyce piece up and out to add, in and down to subtract width.

*Make same change to back piece.

Note: The numbers correspond to the measurements on the illustration on p. 57.

TIP

For a quick fitting, cut out major pattern pieces with lightweight nonfusible interfacing and baste together. The mock-up garment can be tried on to make fitting adjustments before cutting out the fabric.

After sizing and other fit concerns have been altered, review your choice of design options for other pattern changes that need to be made. After fit and design changes are made, it's time to cut out the pattern.

Chapter 4

Basics for Sewing, Repairing, and Maintaining Outerwear

This chapter will give you the information you need to make any garment go together more easily and look better. You'll find tips on construction techniques, presser feet, needles, seams, closure repair, and even long-term garment maintenance. Essentially this chapter is a nuts-and-bolts reference to help you make outerwear that you'll treasure because it wasn't hard to make, it fits your body, and it has all of the features you need.

Cutting the Fabric

When you are ready to lay out your pattern, there a few things to determine about your fabric. Does it need to be washed first? Which side is the right side? Does it have a nap? How should you keep the pattern in place while cutting out a waterproof and breathable (w/p/b) fabric? How should you transfer pattern markings?

Prewash or Pretreat?

Outerwear synthetic fabrics don't need to be washed for shrinkage, but in some cases it is advisable to prewash because, as you'll find more in the Laundering and Long-Term Maintenance section below, dry cleaning can damage some laminates and be detrimental to the durable water-repellent finish (dwr) that is added for surface repellency. One reason to prewash fabric, primarily knits, is to

remove the sizing that is applied during the manufacturing process.

Some fabrics dyed to obtain very bright colors may have an excess of color, and when washed, they may bleed or "crock," causing the excess dye to stain the surrounding fabric. This was a painful lesson for me to learn when I washed a completed insulated white parka that had some dark neon pink! The colors that are the most susceptible to bleeding in just about any fabric are reds and purples.

Make sure that you really *look* at your fabric before you cut the pattern out! Even better, really *look* at your fabric before it is cut in the store. It's easy to not notice a slub or stain in the fabric until it's on the left-front upper pocket, and you'll be lucky if it's there because then all you have to do is remake the pocket! If there is a problem in the fabric, buy extra to work around it. Heck, buy extra anyway, it gives you the freedom to add more flaps, add a self-fabric edge to the lining, make mittens, whatever. Also check the wrong side of waterproof and w/p/b fabrics to make sure there is no damage to the membrane.

Right Side, Wrong Side, Nap or No

On most shell fabrics it is easy to determine which side is the right side, because most coatings are on the wrong side. Fabrics that don't have a coating on either side may work

Consider This

Color, line, and texture are easily intermingled in outerwear. This one-piece ski suit has seven different fabrics with different textures, six different colors, and a chopped up asymmetrical line. Collecting small pieces of fabrics that you like (as shown here) is a good way to get inspired to atypical and unpredictable designing.

Water Sprinkle Test

On a treated fabric, water sprinkled on it should bead up. If one side repels moisture better than the other, use it for the outside of the garment. Some fabrics with decorative laminates on the outside may not cause the water to bead up, but the water shouldn't go through the membrane, either.

equally well. Check by testing water repellency to see if one side is better.

It can be tough to determine where the coating is because there may be only a slight variation of texture to indicate a light coating. Look at the selvage edge, which may show the edge of the lamination separate from the fabric to which it is adhered. Stabilize coated/laminated fabrics with nonfusible, nonwoven medium- to heavyweight interfacings or with self-fabric.

TIP

There isn't a surefire way to tell what type or brand of coating you are looking at if it's not labeled, but if it has an opaque, white skinlike membrane that doesn't feel like plastic, it is more likely to be a Gore or Gore-Tex® type of lamination.

Some people have difficulty telling the right side of double-faced fleece fabrics. Unbonded knit fleece fabrics will have a selvage edge that rolls to the right side, while the crossgrain cut rolls to the wrong side. Other fleece and pile fabrics are usually

more obvious because one side may be a flat knit or have another fabric bonded to it, in which case it has a specific function. Use the water-drop test for these fabrics as well.

When it's absolutely necessary to interface fleece fabrics, a medium-weight nonfusible, nonwoven interfacing is the best option for thicker weights. Lightweight wicking knits, microfleece, and flatter napped fleeces can use a low-temperature fusible knit, but the edges of the interfacing should be secure in the stitching line in case the bond of the fuse is released.

Knit wicking fabrics sometimes have a variation of texture on one side versus the other. I have found that usually the softer texture is meant to go next to the body to pick up the moisture and move it away from the body. Where there doesn't seem to be a difference, use the selvage curl test for fleece to find the right side, which faces out.

When a fabric has nap, the fibers on the surface of the cloth lie in only one direction, and among outerwear fabrics, nap layout (pattern placement to accommodate directional nap) is usually only applicable to some fleeces and especially pile. Pile often has a definite direction in which the nap (pile) lies. Most often, pattern pieces are placed so that the nap lies toward the bottom of the garment. Fleece may show directional nap initially, but after a wash-and-wear or two, the direction of the nap disappears. Flat knits and wovens shouldn't need a nap layout unless they have a directional print, which is more likely in a fleece or pile as well.

Pattern Layout and Marking

When working with woven shell fabric and flat knits, lay the fabric right side up so that as the pattern is arranged on the fabric, you can recheck for any flaws. I generally prefer cutting out patterns with sharp scissors rather than a rotary cutter because there is more precision with scissors, but a rotary cutter can be useful for straight cuts on flaps, for cutting bindings, and for making fleece cord (see p. 113).

(see p. 113).

> **TIP**
>
> If you want to preserve all sizes on a multi-sized pattern, fold under the sizes not used instead of cutting them off. Clip at the inside curves to make it easier to fold pattern sections back.

You can pin patterns to all outerwear fabrics as long as the pins are in the seam allowance. Weights can be used to hold the pattern without the use of pins, but on thick fleece and pile, it's easy to distort the edges of the pattern piece as the weight sinks into the pile. Low-tack transparent tape can be used on shell fabrics with membranes to hold the pattern while cutting and as a substitute for pinning while assembling.

Thicker fabrics (like pile and fleece) will be cut more accurately if the pattern pieces marked "Cut on fold" are cut as a single layer of fabric instead. To do this, either make a full pattern or flip the pattern on the foldline when cutting out.

Seam Types and Edge Finishes

The look of professional-quality sewing is often in the stitching details. Flat seams and firm edges with neat rows of topstitching will give your work the appearance of "handcrafted" instead of smacking of "homemade."

To make the work hold up better in the long term, here are a few general stitching and sewing tips.

- Back-tack all seams and topstitching. It is amazing how quickly a seam can come loose.

- Basting, of course, does not require back-tacking and should be the longest stitch possible for easy pull out.

- When stitching corners and tight curves in a seam that will be turned (like making a flap or tab) shorten the stitch at ⅜ in. before the corner until ⅜ in. after the corner pivot.

- Trim seam allowances when possible. If the fabric being trimmed doesn't fray (coated/laminated, fleece, and knits), trim very close (1/16 in. to ⅛ in.) to the stitching line if called for. Leave seam allowance intact on fabrics that are prone to fraying, but clip the curves (perpendicular to the cut edge) and across corners. After turning to the right side, an easy-fray fabric should be topstitched very close to the seamline to catch the seam allowance in the topstitching. In addition to topstitching, you could sear the edges as well (see p. 97) or use an overlock stitch (see below).

- Clip thread ends even on inner layers, especially with light-colored fabrics. Threads may show through the fabric after the garment is finished.

- Use extra care when stitching with contrasting thread because the eye will be drawn to any irregularity in the stitching.

- Don't use Fraycheck on exposed seams. It doesn't absorb into synthetic fabric well, and may end up looking like glue or slug slime (so does liquid seam sealer on the fabric surface, by the way.)

- Clip straight into inside corners as on a zipper box (see pp. 155 and 160) so the corner will lie flat after turning.

- Stretch fabrics require stretching the fabric when stitching a straight stitch. Some may even require stretching while using a zigzag. Stretch a sample completed seam. If threads break, stretch the fabric more while stitching. If the seam ripples, don't stretch quite as much and/or make the stitch longer. Stitch length for outerwear knits in general (especially fleece and pile) should be fairly long to avoid rippling seams.

- Stitch length for coated and laminated fabrics start at a midrange and get longer. Short stitches may weaken the seam by causing a perforated paper effect and make it easier to rip.

- Work with samples of the fabric to find the results you want. If one thing doesn't work, try something else.

- "Finger-press" seams (use fingers to firmly press seams open or to one side rather than using an iron) to quickly flatten seams for stitching or seam sealing.

Standard Sewing Machine Seams

A sewing machine that provides only a few straight-stitch and zigzag variables has everything you need to sew adequate seams for just about any outerwear fabric. The chart below provides a quick look at seam options, their general stitch length and

Standard Sewing Machine Seams

Seams	Straight stitch	Straight stitch w/ topstitching	Flat-felled or false flat-felled	Triple stitch	Zigzag	Honeycomb or zigzag lapped/ butted seam	Double needle for seam and topstitch	Needle types
								Needle types: U=Universal S=Stretch M=Mocrotex/sharp D=Denim/jeans T=Topstitch/metallica
Uncoated shell (nonstretch)	(M) Also use in French seam	(M)	(M)	(L) Topstitching	Clean-finish cut edges	Not recommended	(L) Topstitching heavy fabrics	U, M
Coated/laminated shell (nonstretch). Trim seam allowances to seam-seal	(M) - (L)	(M) - (L)	(M) - (L)	Not recommended	Not recommended	Not recommended	(L) Topstitching heavy fabrics	U, M, D
Lycra knits (superstretch)	Stretch while stitching (S) - (M) two rows	Not recommended	Not recommended	(L) Heavyweight	(S) (N)	(L) (W) Heavyweight	(M) - (L) (W) Topstitching (N) Seaming	U, S
Fleece/pile and bonded knits (moderate stretch) (Slight stretch while stitching)	M) - (L) Trim seam allowance to ⅛ in.	(M) - (L)	(M) - (L)	(L) Heavyweight	(S) (N)	(L) (W) Heavyweight	(L) (W = 4mm) Topstitching (N) Seaming	U, S, T

Key:
Stitch length: (S)hort, (M)edium, (L)ong
Stitch width: (N)arrow, (A)verage, (W)ide

width settings, and the appropriate type of machine needle for the fabric. Your sewing machine's manual should also offer additional information on settings for each function, though the name given in your manual may differ from that listed here.

Simple seam/straight stitch Fabrics that are low fraying or nonfraying can be easily joined using a simple seam, trimming the seam allowances accordingly. Before sealing a simple seam, trim seam allowances and finger-press open. Stretch the fabric, front to back over the sole plate, while sewing a straight stitch in stretch fabrics. Also, in stretch fabrics, stitch a second pass 1/16 in. from the first pass to reinforce high stress areas.

French seam A variation of the straight seam is a French seam. It provides a very clean finish, useful for hiding rough edges in a single layer microfiber shell. With *wrong* sides together, stitch seam close to cut edges. Open seam and press flat. Turn seam so right sides are together with the cut edges enclosed in the seam allowance, and stitch at the seamline.

Flat-felled and false flat-felled seam A flat-felled seam is best described as the type of seam that is used on blue jeans. It is sewn with the wrong sides together at the seam line, the seam is opened flat, and one seam allowance is trimmed. The other seam

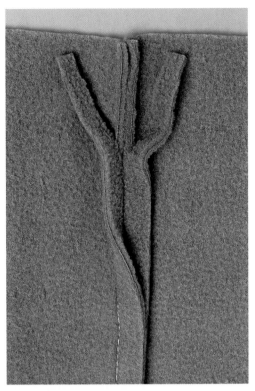

Simple seam/straight stitch (wrong side)

French seam (wrong side at top)

To make a flat-felled seam, place the pieces wrong sides together, matching at the seamline. In this example, the green top seam allowance was trimmed before stitching, but it can also be done after stitching. Stitch at the seamline. The bobbin thread of the first stitching pass will be seen on the right side of the finished seam.

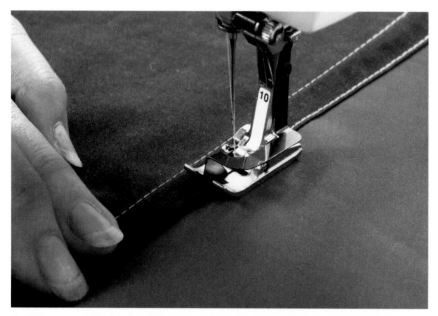

Fold the seam flat with the right side of the fabric up. Fold the cut edge of the remaining seam allowance under and topstitch to finish. The edgestitching foot shown here works well with the needle offset to the left, or use a felling foot, which will roll the edge as you go.

allowance is folded over (felled), the raw edge turned under and secured with a second pass of stitching on the right side of the fabric.

Though a true flat-felled seam is very strong, I find that a "false" or "mock" flat-felled seam has the strength I need for 98 percent of my sewing. I use it for just about any woven or moderate-stretch knit. A false flat-felled seam is easier to use when stitching on a curve and for seam sealing than a true felled seam. Stitch a standard seam using ½-in. or wider seam allowance. Trim one side of the seam allowance close to the stitching line. Open the layers of the garment flat. Fold the remaining seam allowance across the seamline on the wrong side, then edgestitch through all layers close to the seamline (on the right side).

This finish can be referred to as a topstitched seam when only one row of topstitching is used. By adding a second row of topstitching next to the seam line through all layers, the seam has the appearance of a flat felled seam and the extra strength that the additional stitching line adds.

Triple straight-stitch seam A very strong, flexible seam, the triple straight stitch is available on many midrange machines. An excellent stretch seam for firm and heavy Lycra fabrics such as bonded fabrics and wool/nylon/Lycra blended ski-pant fabric. The stitch should be as long as possible for the best seam flexibility.

Zigzag and other stretch seams Once width is added to a stitch, its ability to stretch increases. Depending on the fabric and type of seam, the stitch may be too stiff, the seam may ripple, or the fabric may not return to its original shape. A zigzag-stitched seam doesn't lie very flat when seen from the right

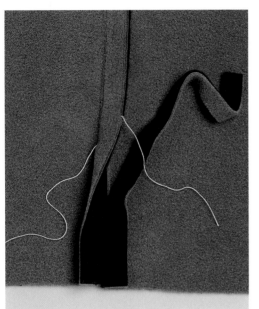

False flat-felled seam (wrong side)

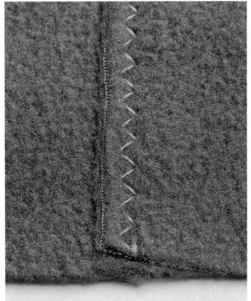

Lapped seam

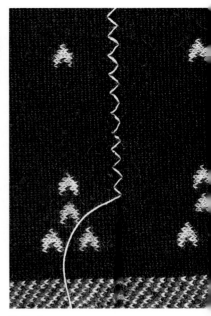

Butted seam

side, but when sewing lightweight Lycra fabrics or meshes, it is the best alternative to an overlock (below) to avoid rippling in the seam. Use it for hems and edge finishes also.

A lapped or butted seam using a zigzag, honeycomb, or similar stitch is useful for seaming neoprene, bonded stretch fabrics, and fleece (nonfraying, stretchy, and thick). A ⅛-in. seam allowance is all that is needed for a lapped seam, and no seam allowance is needed for a butted seam. To sew a lapped seam, the cut edges of the fabric are placed with the edges overlapping ¼ in. and stitched with a zigzag or honeycomb stitch. An edge-stitching foot will aid in making a butted seam; The cut edges are placed side by side, and the two edges are pushed toward the center guide while stitching.

Serger/Overlock Seams

Don't mistake the "overlock" stitches offered on a standard sewing machine as an effective substitute for the real thing. Though not required for good results, an overlock

machine can simplify the sewing process and provide a more professional finish. Two areas where an overlock can be particularly effective are sewing stretch seams and sewing fabrics that need a clean-finished edge to avoid fraying. The additional feature of a differential feed is particularly useful when sewing bulky fabrics like fleece and pile or bonded knits. The differential feed allows the feed dogs to feed more evenly. The feed dogs walk (or run) independently with a left, right, left, right motion.

Overlock seams for shell fabrics When seaming fabrics that tend to fray, a four- or five-thread overlock stitch at the widest settings is adequate, although I often add topstitching to the seam, with the seam allowance folded under. The narrower two- or three-thread overlock can be used to clean-finish the cut edges of garment pieces before assembly.

Serger (Overlock) Seams

Seams	Two- or three-thread flatlock with securing stitch	Three-thread overlock	Four- or five-thread overlock	Coverstitch

Uncoated shell (nonstretch)	Not recommended	Clean-finish cut edges (M) (W)	(M) (W)	Not recommended
Coated/laminated shell (nonstretch)	Not recommended	Not recommended	Not recommended	Not recommended
Lycra knits (superstretch)	(M) (W)	(M) (A)	Not recommended	(M) - (L) (A) - (W)
Fleece/pile and bonded knits (moderate stretch)	(M) (W) Dif.: 1 - 2	(M) - (L) (W) Dif.: 1 - 2	(M) - (L) (W) Dif.: 1 - 2	(L) (W) Dif.: 1 - 2

Dif. = Differential feed. See the key on p. 70.

Improve a flatlock seam by keeping the cut edges of the fabric slightly away from the knife. This will allow bulky fabrics to lie flatter within the stitching. A straight stitch through the center of the finished flatlock will strengthen the seam (stretch the seam slightly while sewing the straight stitch) and minimize snags in the thread.

Stretch overlock seams Most sergers can be set for a two- or three-thread flatlock. These seams are flat and flexible with no seam allowances. Check the manual for tension settings, but the basic configuration is to have one needle thread, with its thread tension set at or close to the loosest possible setting. To reduce the fabric bulk within the stitch, place the wrong sides of the fabric together with the edges of the fabric slightly inside of the cutting blade.

After stitching, the two layers are folded flat as shown in the photo at left. For a more secure seam, stitch through the center of the seam with a straight stitch, using a presser foot that doesn't have a thread slot at the front to avoid snagging a thread (such as a zigzag foot with a side slot). For superstretch fabrics, a three-thread overlock seam provides the most secure stitch with the best stretch. A four-thread has less stretch but is more secure, perfect for moderate-stretch knits.

The newest feature in overlock machines is the coverstitch. It can be used as a seam, but more often it is used as a seam-finishing

method or an edge finish (see below). As a
seam finish, a standard seam may be used,
then "topstitched" with the coverstitch.
The threads that cover the bottom of the
stitch enclose the seam allowances for a flat,
stretchy finish on the inside of the garment.
Several steps are involved to change from
an overlock to the coverstitch function, so
plan the construction process ahead to
avoid going through the switchover more
than once.

Edge/Hem Finishes

A telltale sign of quality often comes from a
garment's neat-looking edge or hem. When
sewing outerwear, it's beneficial to have a
variety of edge finishes to choose from. A
hand-stitched hem is not an option!

A simple straight-stitched hem is clean
and to the point but should be used primarily for shell fabrics and heavier weight
knits. A double needle provides the best
alternative for straight stitching with stretch
fabrics in all weights, using a long stitch setting with a wide needle (4mm). Keep in
mind that the bobbin side of a double-
needle stitch is a zigzag. Zigzag or blind-
hem stitches can also be used for a flexible
edge in superstretch fabrics. The honeycomb
stitch (or a similar stitch) finishes mid- to

A flatlock stitch is ideal when using bonded stretch fabrics, such as shown in this
Willamette Racing Suit (Green Pepper). The flatlock has less bulk for better comfort
and streamlined fit. The garment edges have been finished with a three-thread overlock instead of a hem, and the zipper was easily installed under the serged edge
with a couple of rows of topstitching.

heavyweight fleeces very nicely. The coverstitch is the optimum in edges on knits.
Although some recommend its use for
finishing woven shell fabrics, I feel it's
unnecessary.

Bindings are a favorite of mine for edges.
Using bias from a complementary woven
fabric or firm knit fabric as binding, one can
finish shell fabrics with stitch-in-the-ditch

Alternatives for Hem and Edge Finishes

	Straight stitch	Double needle	Coverstitch	Stitch-in-the-ditch binding	Topstitched or double binding
Shell (nonstretch)	(M)	(M) - (L) (A) - (W) Mid - heavyweights	Not recommended	(M) with nonfraying bias binding	(M) with bias binding
Stretch*	Stretch while stitching (L) Heavy weights	(M) - (L) (W = 4mm)	(M) - (L) (A) - (W) Dif.: 1 - 2	Stretch while stitching	(M) - (L) Use crossgrain knit binding. See p. 95 for gathered-on stretch binding.

*Other options not shown: zigzag, blind-hem, honeycomb stitch, and mock rib. See the key on p. 70.

The best stretch hem for knits, along with a coverstitch, is a double-needle hem. With a single shank, the double needle works in standard home machines that have a zigzag stitch. To avoid a rippled hemline, keep the stitch length medium-long to long.

(see the bottom photo on p. 95), double binding (see Glossary on p. 180), or a standard topstitched binding. Binding works very well on moderate-stretch knits, especially mid- to heavyweight fleece and pile, but use a crossgrain-cut knit fabric, nylon/Lycra, or a microfleece. A mock rib finished with fleece cord is also an excellent way to finish a light- to medium-weight fleece edge (see p. 114).

Seam Sealing

For many years, the advantage of buying a waterproof garment rather than making it has been factory seam sealing. The long drying time, the smell, and sometimes the mess of home liquid alternatives were enough to deter many people from making their own. Fortunately, times have changed and there are better alternatives. There is a possibility in the near future of a thread that will create a self-sealing seam! (I've heard rumors.) Look for it as a way to greatly simplify the sealing process.

Seam Sealing with Liquid Sealer

Liquid seam sealers are still a good alternative for general applications, resealing, large areas, or hard-to-get-to areas. Liquid sealers have been improved so that cracking is not as bad as it once was. Some liquid types are specific to certain fabrics (Aqua Seal is recommended for neoprene) and functions, so check the label for the use. General instructions usually list cleaning the area with a pretreatment or isopropyl alcohol, then applying the sealer. Two application methods are shown in the photos at lower right.

Work in a well-ventilated area because of fumes. Apply liquid seam sealer to the partially complete garment before the lining is closed. Hang the garment inside out and avoid having the sealed areas come in contact with other areas of the garment, as they will stick together. It may take several hours to dry.

Seam Sealing with Tape

Applying seam tape is process-oriented, like pressing a cotton shirt as you make it. As you finish each seam, seal it before you move on to the next process. The tool that makes this process work is the Teflon pressing sheet (available in the notions area of most fabric stores) or a Teflon iron slipper. To make the pressing easier, have on hand a sleeve pressing board, pressing ham, and a fabric glue stick.

Depending on the seam tape that is available, it may be clear, white, or have a tricot backing on one side (used for three-layer Gore-Tex® that has a finished backing on the inside). Tapes are usually about ⅞ in. wide, but on occasion, you may find wider tapes. I found a 3-in. wide roll that I find handy for sealing drawcord casings.

Identify the adhesive side, which is usually the shinier side. If you can't tell, place the end of the tape between two scraps of fabric and press to see which side adheres. I use a wool setting when seam-sealing, but irons aren't all the same. Set your temperature between synthetic and silk to start. If the

Some of the tools for sealing seams include, from the left: Teflon pressing sheet, tube-style liquid sealers with applicator brush, liquid sealers in bottles with sponge-tip applicators, and seam-sealing tape on a roll.

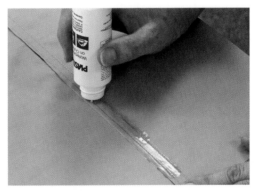

Application of liquid seam sealer with a sponge-tip applicator.

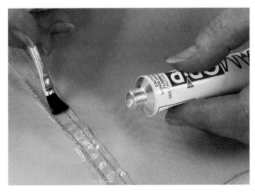

Application of liquid seam sealer with a brush.

glue on the tape doesn't adhere within five seconds, increase the temperature gradually until it does. There is a thin melted line at the edge of the tape when it is adhered.

A padded sleeve board works well for seam sealing. The size and shape allow the garment to slide easily over it and the extra folds of the garment fall out of the way while pressing. The curved end can be used when sealing curves like the neckline and armscye.

Straight seams are very easy to seam-seal:

1 Trim any excess seam allowance so the tape will adhere close to the stitching lines. Flat seams are best when using seam-sealing tape. Examples are flat-felled, false flat-felled, or a basic seam with $\frac{1}{4}$-in. seam allowances (pressed open with a low-temperature iron or finger-pressed).

2 Place the tape, adhesive side down, onto the wrong side of the seam, centering it

so that the tape is sealed $\frac{1}{16}$ in. to $\frac{1}{8}$ in. on either side of the seam and seam allowances (the seam and seam allowances should be completely covered by the tape). Hold the end of the tape down, because it tends to curl as the heated iron comes close.

3 With the pressing sheet on top, press the entire seam, using a press-and-lift action rather than sliding the iron. Don't pull the tape while pressing.

4 Once the tape is anchored along the length of the seam, go over it again, using normal pressing and the Teflon pressing sheet, until all the tape is completely adhered. If the tape doesn't appear to be sticking, it may be upside down. Peel it off the pressing sheet and turn it over. If it's positioned correctly, try a higher temperature.

A shaped Teflon slipper can be put on the iron and used on its own or in conjunction with the pressing sheet, as when spot-sealing along the tape or the trough next to the seam ridge. Use a press-and-lift action, especially when using the slipper on its own. The pressing sheet and slipper are less important on fabrics with a three-layer lamination (with a tricot or lining layer already adhered to the exposed membrane). The seam-sealing tape for them has a light fabric as a backing.

For sealing curves like armscyes and necklines:

1 Place the garment so the seam curves to one side completely. This is where a pressing ham or the padded end of a sleeve board will come in handy.

2 Make short clips in the edge of the sealing tape for more curve.

TIP

For small detail areas or curves, the Clover Mini-Iron, which has a 1-in. by 1$\frac{1}{4}$-in. pressing plate, makes pressing and seam-sealing easier.

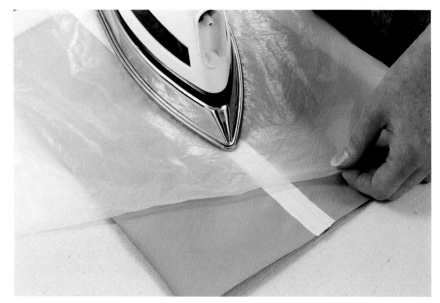

Applying seam-sealing tape on a straight seam using a Teflon presser sheet. A Teflon iron "slipper" is also useful.

3 Use the tip of the iron (or Mini-Iron) or a small spot of glue from a fabric glue stick to spot-tack the tape to the curve before pressing.

4 Seal one side of the curve.

5 Turn the curve the opposite direction and seal the other side.

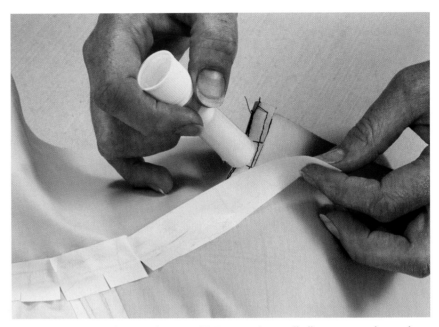

When sealing a deeply curved seam with tape, make small clips on one edge and use a fabric glue stick to hold the tape in place before pressing.

> **T I P**
>
> For a less-expensive substitute for fabric-backed seam tape, try using Ultrahold Heat'n'Bond or Steam-a-Seam (The Warm Co.) adhered to the laminate side of a lightweight fabric with a Teflon membrane. Cut it in strips on the grain of the fabric (the direction with the least amount of stretch) and peel off the paper backing. The Heat'n'Bond is not meant to be sewn through and will gum up the machine needle, so do all the seam-sealing last. Test first; it doesn't work in all cases.

If the tape is adhered in error, don't pull it away from the laminate as the laminate may pull off with it. Cut off any loose ends and seal the remaining edges. If it is necessary to take out a seam that has been tape-sealed, you will probably have to cut through or cut off the seam.

Sewing Techniques

Many custom sewers avoid working with outerwear fabrics because they assume the fabrics are difficult to handle. But with a little information and a tool or two, these fabrics can become favorites.

When pressing a curve, press one side, then turn the curve the other direction to press and seal the remaining side.

A pressing ham or the end of a sleeve board facilitates many narrow and curved seam-sealing processes.

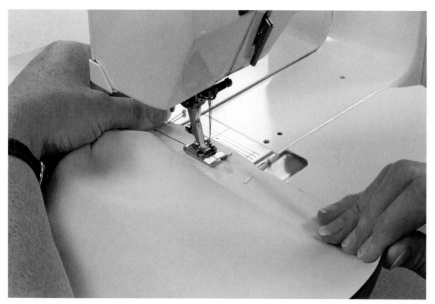

As with most outerwear fabrics, holding the fabric taut across the throat plate may take care of many laminated/coated fabric feeding problems. Urethane coatings will probably need a special foot to aid the fabric in feeding through the machine.

Taming Difficult-to-Sew Fabrics

Sliding Slip-and-slide fabrics like taffetas and satins can slide around while stitching. Pin the layers in the seam allowances and hold the fabric firmly over the machine's throat plate, front to back, while stitching. A glue stick or basting tapes like Washaway Wonder tape or Steam-a-Seam fusible tape may be helpful on occasion.

Fraying Fraying can often be taken care of by searing the fabric edge (see p. 98). Use a hot tool or candle flame to sear fabrics and synthetic cord, tape, and webbing. I also keep a cigarette lighter in my sewing room for quick searing on cord ends.

Elastics The weight and stiffness of a fabric greatly affects how much elasticity remains after the elastic is sewn in place. Start with a firm elastic with good return and minimize the amount of stitching in the elastic. The more stitching, the more the elastic will stretch out of shape.

Laminates/coating Stitching on coated and laminated surfaces can cause the presser foot to grip the fabric, creating an uneven feed. This doesn't seem as big of a problem with Teflon laminates like Gore-Tex®, which can usually be sewn by simply holding the fabric firmly across the throat plate. Urethane coatings, which often appear shiny or simply feel more like plastic, grip the presser foot more easily. Some presser feet that might help are a rolling presser foot, a walking foot, a Teflon foot, or a foot with adhesive-backed Teflon applied on the contact area. As a quick fix, tape the contact area on the bottom of a regular presser foot with dull finish Scotch tape or cover the stitching with a strip of toilet paper that can easily be removed after stitching.

When cutting coated/laminated fabrics, cut as true as possible to the grain indicated on the pattern. It will make shaping from a straight to a curve much more accurate.

Easing Easing in stiff and thick fabrics at sleeve caps or other shaped areas is difficult. Remember to keep the side that needs to be eased (the longer side) on the bed of the machine while stitching. If the two pieces are shaped differently, such as an outside curve to a straight piece, put the curved piece on the bed of the machine and, with your hand under the top straight piece, guide the curve into the stitching line. Clip inside curves to the stitching line for matching to straight edges (as in the collar/neckline).

Working with Insulation and Batting
Though there is a wide variety of insulative bats available, the process of sewing them is relatively the same. The main variable in constructing a garment is whether or not to

Down

To insulate with down, you need to create chambers to contain the down fibers for even heat retention. Most often channels are stitched through the two layers of fabric. For arctic wear, a more consistent warmth is obtained by sewing baffles (walls) between the inner and outer layer so that loft is maintained throughout. Downproof fabric is needed to prevent the down from bearding through.

Working with down is somewhat specialized because of the need to manage the down (which easily floats away on a sigh) and to distribute it evenly throughout the garment. If you would like to work with down and can find the necessary quantities—it is not easily available—try small projects first. When filling the channels or baffles, I suggest confining yourself to a small area, such as a shower stall or bathtub.

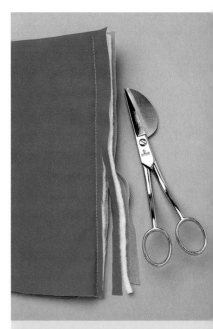

use quilting lines. The basic instructions for interlining with insulation is much the same as using interfacing:

1. Cut the insulation pieces the same as the garment or garment-lining pattern pieces.

2. Baste insulation to the wrong side of the shell or lining pieces within the seam allowance to avoid making holes in the piece.

3. Trim the excess batting from the seam allowance, and treat as one piece when assembling.

Considerations for using insulation

- When using insulation in a w/p/b garment, attach the insulation to the wrong side of the lining pieces so that the shell can be seam-sealed.

- If the shell has a lot of pieces, insulate the lining, which is usually made of larger pieces. Prequilted shell/lining insulated fabrics are sometimes available, and pattern pieces can be cut all in one. Be sure

that the fabric and insulation quality is appropriate for use in outerwear.

- Stretch fabrics should be insulated with stretch insulation (Flex, stretch fleece, or stretch needlepunch).

Stitching

- If the insulation is not secured with its own quilting lines (as on the Thinsulate samples shown in the photo on p. 24), garment pieces should be quilted to the insulation at intervals indicated on the chart on p. 22.

- Make sure that any scrim or remay is between the bat and the outer shell fabric to prevent fibers from "bearding."

- If possible, stitch basting and quilting lines in the same direction, from one side of the pattern piece to the other.

- Appliqué/pelican scissors are very useful for trimming batting from seam allowances. Or, on a rotary mat, fold back the top fabric of the seam allowance with a clear ruler so that the batting seam

allowance can be trimmed using the rotary cutter.

- Loosen the upper thread tension if possible to prevent insulation from being too compacted at the quilting lines.

- Compacting the insulation in front of the presser foot with your fingers, using a "stilletto" or other sewing pick can help thick layers feed more easily.

Closure Installation and Repair

Often the first things to give out on a piece of outerwear are the zippers or snaps. If you can install and repair them yourself, you may be able to save your favorite parka from the trash can, or refurbish that great pair of ski bibs you found at the thrift store.

Zippers

I used to refer to zippers as a necessary evil. As I've learned how to make repairs and size adjustments to zippers neatly, they seem less an instrument of evil and actually more fun because I can mold them to my will.

Perfectly matching zipper and fabric colors is almost impossible to do in all but the most basic colors. If you find the perfect color in a zipper that is too long, buy as many as are needed for the project and then alter them as required (as shown below). If a separating zipper is needed, though, you must buy one that has the right separating configuration. When cutting off zippers, save the stops and sliders, which can be added to any excess zipper chain to make additional zippers. Additional sliders and stops may have to be silver or gold tone rather than matching the color of the zipper.

If you are lucky enough to find zippers in the correct length, you still need to double-

Zipper Terminology

Understanding the parts of a zipper will help you get the zipper you need and repair some zippers that are still sewn into a garment.

Zipper slider (or pull) The part that slides up and down the teeth (or coil) to open and close the zipper. The size of the pull and teeth are often printed on the back with a letter indicating style. Use this number to order replacement pulls. To replace a damaged slider, it must match the brand, size, and style of tooth or coil. Reversible sliders are also available, with tabs on the front and back or a single tab that goes over the top.

Slider or pull tab The tab attached to the pull for grasping to operate the zipper. For pockets, use a dangling tab if possible. Extenders are available for this as well.

Bottom separator Molded into the bottom of the zipper chain during manufacturing. If damaged, that side of the zipper must be replaced.

Bottom slider or pull Refers to a slider that comes at the bottom of a two-way separating zipper. It will separate when both pulls are completely at the bottom. I've heard many people say they don't like this type of zipper because it is more difficult to operate. The pulls must be all the way to the bottom to zip up. Replacement pulls must match brand, size, and style to work.

Top stop The part clamped to the zipper tape on either side to stop the slider from coming off. When replacing stops, be sure the stop is large enough, in the correct position, and clamped firmly in place.

Bottom stop A staplelike stop that straddles the zipper teeth to create a closed end on a nonseparating zipper.

Teeth or coil The interlocking parts of a zipper. Tooth-style zippers are usually molded and clamped over the inner roll of the zipper tape. Coil zippers have continuous coils of teeth that are connected to each other, with the zipper tape woven around the coil. Coil zippers are more flexible than tooth zippers. Talon tooth-style zippers are a cross between the two, with molded teeth on a continuous cord and the zipper tape woven around the connecting cord. The teeth and coil of a zipper chain are available in various sizes. The most common size in outerwear is a #5 tooth. Smaller sizes, like #3 and #4, may also be used, and #8 and #10, which are very large, are best for only the heaviest applications. The slider must match the size of the tooth/coil and should usually be the same brand (there are some crossovers; see zipper part suppliers in Resources on p. 182). To determine the size of an existing zipper tooth or coil, measure the width of the zipper when closed. Examples of a few types and their widths are #5 coil = ¼ in., #5 tooth = ³⁄₁₆ in., #8 coil = ⁵⁄₁₆ in., #10 coil = ⁷⁄₁₆ in., and #10 tooth = ⅜ in.

Zipper tape The woven polyester cloth tape to which the zipper teeth or coil is attached. It should never be trimmed with scissors because it frays easily. If it is necessary to cut the ends, use pinking shears. Fold excess tape ends into the seam when stitching in place.

Zipper chain Continuous zipper material. It can be purchased without hardware and made into nonseparating zipper units by adding sliders and stops. Use zipper chain to make a center-opening zipper with two pulls.

Slide path Refers to the area next to the teeth or coil on the tape. It should not be obstructed by stitching so that the slide operates easily. (This term may be found in this book only.)

Separating zipper A zipper that separates at the bottom when unzipped, such as in a front-closing jacket. Can be found as one-way separating (one pull) or two-way separating (two pulls). The extra pull can zip open from the bottom for ventilation while the upper part of the zipper is closed.

Nonseparating zipper A zipper that does not separate at the bottom when unzipped.

Anatomy of a Zipper

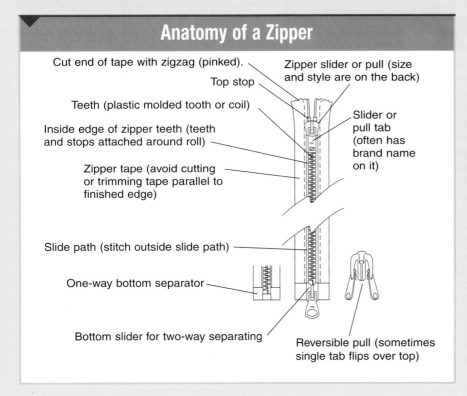

Cut end of tape with zigzag (pinked).

Top stop

Teeth (plastic molded tooth or coil)

Inside edge of zipper teeth (teeth and stops attached around roll)

Zipper tape (avoid cutting or trimming tape parallel to finished edge)

Slide path (stitch outside slide path)

One-way bottom separator

Bottom slider for two-way separating

Zipper slider or pull (size and style are on the back)

Slider or pull tab (often has brand name on it)

Reversible pull (sometimes single tab flips over top)

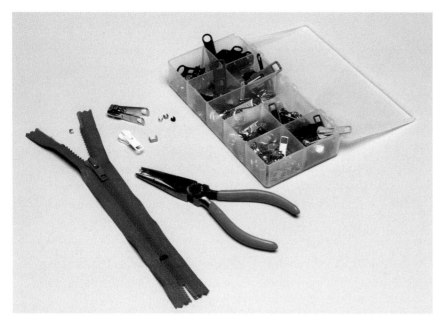

Using needle-nose pliers, wire cutters, and purchased stops, a zipper can be altered to any shorter length and damaged pulls can be replaced. This zipper shows teeth removed at the top, a new stop on the left, and a new bottom stop added before extra teeth below it will be removed. A brass reversible zipper pull is shown at left/center top.

Shorten any zipper at the top by folding out excess length at a 45-degree angle into the seam line. Bottom stops can be made with a bar tack or a folded rectangle of fabric stitched across the desired end of the zipper. The zipper at left is depicted right sides up to show the folded-out excess, but in most applications it would be right sides together with the fabric.

check the measurement because a 22-in. zipper may actually be 22½ in. from stop to stop. Pocket zippers are often off the measurement by ¼ in. or so. The garment should be checked to see if there is enough room for that extra bit. The zipper may need to be altered or the length of the zipper box be adjusted to accommodate it.

Shortening zippers With purchased metal zipper stops (available individually and in zipper repair kits), zippers can be adjusted to any length. Zipper sliders/pulls are also available separately or in a kit.

The easiest ways to shorten a nonseparating zipper as you're stitching it in place are to either replace the bottom stop by sewing a bar tack across the zipper at the desired length, or by stitching a folded piece of fabric, thin webbing, or nylon tape across the coil. When trimming off the excess zipper length, leave an extra ¾ in. to stitch into when installing the zipper. To shorten a separating zipper without using a top stop, fold out the excess zipper tape/chain across the seam allowance while stitching the zipper in place. Stitch carefully between zipper teeth to avoid a broken needle as shown in the photo at left. Cut off the excess zipper tape 1 in. past the stitching.

To shorten a zipper using a metal stop, first remove the factory-installed stop at the end of the zipper. Then:

1 If you are shortening a zipper significantly, mark the correct length and then begin removing five or six teeth above the mark.

2 Use wire cutters to cut through plastic stops and molded teeth. Heavy scissors will cut through coil only (don't use your sewing scissors). Cut only the part of the tooth, coil, or stop that extends beyond the edge of the tape. If the zipper tape is cut, it will fray, which may ruin the zipper.

3 After the protruding part of the teeth is removed, turn the wire cutters parallel to the tape to pinch off the top or bottom of the remainder of the tooth. Metal stops are cut and pried off, similar to what is shown in the bottom photo.

4 For coil zippers, use a pair of needle-nose pliers to clean up the tape by pulling excess bits of plastic away with the pliers.

5 After removing the teeth/top stops, install a new slider if necessary (see below), and pinch on new stops just above the last teeth. Cut off excess tape and teeth using pinking shears or clipping in a zigzag pattern. Apply the new metal top stop over the roll on the inside edge of the zipper using needle-nose pliers. Attach it from the inside edge of the tape, then turn the zipper around and press the back edge firmly around the inside roll.

Slider replacement If a new slider is needed for a separating zipper, pull off the old one and slide the new one on before putting the new top stops on. You can change a regular

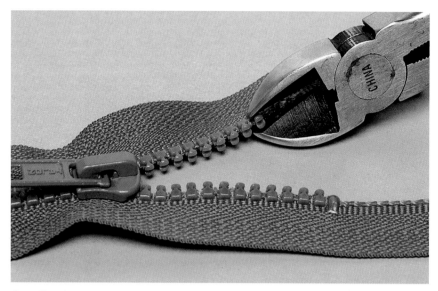

Cut off ends of teeth. Avoid clipping into the zipper tape, which causes fraying and may ruin the zipper.

Cut parallel across top of individual teeth, then pick excess teeth out of the zipper tape with needle-nose pliers.

zipper to a reversible zipper by changing the slider.

When replacing a slider on a nonseparating zipper, I prefer to cut through the bottom stop. I find it is easier to get the slider on from the bottom and pull it in place, rather than push it on backward from the

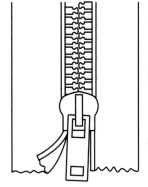

Replacing a Nonseparating Slider from the Bottom

1. Remove bottom stop and old slider.

2. Pull the slider on one side at a time to where the teeth start.

3. When the bottom of the tape is even, grasp both sides of the tape and pull the slider in place.

top (which can be done with closed teeth). Cut through the bottom stop with wire cutters and remove it just as you would a top stop. If it is metal, it can be bent backward to expose the tines and pried out of the tape. After the stop is removed, pull off the old slider. The tape will be separated. Pull the new slider on one side of the tape to where the teeth start, then insert the other side until the two sides are even. Grasp the ends of the tape firmly in one hand, the slider tab in the other, and pull the new tab on.

To complete the repair, add a new bottom stop. The metal stop looks like a staple and is pushed through the zipper tapes on either side just below the last tooth or just over it. The tines on the stop should be over the inside roll of the zipper tape. Use needle-nose pliers to push the stop through the tape with the top of the pliers over the stop and the bottom of the pliers under the zipper and between the area where the tines will come through the tape. After the stop is in place, bend the tines on the back to the center with the pliers.

Replace or repair? When deciding whether to replace or repair a zipper, determine if you can replace a stop or pull as discussed above and if you can find the right size and style of the replacement part. If the zipper teeth or coil are still intact, you only need to replace the pull (and new top stop) to have a functioning zipper. You can also take apart another zipper for parts if it is the right size or style.

If teeth or coil are damaged, you will have to replace the zipper. If only one side is damaged, and if it is possible to match the same size and style, then only one side of the zipper has to be replaced. This is also true of damage to the separating area, though often both sides are simply worn out and should be replaced.

Grommets and Eyelets

Grommets and eyelets are terms that are often used interchangeably, but for description here, grommets have two pieces: one piece with a shank and another that is a washer placed around the shank before the grommet is set. Eyelets, like those used on shoes, are one piece of metal with a scored shank that curls to the wrong side of the fabric when set. Eyelets are not as durable and should mainly be used for low-stress areas and small-diameter cording.

Snaps

Snaps have a great range of types. The prong-style, sometimes called gripper snaps or jersey-style snaps, are easily available in fabric stores with a good notions supply. In the largest sizes and longest tooth most commonly found, they are suitable only for single-layer fleece applications or lighter. In thicker fabric layers, there isn't enough to hold them in place.

Spring snaps (called anorak-style by Prym) have become much more available in the past few years and are a good in-between size. The size and durability of this snap is very good for most outerwear except for the most heavy-duty applications.

For the best durability and firm snap pressure (also called "snap action"), the heavy-duty or durable dot snaps are the universal choice. Spring snaps and heavy-duty snaps are the most practical for all but the lightest weights of outerwear. They require cutting a hole in the fabric because the snap shank goes through the fabric. Both types consist of a cap with a shank (metallic or colored-enamel caps) that attaches to a socket (female part) and a post back that attaches to the stud (male part). Reversible snaps can be made by using a cap to attach the stud.

Structural support for hardware To avoid having a lightweight or stretch fabric rip or stretch away from a snap shank, use a square of a nonwoven interfacing (or other stable fabric) to reinforce the snap area. The addition of free-motion stitching in circles (see

At left, grommets with shanks in two sizes and flat washers to finish the application. The prong-style snaps (second from left, also called gripper or jersey) show the socket piece in front, stud in middle, and gripper rings and caps at back; the heavy-duty snap (third from left, also called durable dot) and the parallel spring style snap (at right, also called anorak style) have the post pieces in front, studs, sockets, and then caps in back.

the photo at left on p. 104) around the hole will further reinforce knits.

A leather punch can be used to cut a hole for the snap, especially when reinforcing with a darning stitch (prong style snaps do not require a precut hole), but small clips can be used when working in only one or two layers as shown in the top right photo on p. 88. Make the hole smaller than the shank of the snap so the snap isn't loose in the hole.

General snap application To attach a snap to a pocket and flap:

1 Mark the snap location on the connecting layers.

2 Make tiny clips with and against the grain.

3 Apply the cap and socket to the flap.

4 Apply the post and stud to the pocket.

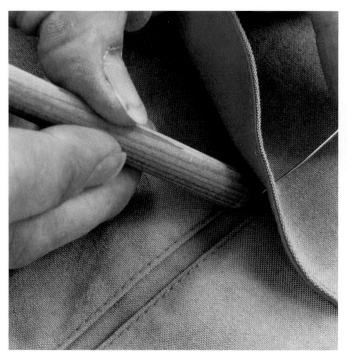

After reinforcing if necessary, mark the snap location using a pin through the outer layer and marker or chalk.

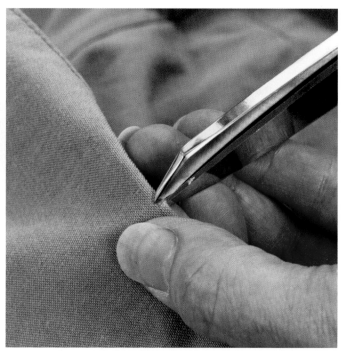

Use a hole punch or small clips on the grain and crossgrain to make a hole for the snap. The opening should be smaller than the post of the snap, so that the post is tight in the opening.

Apply the stud of a spring-style snap.

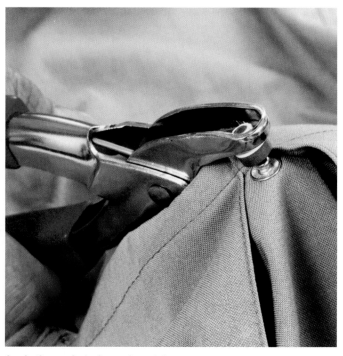

Apply the socket of a spring-style snap.

Removing hardware It's sometimes necessary to remove a snap because it's damaged or in the wrong place. Wear safety glasses. You may be able to remove a snap that isn't set well by using two sets of needle-nose pliers and grasping both sides by the edge of the snap part and pulling them away from each other. This is more often possible with prong-style snaps, which can also be removed by using a thin screwdriver between the parts and turning to pry them loose.

With post-style snaps, it is usually necessary to bend or pinch the inner piece—socket or stud—up away from the fabric to expose the shank. This may require completely mangling the part, but so be it, as long as you don't harm the garment underneath. Electrician's pliers are wide enough to get a grip on the edge of the part and do a good job for this.

After exposing the shank, slide the electrician's pliers or heavy-duty wire cutters under the bent part and cut through the shank. The two pieces should come apart with a little bending of the sharp edges. If the fabric underneath has been harmed or the opening stretched out too far, reinforce the area with a small patch before applying another snap.

Grommet or eyelet removal can be approached similarly by bending both sides up away from the fabric and cutting through the shank. A single-sided eyelet may only need to have the back side squeezed together to remove.

To remove a snap, bend it up and away from the fabric with a pair of pliers.

Use the cutting edge of the pliers to cut through the snap shank.

Laundering and Long-Term Maintenance

Now that you have a good product from your investment of time and money, good care and maintenance are what stand between you and another round of investing more time and money (or lots more money.) This isn't the hard part, because the hard part is over. Treat these durable garments with some respect for what they do for you.

Cleaning

Almost every outerwear garment and fabric described here should be washed in a washing machine and dried in a dryer. One exception is the wool-blend fabric used in ski pants. Even it can be gently machine-washed in cold water with Woolite and hung until it is almost dry (finish off in a tumble dryer with no heat.) Other varieties of insulated, w/p/b, and down garments should be washed with mild soap or one of the specialty formulas as in the photo above to maintain the best water repellency, then tumbled dry on medium heat. Water-repellent treatments are reinforced in the warmth of the dryer and down particulates fluff to get the best loft.

After I wrote an article about down comforters, a furor arose about my suggestion to wash the comforter in mild soap and warm water. Many people wrote in appalled at the idea. However, my source at the American Down Association had assured me of the appropriateness of this method. After all, we are taking about *water fowl!* The important factor for washing a down article is not to wash it too often, and to use a mild soap like Ivory or a special down detergent such as Nikwax Loft Down Wash. Just shaking and

Specialty soaps for outerwear and gear.

airing out the garment, especially in sunlight, will also help keep it lofty and clean.

Coated/laminated fabrics may need to be spun dry more than once to remove the most moisture.

Fleece garments are best turned inside out in the washer and dryer to minimize agitation and the "worn" look (unless that's your intent). For ready-to-wear, it is best to follow the manufacturer's instructions; however, when purchasing an outerwear garment, it should be a concern if the label instructs dry clean only. Some reports indicate that garments that were dry-cleaned were less effective in the long run: They lost their water repellency and had to be retreated. Also, many microfilm insulations, laminates, and coatings are damaged by dry cleaning.

Dry down articles at a medium (not hot) temperature until they are completely dry. A clean tennis shoe or a ring product can be added to the dryer to aid in fluffing the particles. When dry cleaning, be sure that a mild petroleum-based product (such as Stoddard's) is used, which is preferable to ordinary commercial fluids that destroy the loft.

Reapplying Water-Repellent Finishes or Coatings

When moisture no longer beads up on the fabric surface, it's time to reapply water repellent. The items shown in the photo at right are only some of the products specifically designed for use on outerwear. They are applied either directly or in the washing machine followed by a warm dryer. The garment should be clean before treating to get the best results.

Revitalizing Fleece

Some wouldn't dream of trying to make worn fleece look new, because it's like a badge of honor that shows an adventurous spirit. If you do want to revitalize the look of the fleece, use a wire pet brush (preferably unused) or a wide strip of hook tape (one side of hook-and-loop tape) wrapped around your hand to brush the fibers on the fleece. Hold the top of the garment in one hand and brush downward with the grain. It takes a few minutes to accomplish, but you will end up with a much softer, fleecier appearance.

Hook-and-Loop Tape

When laundering an item with hook-and-loop tape, close the tapes together to minimize catching on other fabrics. One piece of hook tape can do a lot of damage in the laundering process.

Hook tape picks up a lot of debris—threads, hair, and fibrous plant life—that sometimes makes it inoperable. Clean out the excess material with a large and preferably dull needle by pushing the needle sideways under the hooks and lifting the fibers out.

A selection of spray-on and wash-in water-repellent treatments. The Tectron product on the left also helps prevent the damage ultraviolet exposure can cause to fabrics, which can be significant for skiwear or boating attire.

Storing Your Garments

The main concern for storage is to get wet garments hung up to dry after use. Shake out excess moisture and hang loosely so air can circulate around the garment to dry. Lofted garments should be stored lofted if possible, whether down or synthetic. If an item is put away seasonally, store it in a breathable (cotton) bag so air circulates and dust is kept out. Store all garments completely dry and in a dry environment.

Though good down will reloft after being compressed, down-filled garments, comforters, and sleeping bags benefit from being stored uncompressed. This is also somewhat true of objects filled with technical high-loft. A simple cotton sack or inexpensive storage bag is useful for storing such items, allowing them to stay lofted and dirt- and dust-free when not in use, though they also can be hung in a closet to stay lofted.

Chapter 5

Simple Ways to Redesign Outerwear

After seeing all of the features outerwear can have, you're probably realizing what yours is missing. In this chapter you may find a way to improve what you already have with a simple change or two. Whether the problem is a cuff or a bad color, don't assume you need a new coat or a new pattern. Try a few basic changes instead.

Waistbands and Cuffs

The areas where a garment firmly meets our skin are the first we notice if the fit or fabric feel isn't right. They're also places that get a lot of wear, so it pays to know how to adapt them to your body.

Stretch Panels

Let's face it. Bodies can change a lot, but a growth spurt or weight gain doesn't always have to make last year's clothes unwearable. Strategically placed stretch panels can make a waistband comfortable again or allow you to reuse a pattern you love.

Heavyweight nylon knit and bonded stretch knits are the best fabrics to use for stretch panels. At a back or side seam, open (unstitch) the seam. The fabric for the panel should be twice as long as wanted, as you need to fold it in half to get a stretchy finished upper edge. Insert the doubled panel and sew to each seam allowance. Clip the garment seam allowance at the end of the first stitching line. The shaping can be

adjusted so that it is narrower near the waist, or you can have reinforcing elastic added inside the fold for extra waist shaping. An insert that intersects with the waist should have a firm stretch so the waist will stay up.

Ribbing

For a quick way to lengthen a sleeve or hem or just to add a soft edge, try ribbing. You don't need a special ribbed fabric for ribbing anymore. Ribbing can be a stretch fabric made into a tube, folded over and stretched while stitched to an edge for a flexible finish. For cuffs and necklines of inner knit (stretch) layers, I often use ribbing that is made out of the same fabric as the rest of the garment (self-fabric). Stretch binding (see below) is another good option.

To make a tubular stretched edge (self-fabric ribbing):

1 Cut the relaxed "ribbing" twice the desired width plus two seam allowances, and the length 10 percent to 25 percent shorter than the garment edge (or more, depending on how much of the edge you want to draw in and the stretch of the ribbing). For a continuous edge, place the short ends of the ribbing right sides together and stitch.

2 Turn the ribbing wrong sides together lengthwise, matching cut edges.

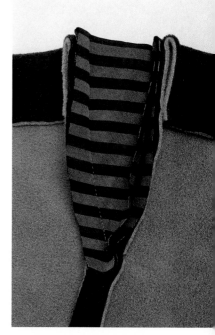

A stretch panel in the form of a long triangle (a diamond shape folded at the center) can be sewn into the center-back seam and stitched to each seam allowance. The top of the triangle forms a stretchy finished edge.

3 Divide the ribbing tube into four equal parts with pins at the cut edge. Divide the garment edge into four equal parts and match with the tube, right sides together, placing the ribbing seam to the back. Stitch the two together while stretching the ribbing to match the garment edge.

Stitch-in-the-Ditch Binding

For a fast, great-looking hem or cuff, try my favorite simple, bound-edge finish that I call stitch-in-the-ditch binding, which is made by using crossgrain strips of knit fabric. This binding process can produce either a flat edge finish or, when used with a Lycra-blend fabric, can create a flexible, gathered edge for cuffs or hem edges. Either way, it produces a comfortable, attractive finish.

There is a big advantage to using this binding technique, as it generally gives better results than other types. Both stitching lines for application are sewn in the same direction. In other binding techniques, the stitching lines usually run in opposite directions. Because you must stitch once on each side of the garment edge, this causes the binding to twist as the presser foot pushes it during the stitching process.

1 Start by deciding how wide you want the finished binding to be. A standard finished binding width for most of my projects is ⅜ in. Multiply that by four, which equals 1½ in. for the minimum width that the binding should be cut. The binding can be cut wider because the excess width will be cut off.

2 To cut binding strips, true up the end of the fabric so that there will be a straight, perpendicular cut from the selvage edge.

3 Cut straight strips of the crossgrain to the desired width. In fleece, most hem edges and sleeve edges are on the crossgrain and have some stretch to them. If the edge you are binding is a vertical, more stable edge such as a front-zipper edge, you can cut the binding on the grain, which has less stretch to cope with where you don't want it.

4 Place the binding on the garment edge, right sides together. Keep the edge of the binding back from the garment edge just slightly so you can see it easily. This makes it easier to keep the edge straight and reduces bulk right at the edge.

5 Begin stitching, making your stitch length long (especially for fleece), using a ⅜-in. seam allowance for the garment edge (the binding will be slightly narrower). If the garment edge has some crossgrain give, slightly stretch the two layers of fabric together, front to back over the throat plate, while stitching. For a gathered stretch binding, the Lycra binding is back-tacked at the beginning of the stitching line, then it is stretched separately before the two layers are held together for stitching. It would be nice to be able to tell you how much to stretch the binding, but every fabric combination is different. Try a sample first to get some idea of the stretch before you stitch on the garment edge. Start by stretching twice the length (stretching a 4-in. section to 8 in.) while stitching and see if you need to stretch the binding more or less to gather as you prefer.

6 Wrap the unfinished edge of the binding to the wrong side, so the edge of the garment and binding seam allowance are encased in the binding, not pulled to the back. Back-tack, then stitch-in-the-ditch between the binding and the garment, which is the previous seamline. If necessary, stretch as before.

7 Trim any excess seam allowance from the binding on the back side.

8 Join the sleeve or side seams to finish the ends. Fold the seam allowances away from the seamline and bar-tack over the seam with a wide stitch.

There is a wide variety of types of fabrics to use for this kind of binding. Knit nylon or poly-Lycra blends, like those used for swimsuits or cycling outfits, are used for a gathered stretch edge. When making this edge, the binding should be cut so there is 100 percent stretch going the length of the binding. To buy the least amount of fabric, a tricot knit will work best because it has stretch in all directions. An accurately cut one-eighth yard of fabric (4½ in. by 60 in. wide) will yield three 60-in. strips of binding (see below for cutting). Stretch fleece can be used as a binding fabric but because of the bulk, it won't gather as much at the edge.

For a flat edge binding, I use microfleece and the stitch-in-the-ditch method in many situations because it's functional, soft, and a

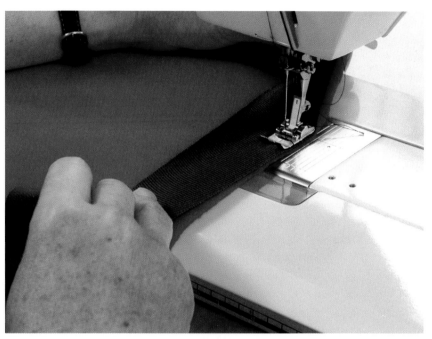

To gather a bound stretch edge, the binding is stretched independent of the garment edge before stitching. Hold the fabrics taut, front to back over the throat plate.

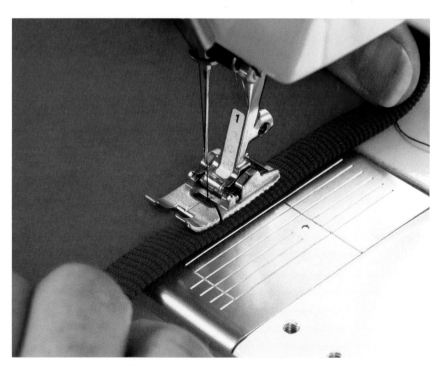

Roll the binding around the garment edge to stitch-in-the-ditch of the previously sewn seam, stretching all layers while sewing. The edge-joining foot makes this process easier.

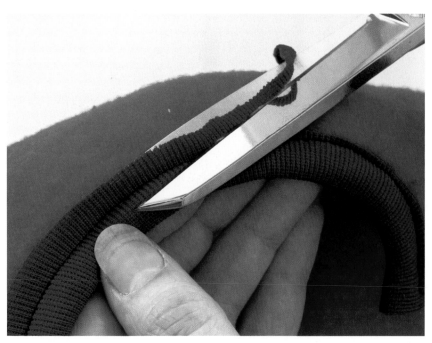
Trim seam allowance from wrong side of stitch-in-the-ditch binding.

Sew the underarm seams after the cuff edge is finished. Minimize the bulk of the seam allowances by finger-pressing them open and making a wide bar tack at the binding join. Trim the seam allowances close to the bar tack.

good match to the weight and texture of a fleece or fleece-and-shell combination garment. Other moderate stretch knits can be used, so try a sample to see what effect you get. The key is to make sure you match the weight of the binding fabric with the garment fabric. I would avoid cotton or cotton blends because they absorb moisture too easily and wear out quickly.

For the easiest application, apply this kind of binding before joining seams that make the edge circular, such as a sleeve seam or a continuous hem edge. After the binding is applied, the ends can be hidden in the seam (as mentioned in step #6 above). To finish an exposed end of binding, the end of the binding, about ½ in., is wrapped to the wrong side on the first stitching pass as shown in the top illustration on p. 102.

Overlays: A Valuable Design Tool

The beauty of overlays is how easily they can transform a garment. You don't have to tear apart a coat's seams, use a lot of fancy stitches, or go hunting around for a perfect pattern. You can quickly design useful and decorative features and sew them right on the garment, which can save you a lot of time and money. What I refer to as overlays can also be called appliqués, panels, patches, and, sometimes, trims. For a definition here, we'll refer to an overlay as a piece of fabric that is applied to the surface of a garment.

Overlays can protect high-use areas, like elbows, knees, and the seat. They can also provide weather protection in specific areas like the shoulders or can be used to add a pocket to stow keys or warm your hands or give an ordinary jacket an extraordinary touch. You'll be amazed at how overlays allow you to simply and quickly customize a coat.

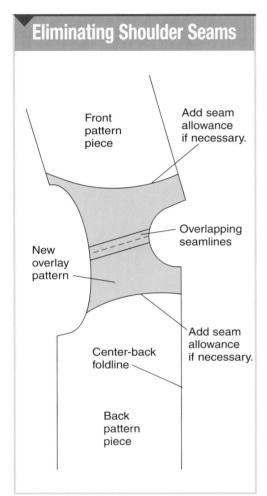

Eliminating Shoulder Seams

Front pattern piece

Add seam allowance if necessary.

Overlapping seamlines

New overlay pattern

Center-back foldline

Add seam allowance if necessary.

Back pattern piece

Overlays can be strictly functional, decorative, or a little of both. The scene created on this jacket was made by using Taslan and Supplex fabrics, fleece cord, braid trim, and "rat tail" (rayon cord trim) overlaid and stitched to the base layer.

Designing a Basic Overlay Panel

Use the garment's main pattern pieces to decide the shape of the overlay and then draw your shape on the pattern. If you want a large piece that extends over seamlines, overlap the pattern pieces at the stitching line. Once you've determined the final design, transfer it to the overlay fabric and cut it with a hot tool (see below) or, if the cut edges are being turned under, add seam allowances before (or while) cutting out the pattern piece.

Searing: Overlays and the Cutting Edge

Thanks to the low melting point of synthetic shell fabrics, cutting overlays is a simple job with the use of a hot tool such as a wood-burning tool. By using a hot tool on nylon and polyester, specifically, you can cut and finish the edge all in one step with no raw edge to hide. The fine tip allows you to draw graceful, curved designs freehand, and the heat-finished edge prevents fraying. Once the overlay design is cut, it can be placed (and pinned in some cases) to the base fabric and straight-stitched, zigzagged, or otherwise stitched in place.

Using a hot tool There are various hot tools (wood-burning tools and some fine-tip soldering irons) and tips that can be used for this process, but I've found a wood-burning tool seems to maintain a good temperature.

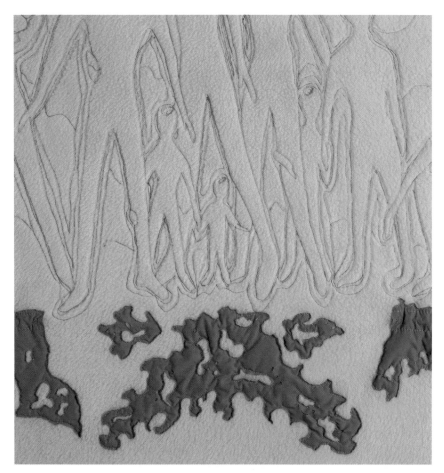

Intricate details in overlays can be easily done by using a hot tool to cut out designs from synthetic fabrics. Use pins or temporary adhesive spray to hold the overlay in place while stitching to the base garment. Free motion stitching was used to apply these detailed pieces.

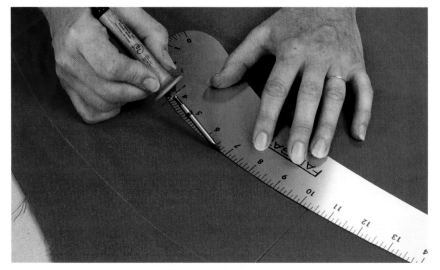

Use a metal ruler or curve to guide the hot tool. A scrap of wood molding can also be used for straight edges.

Besides the wedge tip that hot tools usually come with, I like to use a stencil-cutting tip, which is very thin and sharp, or a chisel tip. These sharper tips can provide very tight detail. Glass seems to be the easiest surface to cut on. An old storm window or mirror will work. Even on a glass tabletop the residue from the melting fabric will clean off later. Do not use a hot tool on Plexiglas, plastic, vinyl, wood, or any other surface that might melt or burn.

TIP

A small wire brush or coarse steel wool is useful for cleaning the nylon residue off the tool while the tip is hot.

There isn't anything complicated about using a hot tool, but it is important to be safe. Keep the work area well ventilated, wear a safety mask if using it for prolonged periods, and always be aware of whether the tip is on and what it is sitting on. I once caused the meltdown of my plastic magnetic pincushion when I wasn't watching where I laid the hot tool.

Test the tool on scrap fabric to see what kind of edge it produces and how fast you have to move the tool. If the tool is creating globs or uneven edges, move the tool faster even if you have to make two passes. A good seared edge will have a bead of melted material along the edge. Be aware that this melted edge can be a skin irritant. If the melted edge is in a seam allowance where it will come in contact with the skin, bind or finish the seam allowance in such a way so that the melted edge isn't exposed.

Hold the tool as you might use a pencil, but pull it, with the point or wedge gliding on the cutting surface. Move the scrap fabric away as you work so that the melted edges don't fuse together as they cool, which can be an issue, especially on thicker fabrics.

The fastest way to sear and cut out overlays is to lay the pattern or design on the shell fabric that is layered over interfacing, and cut through both layers at one time. A nonwoven, polyester interfacing provides opacity for lighter colored fabrics and firmness to lightweight fabrics but is not always necessary. The hot tool can cut with either the shell fabric or the interfacing on top and will slightly melt the edges of the two layers together. If the shell fabric is on top, the design is cut as it will be seen, so it is very simple and straightforward.

On some heavier or light-colored shell fabrics a scorched brown edge may form when seared. I cut these with the shell fabric on the bottom and the interfacing on top so any scorching that occurs won't show. If I'm using a symmetrical overlay design when cutting with the shell fabric on top, I don't have to make any changes. With an asymmetrical design, I lay the right side of the overlay pattern on the wrong side of the interfacing, then cut.

Hot tools also give a straight seared cut on synthetic webbings, cording, and tapes. Trim any loose threads off before searing to avoid burning blobs of goo. Thicker webbings may be too much for a hot tool, but a candle flame or cigarette lighter can give a clean-looking finish.

Attaching Overlay Panels

Overlays are easy to stitch in place. Use pins, basting tape, or Steam-a-Seam to hold the overlay in place while stitching. Fabric with a prefinished, nonfraying edge (seared synthetics, coated fabrics, or knit fleece) can be quickly topstitched with a straight stitch or zigzag. Straight edges on overlays can also be finished by first turning under a narrow seam allowance and then topstitching in place.

Overlays can be fleece on fleece or shell fabrics on other shell fabrics or shell fabrics on fleece. They can be for functional or decorative purposes or a combination of both. Waterproof shoulder panels, casings, and edge finishes can all be made with overlays.

When sewing on coated or laminated fabrics, overlays of any kind should be stitched to the shell layer only so that the stitching lines can be sealed from the wrong side. When using this technique on an existing garment for repair, that may mean unstitching (ripping out) a connecting seam in the lining to access the shell layer as a single layer. On a new garment, stitch all the add-on overlays in place and seam-seal before attaching the lining.

In all practicality, an overlay is one of the best ways to approach a repair where the fabric has been severely damaged. An overlay can be designed for function (as a pocket) or as a simply decorative overlay. In either case a repair can be made so that it is undetectable.

Practical Overlay Panels

This section is dedicated to easy-to-make overlays that improve the function of the coat in areas such as water repellency, warmth, and fit.

Overlays as drawstring or elastic casings

An overlay can be used as a drawstring or elastic casing with traditionally straight edges that can be turned under and topstitched if you prefer a more traditional application or incorporated as a design at the edges, as seen on the cuffs and hood in the photo on p. 100. Casings can be made

Consider This
Prestitched appliqués, like the hot-cut nylon example shown here, can be held in place for stitching by spraying a temporary spray adhesive on the wrong side before placement. A light application of Sulky's KK 2000 will disappear after a day or two, so it is excellent for placement of pockets, drawcord casings, and other overlay pieces.

The elastic casing and hood drawcord casing were made as overlays from the shell fabric, adding interesting detail and reducing the bulk that a self-fabric casing would have provided.

with both hot-cut synthetic fabrics or cut knit-fleece overlays.

A simple drawcord casing can be made with an overlay panel the length and width of the drawstring area with the edges finished (seared nylon or cut fleece). The ends of the drawcord panel can be finished with a narrow hem. If grommets or eyelets are preferred, they should be applied before the panel is stitched in place.

The free-form panel is topstitched at the outer edges. Topstitch two parallel rows at the casing line to serve as a channel for the cording. This type of drawcord casing can be stitched to the right or wrong side of the garment. This is the easiest way to make a curved casing (like one on a hood that curves to give better peripheral vision). Cut an underlay panel that parallels the curved edge, which can then be stitched to the wrong side. The drawcord casing shown in the w/p/b hood construction shown in the top photo on p. 132 uses a slightly curved underlay that matches the front of the hood. Install a grommet in the body of the hood

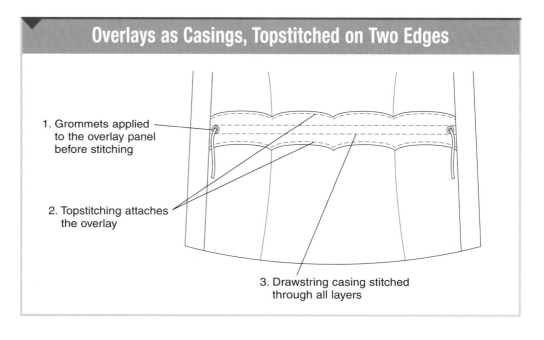

Overlays as Casings, Topstitched on Two Edges

1. Grommets applied to the overlay panel before stitching

2. Topstitching attaches the overlay

3. Drawstring casing stitched through all layers

before the overlay is stitched in place and seam-seal stitching lines before the hood is lined and finished.

Overlays as pockets Patch pockets are simply overlays that are prehemmed at the upper edge and stitched in place. They can be applied in the traditional way of turning the edges under and topstitching to the garment or by using alternate edge finishes. After finishing the opening area with a microfleece binding, the fleece pocket shown in the photo below was edge-finished with fleece cord, using a zigzag stitch, then applied to the garment using two rows of topstitching.

A woven-synthetic patch pocket with a seared edge can be attached with a few rows of topstitching; however, if it will get a lot of use, I prefer to turn the edges under and topstitch it in place (see the bellow pocket on p. 153).

When I added upper pockets to an existing jacket (see the photo on p. 121), I bound the edge of a preassembled overlay pocket

Pockets as overlays can be made as simply as this one in fleece, fusing microfleece binding at the opening and fleece cording to finish the cut edges. The drawcord and collar trim are also twisted fleece.

with a complementary bias binding on all the exposed edges. It was very easy to get the right placement. I could move the pocket around and see what it would look like. Once I determined the right location, I stitched through the shell only and seam-sealed the stitching lines in the waterproof membrane.

For a soft interior on an overlay hand-warmer pocket, the entire pocket can be lined with lightweight fleece (see the photo on p. 92).

1 Cut the fleece liner slightly smaller than the shell pocket piece (¼ in. on all edges).

2 Stitch the shell pocket and lining, right sides together (with shell fabric on top), slightly stretching the fleece to the shell fabric edges. Leave the top of the pocket open for turning.

3 Trim the fleece and pocket fabric seam allowances very close to the stitching line (with high-fray fabrics leave the seam allowance slightly wider), clip across corners if necessary, and turn it to the right side.

4 Hem or bind the top edge (see bias or double bindings in the Glossary on p. 180).

5 Topstitch pocket to garment, first close to the edge and then again ¼ in. to ⅜ in. inside from that.

Overlays as edge finishes for zippers
Applying a front facing to a jacket is a very common way to finish a center-front edge. This concept can be reversed so that the "facing" becomes an edge-finish overlay that is stitched on the wrong side then brought to the right side to finish. One benefit of this overlay is that it conceals the zipper tape between the layers for a nice inside finish.

Consider This
Instead of trying to match a drawcord to the garment, make twisted fleece cord from the same fabric. You will be amazed at how strong it is! See p. 112.

Consider This

Woven fabrics can stabilize and add elegant trim to fleece fabrics. The heavy cotton woven on the collar and back belts was cut on the crossgrain to provide an edge finish around the inside of the hem as well.

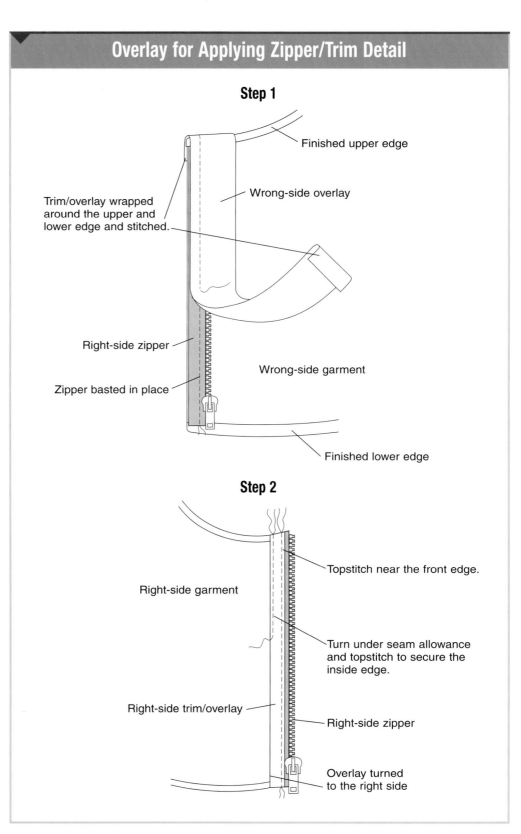

Overlay for Applying Zipper/Trim Detail

Step 1

Finished upper edge

Wrong-side overlay

Trim/overlay wrapped around the upper and lower edge and stitched.

Right-side zipper

Zipper basted in place

Wrong-side garment

Finished lower edge

Step 2

Right-side garment

Topstitch near the front edge.

Turn under seam allowance and topstitch to secure the inside edge.

Right-side trim/overlay

Right-side zipper

Overlay turned to the right side

On knit fleece, a woven fabric can be used to reinforce the front edge for applying snaps or buttonholes.

The overlay should be made with the same shaping as the front edge. If the front edge is straight and the overlay is narrow, then a straight, narrow piece of fabric or trim can be used. If the overlay is wide and/or the front edge is irregular, use the pattern piece to make an overlay design (see the illustration on p. 97).

1 For an easy zipper application, the zipper is pinned and basted, wrong sides together, to the center-front edge (a chin guard can be inserted between the zipper and the garment if desired, see p. 173).

2 The overlay is placed, right sides together, over the right side of the zipper and stitched in place with the same seam allowance as the basting line. When stitching to a fleece garment, try to keep the fleece on the bed of the machine. (In some cases it may be useful to first stitch the zipper right sides together with the shell fabric overlay, then stitch the overlay right side to the wrong side of the garment at center front edge.)

3 If the top and bottom edges of the garment have already been finished (with a bound edge, hem, etc.), a finished corner can be made by wrapping the ends of the overlay or trim to the back side of the work, encasing the raw ends under the overlay, creating a smooth finish. For better control, you may want to do this in two steps: Leave the ends of the trim loose on the first stitching pass, then firmly fold under the end against the upper or lower edge of the garment and stitch just the last few inches in place.

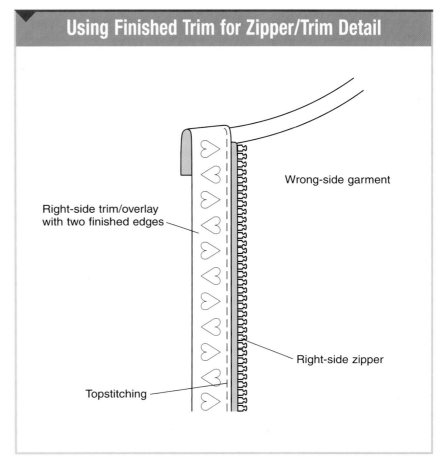

Using Finished Trim for Zipper/Trim Detail

Right-side trim/overlay with two finished edges

Wrong-side garment

Right-side zipper

Topstitching

Trim bulky fleece seam allowances close to the stitching line and clip across corners, then turn the overlay to the right side. Topstitch close to zipper, turn under seam allowance of the remaining edge, and edgestitch in place. Finishing binding at the ends can be done in the same way, only the seam allowance is not trimmed.

When using a trim that has a finished edge on both sides, the trim can be topstitched on the basted zipper edge, with the wrong side of the trim to the right side of the zipper. Just as in the method above, the ends can be wrapped to the wrong side for finishing.

Consider This

Free-motion stitching has many possibilities in surface design. I like using it for attaching detailed hot-cut appliqués, stitched design as on May's coat in the large photo on p. 109, and stippled areas as shown here. Use a darning or quilting foot with the feed dogs dropped and loose pressure on the foot (if possible). Move the fabric in all directions to achieve the desired effect. Practice on a scrap of the same fabric first!

Equipment for Sewing Overlays

For overlays with nonfraying edges, whether fleece or preseared or coated shell fabrics, pin or secure the edge with a glue stick or basting tape, then straight-stitch or zigzag the edge in place. An edgestitching foot, like the Bernina #10 edgestitching foot with an offset needle, will make stitching edges easier. On very curvy, detailed edges, I prefer to use a darning or quilting foot, Bernina #9 and #29 respectively, and to drop the feed dogs and use a free-motion stitching technique. It's much faster and easier to get a detailed edge, as in the top photo on p. 98. In some instances, such as a fleece or heavy knit, the honeycomb stitch is a very nice finish.

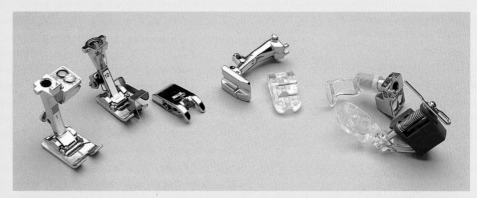

Machine feet that are useful for applying fleece cording, topstitching, free-motion stitching, and reverse-feed stitches (i.e., honeycomb stitch): (left to right) reverse feed with side thread slot (Bernina #1), edge stitching (B #10) and edge/joining foot (Viking), tricot foot used for cording (B #12) and snap-on pearls-and-piping foot, quilting and darning feet (B #29 and V).

Decorative Overlays

What makes outerwear really distinctive, besides well-engineered, functional details, is design. Sometimes decorative and functional, other times, strictly decorative, design can create mood, express personality, and definitely make a statement. Though I've seen plenty of examples of embellishment on outerwear that detract from the function of the garment, the creative overlays in the photos on pp. 92 and 109 are meant to maintain or enhance the function.

Design development A general idea of knowing where you're going with an overlay design takes a lot of the anxiety out of the project. Do you want to add a geometric design? A specific object or shape? Take some time to scout out ideas. Look for appealing images in art books and magazines, children's books, and design books; there are endless possibilities. Then enlarge a line drawing of your pattern on a photocopier and sketch possible design elements. (See the photo on p. 32.) You may not know

Practical and Decorative Overlay Variations

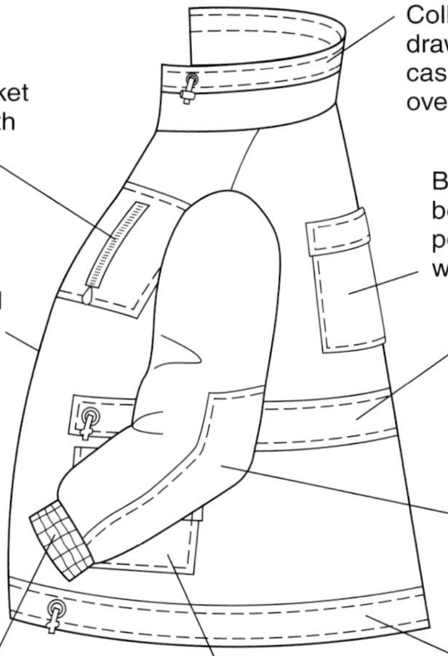

Water-repellent shell

Patch pocket overlay with a zipper

Unfinished front edge

Cuff elastic casing

Patch pocket with flap

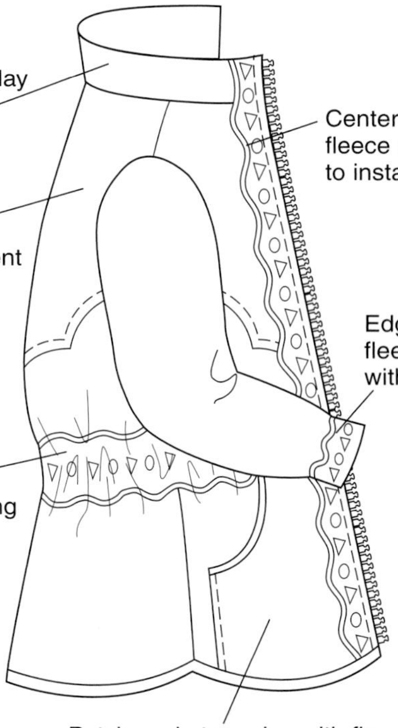

Collar: drawcord casing overlay

Back: bellow pocket with flap

Waist: drawcord casing overlay

Elbow patch overlay

Hem: drawcord casing overlay

Fleece garment

Collar: woven overlay with fleece

Yoke: water-repellent overlay

Waist: elastic-casing overlay

Center-front fleece overlay to install zipper

Edge-finish fleece overlay with cord

Patch pocket overlay with fleece and water-repellent woven shell fabric

For a strictly functional shell, as at left, the waist drawcord casing, elbow patch, and patch pockets can be easily applied by turning under the seam allowance (if the edge is not prefinished) and topstitching in position. Overlays that abut a finished edge, such as the collar, hem, and cuff casings, can be assembled similar to what is shown in the illustration on p. 100. The overlay is left unfinished on outside edges that will subsequently be finished with lining, binding, or other finishing. As the zipper and flap are applied to the center-front edge, the raw edges of the overlays at the front edge will be finished.

how you will accomplish the design yet, but start anyway.

From there, finalize the design on the pattern itself. During this process, think of the techniques that would best interpret your inspiration. Synthetic seared overlays (appliqués), synthetic suede overlays, fleece cording, and some stitching techniques are shown in the illustration above as a variety of simple embellishments with which to paint your inspiration.

As shown in this chapter, overlays are an example of adding function and design at the same time. The overlays on May's jacket (p. 109) could have been straight-edged panels to accomplish added water repellency and wind resistance, but the subtle colors and design express something more about May than pure function.

May wanted a distinctive everyday fleece coat, so I looked for an appropriate overlay design. I located a bamboo design from a book on Japanese family crests. Though I

Mitered Corners on Overlays and Trims

When edges are turned for hemming or topstitching, clean, sharp, 90-degree corners can be made by mitering them with a short stitching line.

1. Mark the desired location of the finished corner on the wrong side, fold the fabric diagonally across the mark to the corner with the right sides together.

2. Stitch perpendicular from the mark on the fold to the cut edges (back-tack to secure ends of stitching) For fleece or thick knits, a narrow strip of low temperature, fusible interfacing can be fused at the stitching line for a sharper corner and the angle can be slightly toward the hem foldline because of the stretch of the fabric.

3. Clip or trim the inside of the corner if necessary, only after checking to see if the miter looks correct from the right side. Turn to right side on hem foldline and stitch in place, turning seam allowances under if necessary.

For angles that aren't 90 degrees:

1. Fold the corner as shown, with cut edges matching and right sides together. Mark the miter seamline from the corner point so that the angle from the hem foldline to the cut edge is at the same angle as the corner fold to the hem foldline.

2. Verify the angle by folding the already folded fabric from the corner mark along the hem foldline.

3. Finish as for step 3 above.

In hem areas where you need to turn under a raw edge to finish, end the stitching of the miter short of the cut edge so a narrow hem can be turned for topstitching.

Flat trims, braids, and fleece trims can be stitched to an edge at the hemline (or fold) as an overlay finish, as in the photos on pp. 92 and 107. In the photo on p. 107, the right side of the collar overlay was seamed to the wrong side of

Mitering a 90-Degree Corner

Step 1

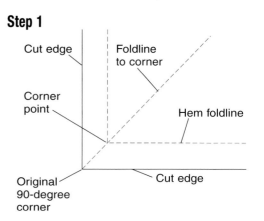

Cut edge | Foldline to corner

Corner point | Hem foldline

Original 90-degree corner | Cut edge

Step 2

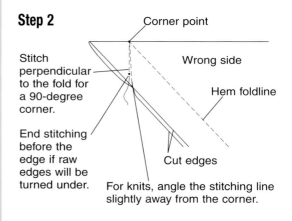

Corner point

Stitch perpendicular to the fold for a 90-degree corner.

Wrong side

Hem foldline

End stitching before the edge if raw edges will be turned under.

Cut edges

For knits, angle the stitching line slightly away from the corner.

Step 3

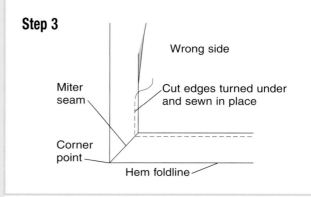

Wrong side

Miter seam | Cut edges turned under and sewn in place

Corner point

Hem foldline

Mitering Angles Other Than 90 Degrees

Step 1

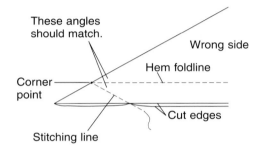

These angles should match.

Wrong side

Hem foldline

Corner point

Cut edges

Stitching line

Step 2

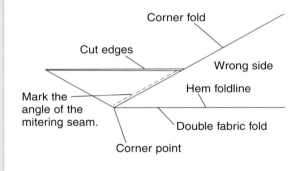

Corner fold

Cut edges

Wrong side

Hem foldline

Mark the angle of the mitering seam.

Double fabric fold

Corner point

Step 3

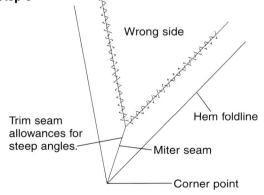

Wrong side

Hem foldline

Trim seam allowances for steep angles.

Miter seam

Corner point

Some fleece fabrics have a different texture on the reverse and face of the fabric. The edges of this coat were hemmed to the right side with mitered corners and finished with black fleece cord.

the garment edge then turned to the right side. When applying trims with two finished edges, topstitch one edge to the hemline fold, and trim away the excess hem allowance. To miter, the trim should be stitched only to the corner where the hemlines intersect, but a short section of trim should remain beyond the corner. Then stitch as shown above, starting at the corner where the trim's stitching lines intersect. The trim is then turned and topstitched in place on the inside edge. (See the photos on p. 108.)

(continued on p. 108)

To attach trim to an outside corner, topstitch the trim, right side up, to the wrong side of the garment at the hemline, letting the excess trim extend beyond the corner.

Cut off the old hem and fold the garment, wrong sides together, so that the trims line up. Miter the trim by sewing diagonally from the corner point to the edge of the trim as in step 2 on p. 106.

Turn the trim to the right side and topstitch the inside edge to the right side of the garment.

To attach trim to an inside corner, topstitch the trim to the seamline on the wrong side of the garment, ending exactly at the seamline corner. Leave yourself some excess trim at the corner.

Stitch a new piece of trim to the second side of the corner, again leaving some excess as a tail. Trim fleece seam allowance and close to stitching line.

Fold the trim so that the right sides are together, then fold out the excess at the corner and stitch the miter. Turn the trim to the right side for a beautifully finished corner.

Using personal color and design preferences are two compelling advantages of the custom-made garment. Overlays increase the potential of the "garment as palette" for greater clarity of expression. May's jacket is well worn because of these factors, though the durability of the fabrics keep it from looking like it.

could have enlarged the design on a copier, I found it quicker to draw the simple shapes freehand on a piece of paper. It allowed me to adjust the scale as needed, then trace the final design on pattern paper.

Three different fabrics were used in the overlays: a coated crinkle-nylon taffeta in a similar color tone to the fleece, which didn't need to be seared on the edges, and two Taslan nylons in celery and melon colors, used with medium-weight interfacing, both

of which were cut with a hot tool. (See sections on overlays and searing on pp. 97–100, for more specifics on cutting, searing, and stitching overlays.) The overlays shown in this garment could have been made from fleece or synthetic suede, too. The finished product would have had a different function and look, but the assembling process would have been very similar.

Consider This

This insulated red parka has black synthetic-suede oak leaves stitched as overlays to frame the zippers. My friend Pat was inspired by a design in a European skiwear catalog and used this idea very effectively. The appliqués were stitched to the insulated shell pieces before the zippers were installed and before the lining was attached. The zippers were then stitched through all layers but the lining.

Consider This

Seamed color blocking was built into this DK Sports pattern, but color blocking can easily be accomplished with any pattern. The reflecting trim on this cycling jacket adds to its functionality.

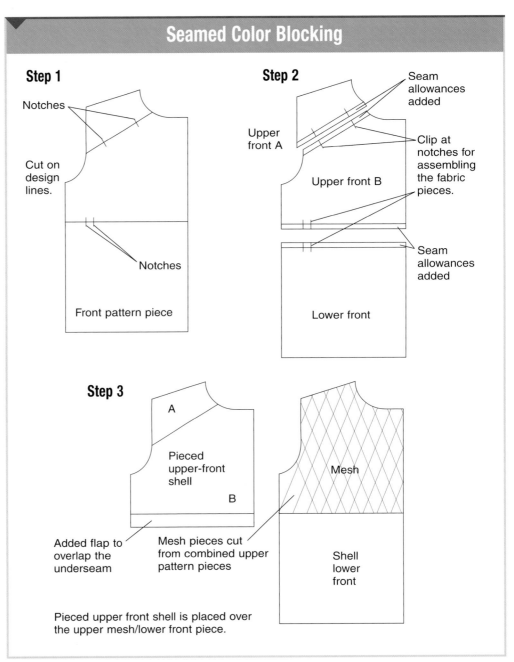

Seamed Color Blocking

Step 1

Notches

Cut on design lines.

Notches

Front pattern piece

Step 2

Seam allowances added

Upper front A

Upper front B

Clip at notches for assembling the fabric pieces.

Lower front

Seam allowances added

Step 3

A

Pieced upper-front shell

B

Added flap to overlap the underseam

Mesh pieces cut from combined upper pattern pieces

Mesh

Shell lower front

Pieced upper front shell is placed over the upper mesh/lower front piece.

Color blocking Hate those neon pink accents on a coat you thought was perfect a couple of years ago? Color blocking may save the day. An overlay shaped like a panel on the jacket, like the chest or yoke, may cover the offending color with one you love.

If you're making a jacket that has a sewn-on yoke panel, you can use color blocking to easily enhance function. Look at the yoke pieces as separate panels and use contrasting fabrics for them. To simplify construction, cut both the fleece and the shell fabric from the selected pattern pieces. The shell panel (water repellent or w/p/b) is placed wrong side to the right side of the under fabric (fleece) of the same pattern piece. Baste or overlock the two pieces together with the bulkier fleece on the bed of the machine and the shell on the top. Trim the seam allowance of the fleece to the basting line, then treat them as one piece throughout the rest of the construction process.

Pockets, flaps, and larger areas of a garment can be color-blocked by altering the pattern. Vented yokes can be added, using the color-blocking method. A separate overlay pattern piece that is slightly longer and finished separately on the lower edge is added to cover the mesh fabric of the upper section as seen in the illustrations on the facing page.

When applying an overlay directly to an already-made garment, be sure that you won't be stitching through any pocket bags or linings unnecessarily. It is best to remove (unstitch) patch pockets or flaps from a garment before applying an overlay, then restitch to the garment after the overlay is in place. Seam-sealing will be needed on the wrong side at the stitching lines when stitching to any coated or laminated fabrics.

Simple overlays as trim Fleece fabrics are often available in prints with borders. Some of them are very busy prints that, when used on their own, are overwhelming. Cutting out patterns or borders, usually printed across the grain, from larger prints provide some interesting options for embellishing. It isn't necessary to "pre-design" this type of project on the pattern pieces. Select and cut borders that will coordinate with the fabric, then play with the placement on the partially sewn garment!

A simple fleece vest can be embellished quickly using borders cut from two other printed fleece fabrics. Using borders for embellishment is easy when placed on a partially sewn garment. Fleece cording adds detail to the edges of the overlays, armscye, and the center-front edge for an easy zipper installation. The neck and hem edges have been finished using stitch-in-the-ditch microfleece binding.

Fleece borders, overlays, and cording are easily positioned and stitched for inexpensive details. Pins or temporary adhesive will hold overlays while stitching. Using an edge/joining foot and suggested feet for cording will speed the process even more.

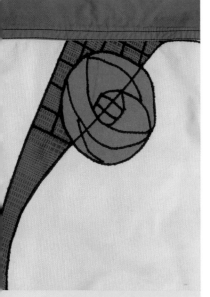

Using Surface Designs Wisely on Technical Fabrics

I f you want a garment with a detailed surface design on a technical fabric, plan your design carefully. A lot of stitching is detrimental to w/p/b and other coated fabrics, so embellishment that requires a lot of stitching should be avoided. But an overlay can be used to create the embellished design and can then be applied to the shell using minimal stitching for easy seam-sealing.

The fabrics in the overlay should be compatible with the fabrics they are applied to. Even with that, an overlay on a w/p/b fabric will probably limit effectiveness in the area of the overlay, most likely its breathability. As a result, it would be wise to limit placement of overlays to areas like the collar, upper body, shoulders, and upper arm so that breathability can be maintained in other areas, unless, of course, you are using the overlay as a repair.

The yellow shoulder yoke is an embellished overlay that was applied to a w/p/b garment without making it any less waterproof.

Consider This

Appliqués often benefit from the line of color that a satin stitch provides, but puncture holes from the needle are detrimental to water-repellent fabrics. Instead, emphasize design lines with fleece cord. A long zigzag attaches the cording and can be seam-sealed if necessary. This panel was stitched first, then underlined with a w/p/b liner. Borrow design ideas from your favorite artists and designers. A simple Mackintosh rose was easy to draw freehand, inspired from one of my art books.

The side seams of the vest in the top photo on p. 111 were eliminated by overlapping the seamlines of the front and back pattern pieces, thus eliminating an unnecessary seam before embellishing (as in the illustration on p. 97). On the right side of the top photo on p. 111, notice how the borders have been placed and pinned. Repositioning is simple, and once you decide what you like, simply zigzag it in place (or topstitch with the needle offset) and finish with cording. (See the bottom photo on p. 111.) Areas where the border curves or turns a corner,

such as at the shoulder or the V at the center back, require a stitched tuck or stitched-down miter at the pivot point (see p. 108).

Fast Finishing with Fleece Cording

In 1994 I was making fleece hats and came up with some very popular designs that had tassels. Though other hatmakers were making tassels from a straight-grain cut of fleece, which has a squarish look to the cord, I really liked the way that the fleece looked when cut from the stretchy crossgrain and deliberately stretched out of shape. Soon I was using fleece cording as braided ties for the hats, contrast color edges for appliqués, and as a soutache braid. The results were impressive, especially considering how easy it was to make and apply the cording without an extra trip to the fabric store for notions.

As I experimented and played with the cording, I found it provided an excellent edge finish for many types of fabric overlays, especially when using fleece. The fleece cording produces a dense line of color to delineate the overlay from the ground fabric without having to use a satin stitch (which requires stabilizing). Using fleece cording, pockets, casing edges, and artistic overlays can be applied quickly and finished without a lot of fuss and prolonged planning.

The cording can be made from knit fleece fabrics with a crossgrain stretch and many other single-knit fabrics. Most fleeces fall in this category, but be aware that you can't make fleece cording from woven fleece, bonded fleece, and some piles (a pile only has nap on one side).

To make fleece cording, cut strips of knit fleece ¼ in. to ⅜ in. wide on the crossgrain (the stretchiest direction). Though I usually recommend scissors for cutting fleece, the easiest cutting tool for this process is a rotary cutter. Use a mat and a graded clear-plastic ruler so the cut is very straight and you can see exactly how wide a cut you are making. The lighter weight the fleece you are working with, the narrower you can cut the strips. Microfleece can make a very thin cording when cut at ¼ in.

To begin, make a straight crossgrain cut, perpendicular to the selvage. If you are using a scrap piece, hold the fabric up to the light to see where the crossgrain is, and true the edge before cutting. Make a second cut ¼ in. to ⅜ in. away and parallel to the first cut.

To make "Rochelle's Fleece Cord," cut crossgrain strips of knit fleece. A rotary cutter and mat makes cutting strips faster.

Stretch the strip of fleece, which has been cut on the crossgrain, to make the cord.

Stretch the cut strip, pulling firmly along its length. Try to remove any stretch left in the fabric. It will become several times longer than its original length and narrower as the cut edges roll to the wrong side.

If the cord breaks while stretching, it may be too narrow, or too narrow in spots along

Consider This

Two colors of fleece cording tied together and twisted using an eye hook in a drill or a bobbin winder (turning to the right) can make a two-color cord that has many potential uses. Or tie two equal lengths of cord together and pin one end of the joined cord into the padding on an ironing board. Twist the joined cord until it starts to kink when not pulled taut. Keeping the tension tight, grasp the joining knot for the two colors and pull the ends together. Begin turning the knot to the right to begin the twisting, then let go, allowing the twist to form. Some retail stores have tools especially for making twisted cord. Knot the end if it will not be stitched in place immediately.

Here, fleece cord is used to finish the edges of mock ribbing (in a mid-weight fleece) made by sewing continuous rows with a wide (4mm or wider) double needle and with the upper tension adjusted to 9 or 10. More complete instructions are in my previous book, *Sew the New Fleece.*

an uneven edge, or the cut may be too far off the crossgrain. To remedy this, double-check the grain against the light, have very straight cuts (which is why a rotary cutter is so great), and add 1/16 in. to the width of the strip.

Cording in quick and practical applications

You have probably already recognized many decorative applications for this cord, as on the jacket in the photo on p. 100, but it is very practical, too. Finishing the edges of pockets and trim overlays, appliqué edges, zipper tape edges, and at hemlines are just few of the ways to use it.

Fleece cord can provide an inconspicuous or decorative edge trim. As a single strand, it can be butted up against the cut edge of a fleece garment and zigzagged in place. The edgestitching presser foot works really well for this when set with a very wide and long stitch. The edge of the fleece and the cord are simultaneously pushed toward the center bar of the presser foot so that the zigzag is stitching equally over the two sides with the cording pulled taut. Match the thread color to the cording to get the look of a solid edge of contrasting color.

Topstitching seam allowances or through elastic casing using fleece cord, as shown in the top left photo on the facing page, is practical in function but provides an opportunity for enhancing color and line. It takes only a little extra time, just long enough to make the cording. A false flat-felled seam or a basic seam can be topstitched with cording and using a long, wide zigzag and a cording foot.

Twisted or braided cord loops make excellent alternatives to buttonholes (see the center photo on the facing page) or hanging loops at the inside of the back collar. (See the bottom photo on the facing page and see p. 12 for a full back view of this garment.) Single strands can also be used to make tassels, cover seam allowances, and sew on buttons.

Whether you are remaking your outerwear or creating something entirely new, these techniques are functional, simple tools to facilitate both spontaneity and more planned projects.

A zip-in fleece liner can be added to many jackets by stitching a reversible separating zipper to the seam allowance inside the center front. In this example, the "joining zipper" is covered with a flap of Ultrasuede and fleece cording trims and hides the overlapping edges.

Consider This

Sulky invisible thread, which is polyester instead of nylon, will not irritate the skin the way nylon mono-filament thread does, and it is especially helpful for stitching on bicolored twisted fleece cording rather than trying to match just one of the colors in the cord. It is also nice for stitching on hot-cut nylon appliqués.

Twisted fleece cord was rolled into medallions to frame the button loop, also made with twisted cord. The large button is sewn on with a single strand of cord.

Free-motion stitching and tassels made from fleece cord, rayon floss, and glass pony beads add distinctive details on this coat.

Design-As-You-Go: Fundamentals and Great Design Adaptations

Even though I've been sewing for years, I don't always know, when I start a project, exactly what I want it to look like in the end. The specific function of the garment is often the beginning point, but an inspiration may come along during the sewing process from a particular fabric, pattern, or even an unusual button. My experience has given me a collection of adaptations that I can use on almost any pattern and many ready-to-wear garments. If I need more flexibility, I can add it. If I need a better pocket, I can make it. This saves me time and money hunting for that elusive perfect pattern or ready-made jacket. Usually I can make these adaptations as I go, without special pattern drafting or painstaking measurements.

The Fundamentals

Before you hunt for a pattern that's just right or spend time creating a special feature, think of what's already at your fingertips. An easier solution may be in front of you. Here are a few basics that make custom work a lot simpler.

Design from Ready-to-Wear

You know that fleece pullover that you just love? The one that cost you $75? You can make an exact duplicate without searching for something similar in an expensive pattern. If the garment is worn out or unusable, cut it apart at the seamlines and use it as a pattern, adding seam and hem allowances where they are needed.

To make a pattern from a ready-made garment without cutting it apart:

1 Tape 1-in. gridded or lined pattern paper (available at fabric stores) over a cardboard cutting board (the inexpensive type that folds up.)

2 Draw grainlines on the grid to use as reference points for the center front, back, sleeve, and other grainline locations.

3 Lay the garment next to the drawn grainline (so the center front or other grainline is parallel). Have the portion of the garment you want to draw lying flat and the rest of the garment either flat underneath it or folded out of the way (sometimes it is piled on top). If possible, pin through the fabric and the cardboard backing at the corners of the garment to hold it in place. (See p. 118.)

4 Draw around the edges where possible. Where the edge of the pattern piece is not exposed, like seamlines at the armscye or neckline, use a pin to puncture the pattern paper through the layers of

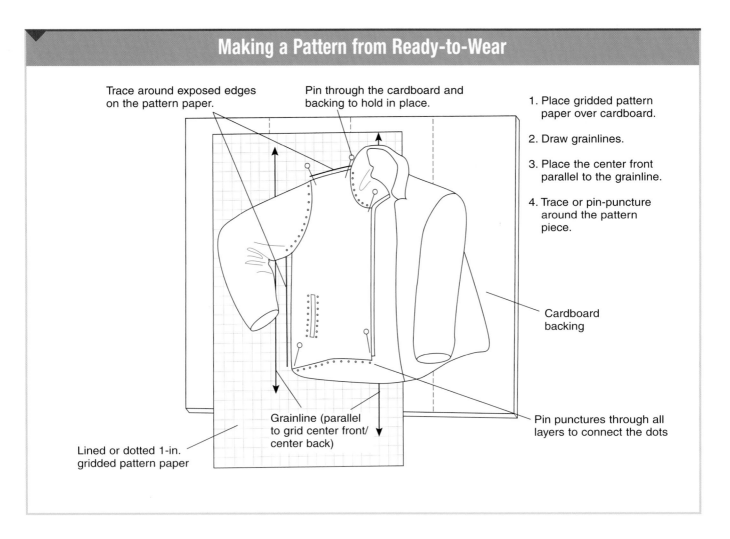

Trace around exposed edges on the pattern paper.

Pin through the cardboard and backing to hold in place.

1. Place gridded pattern paper over cardboard.

2. Draw grainlines.

3. Place the center front parallel to the grainline.

4. Trace or pin-puncture around the pattern piece.

Cardboard backing

Grainline (parallel to grid center front/ center back)

Lined or dotted 1-in. gridded pattern paper

Pin punctures through all layers to connect the dots

fabric into the cardboard underneath. After the garment is removed, the puncture holes can be traced, like connect-the-dots. For sleeves and other circular shapes, trace half of the sleeve at a time.

5 After all the pattern pieces have been drawn, true up the pattern by matching seamed edges and/or measuring the garment and comparing with the new paper pattern.

6 Add seam and hem allowances.

If you are copying a garment with a waterproof membrane, fold the edges of the garment back to determine the seamlines and to avoid ruining the waterproof function of the garment with pinholes. Gathered and elastic edges need to be measured across the piece just outside the affected area to get an accurate length. Elastic can be stretched to capacity for measuring.

This pattern-making suggestion is for personal use only, not for making patterns or garments for resale, which could be a copyright and/or patent infringement. See the Tracy Doyle book in "Additional Reading and Information" in Resources on p. 182 for a book on this subject.

Borrowing Pattern Design Elements

There are times when a design element can be borrowed from an existing pattern rather than created from scratch. Pockets, collars, hem shapes, and cuffs can all be taken from one pattern and applied to another base garment. In many cases you can trace the pocket placement from the original pattern to the new pattern, and the pocket bag or back and flap can be used on the new pattern by following the pattern directions for the original pocket.

Some features are anchored to or are part of the neckline or armscye, such as a collar, hood, or shaped sleeve. In these cases both the original and the new pattern should be of relatively the same size and shape. Transfer the entire neckline or armscye to the new pattern. It's much easier than it sounds! The shoulder seam needs to be overlapped at the seamline on both patterns so the neckline (or armscye) can be traced from the original and then transferred to the new pattern as shown in the photo at right. Match the center front and center back when adding a neckline to a new pattern. An armscye should be placed the same distance from the neckline as on the original pattern so as not to be too low or too high on the shoulder.

Once the shape of the neckline or armscye has been transferred, the pattern pieces for the collar, sleeve, and so forth can be used as if it were the same pattern.

Making a Muslin

If you're terrified of cutting into expensive fabric or making an irreparable sewing mistake, relax and make a muslin. By sewing the basic structure of your garment in an inexpensive fabric, you can check the fit or try a

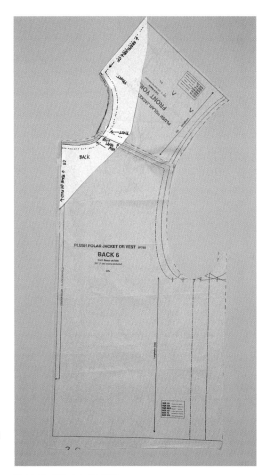

Transferring a neckline.

new technique without the worry. In some cases I feel it's well worth the extra step.

Choose a pattern and make any size adjustments that are needed (see chapter 3). Cut out the major pattern pieces (no facings, pocket pieces, cuffs, or linings) using an inexpensive fabric of the same type of weave or knit, weight, and stretch. Fabrics that are perfect for this are often available on remnant and close-out tables. An alternative to the fabric "muslin" is to fuse a lightweight interfacing to the pattern pieces. Baste or pin the major pattern pieces together. Fit the basted/pinned pieces to the body and adjust as needed.

This is a good opportunity to try out design features and their placements as well. Pockets, vents, flaps, drawcord casings, and hood locations can be drawn on the muslin with a pencil or pen, or pieces of fabric can be quickly cut and pinned in place to represent the general size and shape. The latter choice provides the option of moving the design pieces around for a design-as-you-go option. After placement lines for design features have been added, take apart the muslin and use it as a pattern.

Though well used since it first appeared in *Threads* magazine in 1989 (issue 25), this fleece and Taslan nylon jacket still looks great and is very practical for many weather conditions and activities.

Renew Your Outerwear: A Case History

Seeing design features as separate, adaptable elements opens up many possibilities to renovate an existing garment. One feature of the new outerwear fabrics is that they last and last and last. However, styles, bodies, colors, and needs *do* change. The good news is that the jacket that's been your favorite for five years doesn't have to head to Goodwill. If the fabric and most of the zippers are still in good shape, recycle it by redesigning it. Maybe all it needs is a little difference of color, which can be added as overlays or a few extra pockets. Some extra length added at the bottom or a contrast color added as a hood could rev up that jacket for a whole new start.

The two jackets in the photos at left and on the facing page seem like very different jackets. You might be surprised to find out that they were originally the same shape, practically identical except for the type of shell fabric and color. They were both used quite a bit as the style seen at left; however, the one made with the blue Gore-Tex® fabric combined with a permanent fleece lining, proved to be too warm for most days in our Pacific Northwest climate. I also didn't like the ribbing at the cuff and felt that the shorter length and the bottom ribbing were less useful for rainy weather.

I decided to keep this coat because it fit well and wasn't very worn. The Gore-Tex® fabric was in good shape, but the liquid seam-sealing had cracked and the seams needed to be taped for increased water protection. The base garment had ribbing on the lower edge that I didn't like, but it could be cut off. The location of the pockets limited the location of the extension piece, which made the waistline a little low but still work-

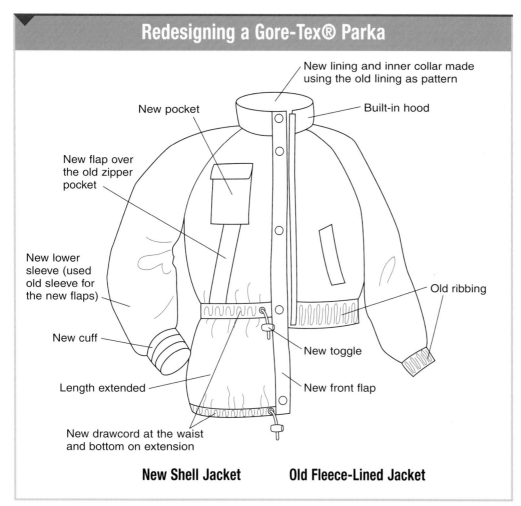

Redesigning a Gore-Tex® Parka

New lining and inner collar made using the old lining as pattern

New pocket

Built-in hood

New flap over the old zipper pocket

New lower sleeve (used old sleeve for the new flaps)

Old ribbing

New cuff

New toggle

Length extended

New front flap

New drawcord at the waist and bottom on extension

New Shell Jacket   **Old Fleece-Lined Jacket**

This Gore-Tex® shell went from being an unused parka to a recycling success.

able. This was an excellent opportunity to redesign.

I "unstitched" the fleece lining from the shell and used it to make a pattern as shown in the illustration on p. 118. I added the black portion to the sleeve by cutting off part of the sleeve, which was then used as a pattern for cutting the new Gore-Tex® fabric. I used the blue sleeve fabric to make a center-front flap. Black detailing was added to the pocket flap and pocket, and drawcord casings finished the ends in place. The waistline drawcord casing was created while stitching the extension in place using a wide flat-felled seam to create the casing, adding

the desired length, and another drawcord was added at the hem. New cuffs finished it off, using a stretch Gore-Tex® panel and an adjustable hook-and-loop tape tab. The center-front zipper on the shell still functioned well so it was left intact.

The mid-weight fleece lining was still in good shape, so it got the remodeling treatment, too. It needed to be taken in so it could be worn easily as a lightweight jacket or as an underlayer, but the shaping of the lower armscye was lost as width was taken out of the side and underarm seam, leaving little rotation in the sleeve. To compensate, I added a gusset from a dense, high-wicking

Attaching a Full Lining

A full lining and shell can be finished easily by machine-stitching only at the outer edges. After placing the layers right sides together, pin at matching points in the seam allowance and then in between those points until it's all even. Be sure flaps are folded away and finished edges are out of the stitching line. An unstitched opening in the center back will be needed for turning the garment to the right side.

To attach the lining to the seam allowance at the cuff, pull the shell sleeve and lining sleeve around the side of the coat so the ends of the sleeves are facing each other, like in a mirror, with the cuff between. Match the two edges so the seams and any pleats are corresponding and pin in place. (See the photo below.) If the two sleeves are fitted inside each other, it is *wrong*, and the sleeve will be twisted when it comes out. With the shell sleeve slightly tucked in the lining sleeve, stitch the two together, using the cuff-attaching stitching line as a guide. (See the top

When stitching the lining to the shell-cuff seam allowance, the cut edges should face each other, as in a mirror, with the cuff in the middle.

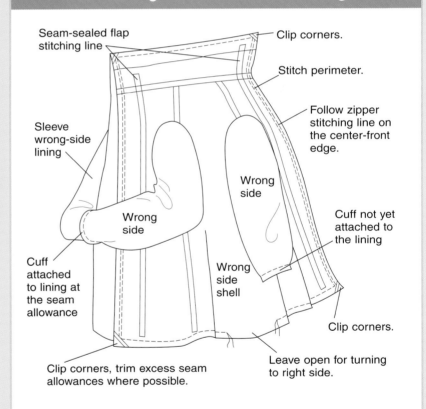

Attaching the Shell and Full Lining

Seam-sealed flap stitching line

Clip corners.

Stitch perimeter.

Follow zipper stitching line on the center-front edge.

Sleeve wrong-side lining

Wrong side

Wrong side

Cuff not yet attached to the lining

Cuff attached to lining at the seam allowance

Wrong side shell

Clip corners.

Clip corners, trim excess seam allowances where possible.

Leave open for turning to right side.

photo below.) Rotate the sleeve and reposition as you circumnavigate the cuff.

After turning to the right side, the lower edge of the sleeve can be topstitched through all layers to help it lie flat (see the bottom photo below).

Stitch through all layers of the shell cuff and lining edges. The edge will rotate on the bed of the machine, not around the free arm.

Topstitching through the layers above the cuff is a personal choice. It is difficult to seam-seal this stitching line.

Lycra mesh for better rotation and added comfort (see the bottom illustration on p. 136). New side-front pockets and pocket zippers were installed for a wider variety of use and a new separating zipper was installed in the center front. A whole new fleece jacket from the lining of the old one!

In both of the resulting garments, design followed the evolution of the garment. Being flexible is part of the fun of designing-in-process. There were only a few times when I actually used a premade pattern piece: making the cuff pieces for the adjustable cuff pattern (see p. 139), using the cut-off sleeve as a pattern, and making a pattern for the lining from the removed fleece lining. Often, just holding the new fabric next to the garment gave me enough information to design the pieces I needed by rough-cutting the fabric, stitching it in place, and then trimming away any excess.

Designer's Toolbox: Building Your Own Custom Outerwear

I have a "toolbox" of techniques I've developed or discovered that allows me to improvise when I don't have a pattern in hand. These are some of the most useful tools I use for customizing outerwear.

Making a Zip-Out Insulating Vest or Jacket

Versatility is a terrific characteristic to have in outerwear, and one way to have it is to make a finished insulating vest or jacket that can be zipped into a shell garment. A vest may be more useful in temperate climates but a zip-out fleece jacket is also nice to have for versatility.

Pattern Comparisons for Zip-In Insulating Layer with Collar

Shell neckline

Inner layer neckline

Higher armscye for the inner layer

Lower/looser armscye for the shell

Lower neckline okay for the inner layer

Both layers close or matching at the upper center front when design includes collar on inner layer

Inner layer (less ease)

Match center front

Shell (more ease)

Inner layer shorter

Adjusting fit for an inner layer The most important detail to remember when you start is that the inner layer should have a slimmer fit than the shell. Compare the inner-layer pattern with the shell-garment pattern to determine if they will fit easily together by lining them up on the center front. On the inner layer, the armscye should be higher and the body narrower, and the neckline should be in relatively the same spot if you want the inner layer to have a collar as well. If the inner layer has no collar, then the front neckline can end below the shell layers, but the back neckline should be close to the same. I prefer to make an inner

layer and outer shell layer from the same pattern pieces with slight adaptations to the pattern.

If you're working with a pattern that includes a lining, the lining pattern may be used for the inner layer pattern if it meets the shell (outer layer) at the center front and isn't cut off at a facing. A lining pattern often has less detail but accurate sizing, though it may need to be shaped to a slimmer fit than the shell, especially when using thick fleece.

How many extra zippers? A zip-in garment can be finished in two ways, depending on how the layers are zipped together, but three separating zippers are needed in either case: one that closes the inner layer, which is also used to zip into the shell (inner zipper), one to join the inner and outer layers (joining zipper), and one to close the shell (shell zipper). For an inner layer that can be zipped-in while worn, as in the case of the orange coat (which zips in to Maddie's blue w/p/b shell, see the left photo on the facing page) two of the zippers need reversible pulls (see Resources on p. 182 for zipper supplies) so that the pull tabs are accessible while zipping in and out of the shell. For an inner layer that is taken off and turned inside out to zip into the jacket, the two separating zippers need not have a reversible pull.

The inner zipper and joining zipper in both cases should be identical, and when they are separated, they should zip to the other corresponding zipper piece without difficulty. If you're having trouble finding identical zippers with reversible pulls, you may be able to replace the pull. See chapter 4 for directions.

Attaching zippers A joining zipper allows you to be able to convert clothing from one

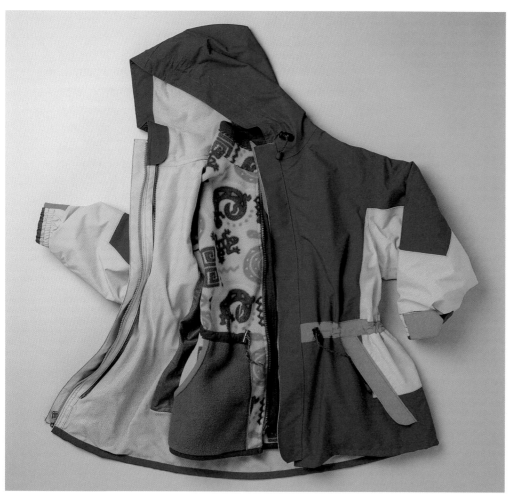

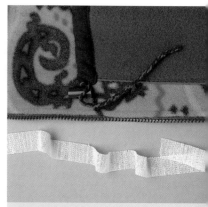

Consider This
To stabilize just the zipper area, cut a narrow strip of fusible interfacing and fuse it to the wrong side. It isn't necessary for it to be fused securely, and you can trim the extra away after the zipper has been stitched in place.

A component system like this one will offer a lot of variability for temperature and weather conditions. This was made using the same process as the version shown in the illustrations on pp. 128–130, though with a couple of variations—a hood instead of a collar and the joining zipper close to the edge of the flap.

type of function to another. The joining zipper method used below can be adapted for zip-off sleeves, pant legs, and coat extensions.

1 Construct the outer shell to the point where the center-front zipper is basted in place and all outer edges are yet to be finished (the lining is not yet sewn in place). When making a single-layer unlined shell, such as a three-layer Gore-Tex® garment, a collar lining (inner col-

lar) will be used for finishing instead of a full lining.

2 Construct the fleece layer and finish its center front with one of the reversible zippers. Separate the remaining zipper (joining zipper) and zip it to its counterpart on the fleece layer.

3 Make zipper flaps (see p. 166) from the shell fabric or a lighter weight coordinating fabric that measures slightly

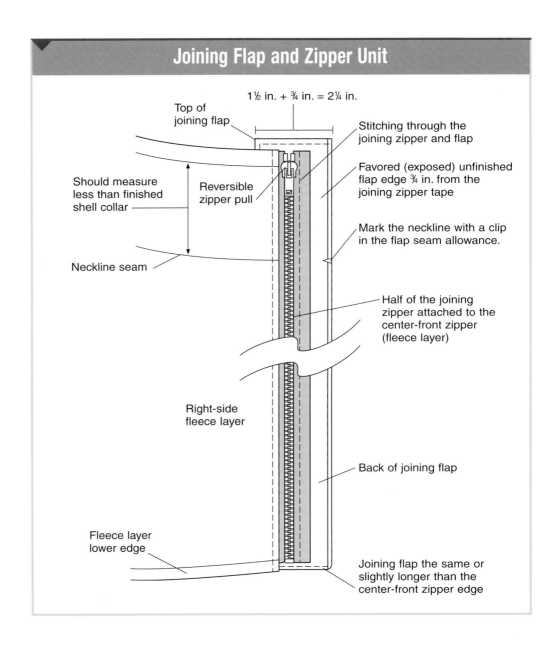

Joining Flap and Zipper Unit

1½ in. + ¾ in. = 2¼ in.

Top of joining flap

Stitching through the joining zipper and flap

Should measure less than finished shell collar

Reversible zipper pull

Favored (exposed) unfinished flap edge ¾ in. from the joining zipper tape

Mark the neckline with a clip in the flap seam allowance.

Neckline seam

Half of the joining zipper attached to the center-front zipper (fleece layer)

Right-side fleece layer

Back of joining flap

Fleece layer lower edge

Joining flap the same or slightly longer than the center-front zipper edge

longer than the center-front edge of the fleece layer and is approximately 2¼ in. to 3 in. wide.

4 Place the prepared flaps on the inside of the fleece layer at the joining zipper with top and bottom edges of the flaps showing evenly above and below the center-front zipper. On the joining zipper tape edge, expose (favor) the flap edge ¾ in.

beyond the edge of the tape. (See the illustration above.) Stitch through the center of the joining zipper tape to attach the flap. Repeat for the other center-front edge. Make a clip in the flap seam allowance at the neckline for matching to the shell layer.

5 To double-check the alignment of the pieces, put on both the fleece layer (with the joining zipper/flap unit in place) and

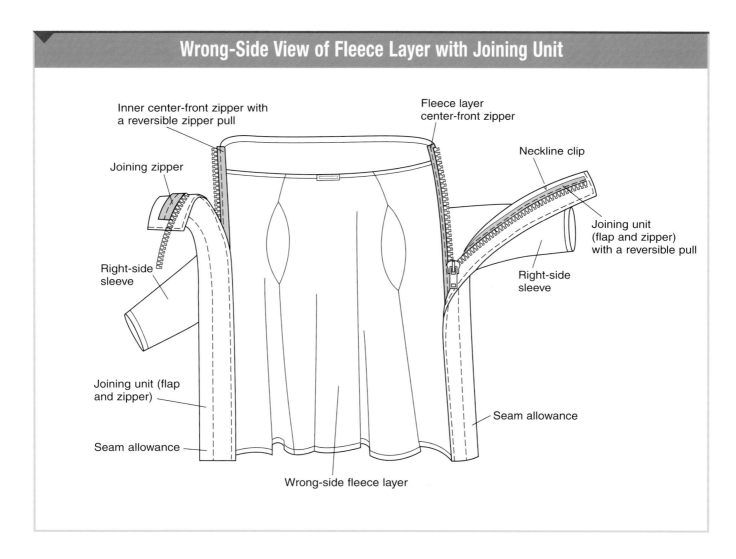

Inner center-front zipper with a reversible zipper pull

Fleece layer center-front zipper

Joining zipper

Neckline clip

Right-side sleeve

Joining unit (flap and zipper) with a reversible pull

Right-side sleeve

Joining unit (flap and zipper)

Seam allowance

Seam allowance

Wrong-side fleece layer

the shell. Check the alignment of the neckline and whether the two pieces hang well together before stitching the joining unit to the shell. The joining zipper/flap unit can now be zipped off from the fleece layer for easier assembly with the shell layer. (See the illustration above.)

6 Place the flap side of the joining unit to the right side of the center-front seam allowance of the shell, matching the neckline clip on the flap with the neckline of the shell. Baste the joining unit, using a ¹⁄₂-in. seam allowance. (See the illustration on p. 128.)

Optional but strongly suggested: An additional inner collar flap is simple to make and covers the end of the joining unit. It provides a neat finish and protection for the face from zipper pulls and intersecting seams at the inside edge of the collar.

1 Make the inner collar flap with a lower edge narrow enough to access the zipper pulls underneath. The length of the flap should be from the top cut edge of the shell collar to just below the shell collar seam (neckline). (See p. 169 for designing a shaped flap.) Finish the lower edges of

An inner collar flap has finished, topstitched shaped edges and enough room for a seam allowance at the cut upper edge. Make one for each side, with right and left shaping.

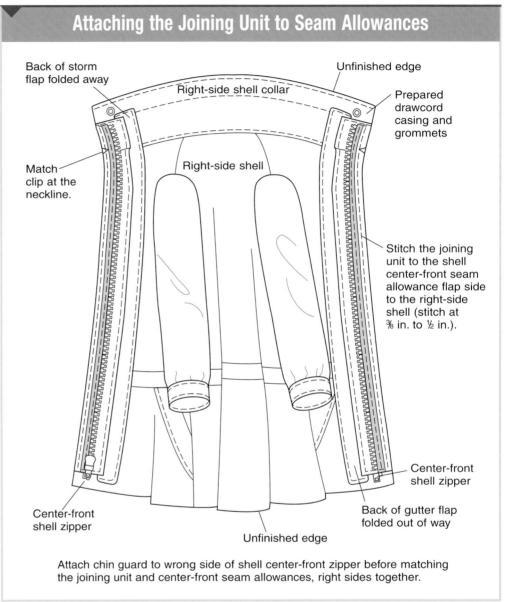

Back of storm flap folded away

Right-side shell collar

Unfinished edge

Prepared drawcord casing and grommets

Match clip at the neckline.

Right-side shell

Stitch the joining unit to the shell center-front seam allowance flap side to the right-side shell (stitch at ⅜ in. to ½ in.).

Center-front shell zipper

Back of gutter flap folded out of way

Center-front shell zipper

Unfinished edge

Attach chin guard to wrong side of shell center-front zipper before matching the joining unit and center-front seam allowances, right sides together.

this flap. The straight edge need not be finished with topstitching as it will be finished in the final step.

2 Place the inner collar flap right sides together with the shell collar, so the vertical straight edge of the flap is parallel to and right next to the center-front seamline (where the center front zipper

of the shell is basted in place). Baste in place at the upper edge only. (See the illustration on the facing page.)

3 Place the lining and prepared shell right sides together, matching at neckline and all cut edges. The front edge of the collar flap and the exterior shell flaps should be folded away to avoid catching them in the stitching lines.

Attaching the Inner Collar Flap

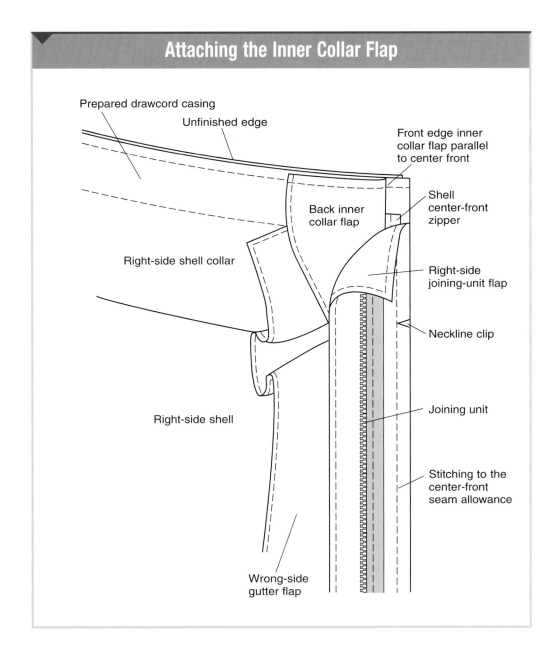

Prepared drawcord casing

Unfinished edge

Front edge inner collar flap parallel to center front

Shell center-front zipper

Back inner collar flap

Right-side shell collar

Right-side joining-unit flap

Neckline clip

Joining unit

Stitching to the center-front seam allowance

Right-side shell

Wrong-side gutter flap

4 Stitch around the lining at the seamline, leaving 10 in. to 12 in. open at the lower edge for turning to the right side.

5 Attach the cuff to the lining as shown in the illustration on p. 130 and in the sidebar on p. 122. Clip corners and trim seam allowances where necessary and turn the garment to the right side.

6 Finger-press around the edge to flatten the seamline. Fold the joining unit to the inside of the garment at the center front. (See the illustration on p. 130.) When working with a single-layer shell, place the inner collar (or collar lining) piece right sides together with the outer collar, stitch, and finish the collar edges in the same manner as above.

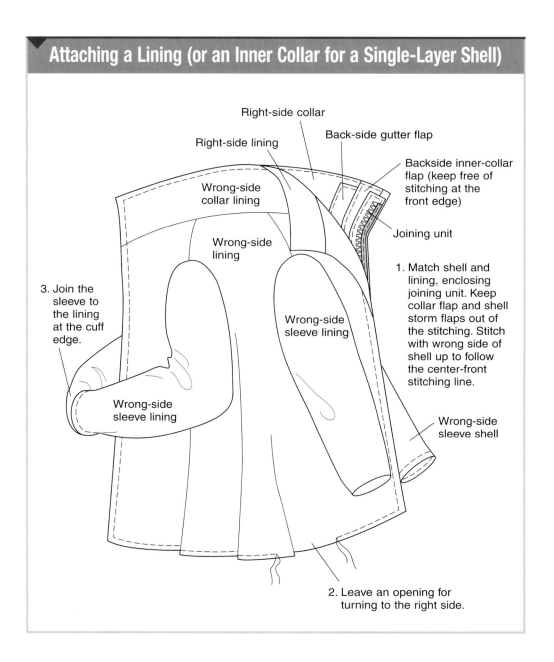

Attaching a Lining (or an Inner Collar for a Single-Layer Shell)

Right-side collar

Back-side gutter flap

Right-side lining

Backside inner-collar flap (keep free of stitching at the front edge)

Wrong-side collar lining

Joining unit

Wrong-side lining

1. Match shell and lining, enclosing joining unit. Keep collar flap and shell storm flaps out of the stitching. Stitch with wrong side of shell up to follow the center-front stitching line.

3. Join the sleeve to the lining at the cuff edge.

Wrong-side sleeve lining

Wrong-side sleeve lining

Wrong-side sleeve shell

2. Leave an opening for turning to the right side.

7 Fold the inner collar flap to the inside of the collar and pin it in place under the topstitching line.

8 Topstitch around the hem, folding cut edges to the inside and closing the opening used for turning. Topstitch both sides of center front and collar and catch the inner-collar flap in the stitching. Keep the shell storm or front flaps (see pp. 170 and 171) out of the stitching line. (See the illustration on the facing page and the photos on p. 132.) To finish a single-layer shell, turn the collar, inner collar flap, seam allowances, and joining unit to the wrong side and topstitch in the same manner.

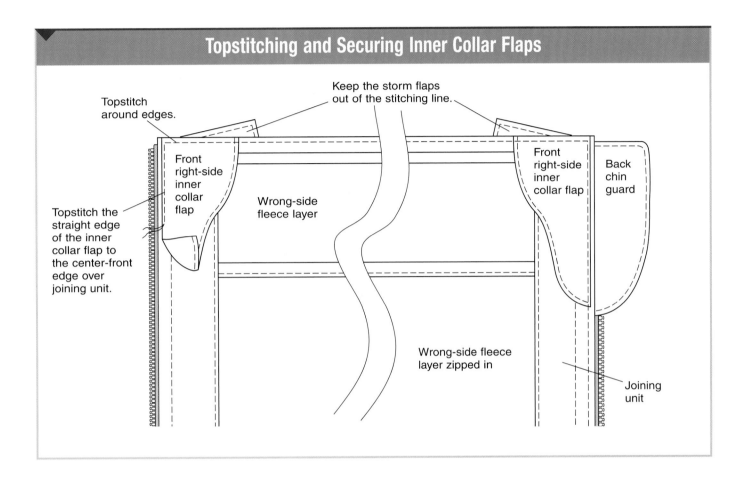

Topstitching and Securing Inner Collar Flaps

Topstitch around edges.

Keep the storm flaps out of the stitching line.

Front right-side inner collar flap

Wrong-side fleece layer

Front right-side inner collar flap

Back chin guard

Topstitch the straight edge of the inner collar flap to the center-front edge over joining unit.

Wrong-side fleece layer zipped in

Joining unit

The barn coat with a fleece zip-in vest shown in the top left photo on p. 115 is a slight variation on these directions. There is a lower neckline on the inner fleece vest, and fleece cording covers the serged edge of the seam allowance of the joining seam.

Sleeve and Knee Design Changes for Articulation

A comfortable sleeve design can make all the difference in the success of a garment. If the sleeves are restrictive, having a minimal range of motion, the garment will not be your first choice when reaching in your closet. Don't let a generous armscye opening fool you into believing that it will give you range of motion. If the bottom of the armscye is too low, it may pull the entire garment up when you raise your arms.

The shape of the knee area on the pant leg has the same issue of fit for movement. A garment will be used much more if the knee bends easily for activities that need flexibility. In shaping for the elbow or knee area for flexibility, some of the same alterations can be adapted for both uses.

Altering a pattern for a curved sleeve A big step toward a comfortable sleeve is getting the right shape. A sleeve that is cut straight, with the underarm seam meeting the side seam, is only going to fit when the arms are at the sides of the body. When the elbows bend (which is 99.9 percent of the time—think about it!), the sleeve is restricting and begins to twist to compensate. The old style of a darted sleeve or a shaped sleeve with the seam in the back fits the movement of the arm bet-

As with the cuff, a hook tab-and-loop piece are sewn at the back neck of the fleece layer in the collar seam. A loop sewn in the lining collar seam of the shell layer allows the tab to loop through and attach to the hook tape sewn on the fleece layer, keeping the two layers together.

A combination of a hook tab-and-loop piece are sewn to the wrist of the fleece layer so that when the components are zipped together, the tab can be brought to the outside of the shell cuff and easily keeps the two layers together.

ter. Some outerwear patterns are available with this shaping, but quite often altering an existing straight-sleeve pattern takes less time than hunting for the right pattern.

To make a curved sleeve from a straight-sleeve pattern:

1 Draw a vertical line through the center of the sleeve. Then draw a vertical line from the back sleeve notch (at the edge of the sleeve cap) to the cut edge at the wrist, parallel to the underarm seamline and the center of the sleeve.

To find the correct position of the elbow for fit, measure on the body from the back of the arm at the midway point between the shoulder and the underarm to the elbow. Using this measurement, find the elbow point by measuring from the back notch down the new line. Draw two horizontal lines on the pattern across sections C and B: one connecting the back seam allowance to the center line at the elbow measurement and the other 1 in. below. Cut the vertical lines.

2 Move the back piece C to the front, so that it is now next to section A. Overlap the seam lines, but do not tape in place yet. Slash through the horizontal lines on both outside pieces B and C. Spread the outside edges of the slashes $\frac{3}{8}$ in. or the desired amount as shown. This will create the curve in the pattern pieces and at the wrist edge that is needed for flexibility.

3 Tape the pieces in place and redraw the new pattern, adding seam allowances at the new seamline. Mark the old underarm seam for matching to the side seam (where the seam was overlapped) and the shoulder point for matching at the sleeve cap.

Making a Shaped Sleeve from a Straight Sleeve

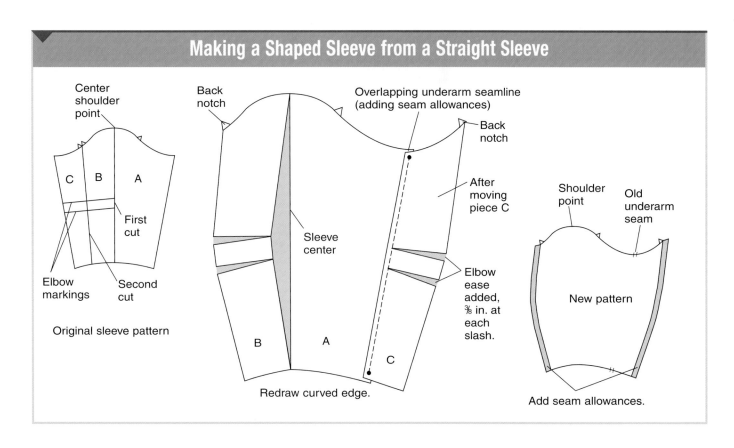

Center shoulder point

C B A

First cut

Elbow markings

Second cut

Original sleeve pattern

Back notch

Overlapping underarm seamline (adding seam allowances)

Back notch

After moving piece C

Sleeve center

B A

Elbow ease added, ⅜ in. at each slash.

Redraw curved edge.

Shoulder point

Old underarm seam

New pattern

Add seam allowances.

Adding a Pleat to a Back Sleeve or Knee

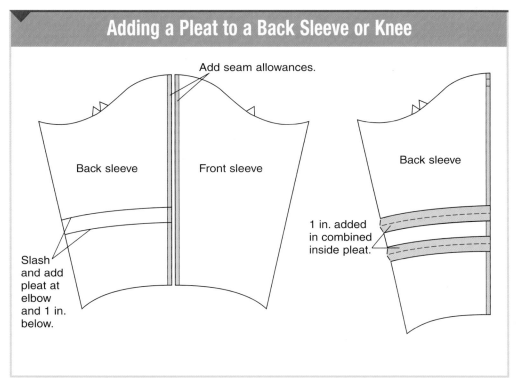

Add seam allowances.

Back sleeve

Front sleeve

Back sleeve

Slash and add pleat at elbow and 1 in. below.

1 in. added in combined inside pleat.

Top/edgestitched pleats.

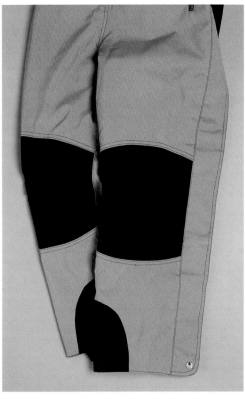

A pleated articulated knee is a feature of the pattern for these pants, the Whitehorn Pants from Storm Mountain. Full side zips and a reinforced seat and inner cuff area make it a very complete pattern.

Pleated back sleeve or knee You can create a flexible sleeve by adding a pleat or two at the back of the sleeve.

1 Cut the sleeve pattern through the center vertically and add seam allowances at the cut edges. (See the bottom illustration on p. 133.)

2 Slash the pattern horizontally across the back sleeve at the elbow and just below the elbow measurement. Add twice the desired depth of the pleat at each slash (the pleat will be ½ in. deep as shown in the bottom illustration on p. 133, so the total added is 1 in. to each slash). When making an adjustment for the knee, use this step on the pant front pattern at the knee area. Additional or deeper pleats may be necessary for the best flexibility of the knee area. Follow the same instructions for finishing.

3 Cut out the sleeve pieces from the shell fabric. Edgestitch on top of each pleat and fold the pleats closed with the insides of the pleats folded up (the inside fold of the pleat can be edgestitched from the wrong side for a firmer pleat), and staystitch the edges of the pleats in place in the seam allowances. After the pleats have been staystitched, the sleeve-back edges should match the original length of the pattern. (A pant front with knee pleats can be assembled as usual after staystitching the pleats.)

4 With right sides together, stitch the sleeve back to the sleeve front at the center, and topstitch through all layers on the front-sleeve edge. The sleeve may now be used as if it were the original pattern piece.

A variation of this process, which defines the axis of the elbow or knee with sewn-down darts to either side of where the pleats would have gone, can be used instead of pleats. The amount added to the pattern for a dart at the slash points should be less than that for a pleat.

Gussets Other interesting ways to shape a sleeve (or pants for that matter) include slashing the pattern at the elbow and putting a gusset in. This can also be used for retrofitting an already made jacket. An added gusset under the sleeve increases flexibility for arm movement. Many types of gussets can be inserted using the method shown in

The darted articulated knees of this racing suit are made by adding a few inches in length to the front-pant pattern at the knee area only, then stitching short darts 2 in. to 3 in. in from the side seam toward the center of the pant front.

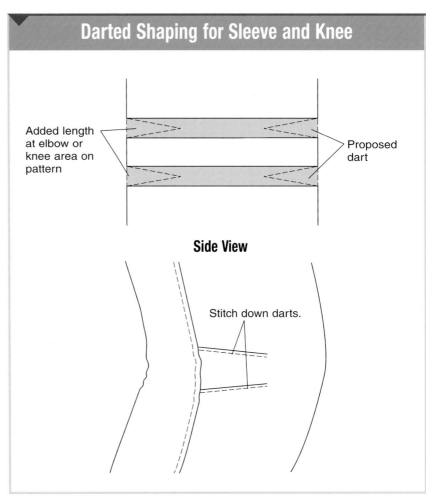

Darted Shaping for Sleeve and Knee

Added length at elbow or knee area on pattern

Proposed dart

Side View

Stitch down darts.

the top illustration on p. 136. For a standard armscye that needs rotation flexibility and over-the-head movement, I recommend a 10-in. long gusset that is 3 in. to 4 in. wide at the armscye seam. A crotch that is too short would benefit from a 6-in.- to 8-in.- long by 2-in.- to 3-in.-wide gusset that is placed in the crotch seam. The shape of a gusset may vary from a lens shape with rounded sides to a diamond shape.

The fabric to use in a gusset is determined by your purpose. If you simply want more room and flexibility, a self-fabric gusset (a gusset made from the same fabric as the garment) will do the trick. This is also

the best choice for an outer layer crotch gusset because a different fabric will draw more attention. If additional stretch is needed, you may want to use a stretchier Lycra fabric. If added ventilation is needed, a wicking stretch mesh is a good choice, as was used in the fleece jacket made from the fleece lining out of the blue jacket makeover, shown in the photo on p. 121.

If the garment has a low armscye, the gusset may need to be turned sideways as in the remade fleece jacket just mentioned. Flexibility needed to be added for overhead movement after taking in the side seam. I

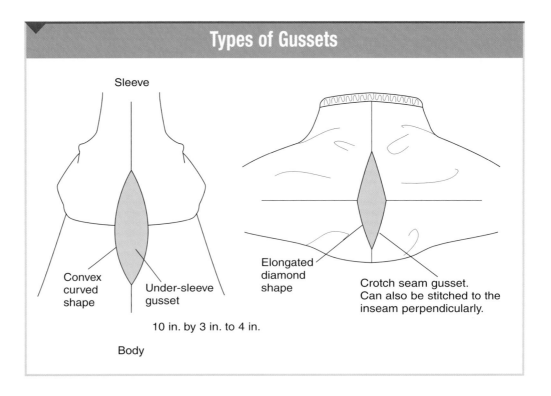

Types of Gussets

Sleeve

Convex curved shape

Under-sleeve gusset

10 in. by 3 in. to 4 in.

Body

Elongated diamond shape

Crotch seam gusset. Can also be stitched to the inseam perpendicularly.

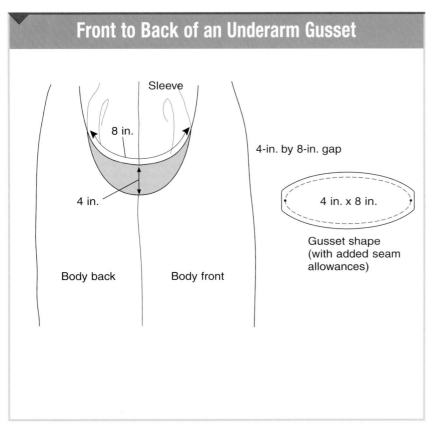

Front to Back of an Underarm Gusset

Sleeve

8 in.

4 in.

4-in. by 8-in. gap

4 in. x 8 in.

Gusset shape (with added seam allowances)

Body back   Body front

unstitched the armscye seam to the front and back notch areas. With the jacket on, I raised my arm to see how much width needed to be added. There was about 4 in. between the side seam and undersleeve.

I drew a gusset that was 4 in. at the center and diminished to nothing at the notch area. The length of the gusset was the same as the notch-to-notch area, about 8 in. long in this case. The notch is located where the sleeve starts to curve under the arm.

1 After determining the finished size and shape of the gusset, add seam allowances.

2 Place one edge of the gusset right sides together with an edge. Stitch from notch to notch as shown. Clip through the body seam allowance.

3 Place remaining edges right sides together and stitch notch to notch. If any part of the seamline still remains open, extend the stitching line beyond the notch. The clipped seam allowance helps the gusset lie flat enough to do this.

Clip your own notch when retrofitting this type of gusset. Most gussets will be inserted lengthwise in an underarm seam or in a crotch seam between points determined at your discretion. They are usually centered on a seam junction in the same way as described here on the armscye/underarm seam junction.

Elastic Cuff with Hook-and-Loop-Tape Adjustable Tab

A cuff can be as simple as elastic in a casing, a straight hem, a bound edge, or a heavy-duty ribbing (nylon, acrylic, or polypropylene) quickly applied to the end of the sleeve. With a little extra time and planning, you can add an adjustable cuff.

A cuff with a hook-and-loop-tape adjustable tab and an elastic panel provides an excellent combination for fit and function. This adjustable cuff has the distinct advantage of adjusting from fitting the wrist to fitting over snow mitts or gloves. If the tab is large, it can be manipulated with a gloved hand. This particular cuff is not as easy to assemble when sized down for children, so for very small wrist sizes think about applying a hook-and-loop-tape tab to an elasticized edge instead, as in the illustration on p. 138, or using a stretch insert in the cuff (see below).

Making the cuff The circumference, width, and amount of elastic can be varied for size and design according to preference, but, as an example, the pattern and measurements

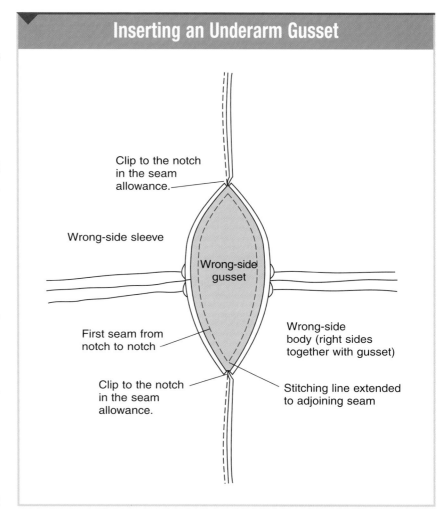

Inserting an Underarm Gusset

Clip to the notch in the seam allowance.

Wrong-side sleeve

Wrong-side gusset

First seam from notch to notch

Clip to the notch in the seam allowance.

Wrong-side body (right sides together with gusset)

Stitching line extended to adjoining seam

here are sized for a medium to large adult. If you need to add extra width (beyond the 12⅞-in. circumference) to the cuff for larger sized hands/wrists, add extra width in the elastic casing pattern piece (or alternative stretch panel) as shown on the pattern on p. 139. Additional length will be needed in the elastic as well.

Make the cuffs ahead so that they can be applied as easily as a ribbing cuff. The grid on p. 139 shows the pattern with tab placements for a right-hand cuff. The left is the opposite of that placement. While this may

TIP

When working with small cuff sizes, turn the sleeve inside out and stitch while working through the opening of the cuff. It is much easier to manipulate the edge. This is also true when machine sewing a lining on at the sleeve hem.

Adjustable Cuff Variations

Loop tape sewn
to elastic cuff

Hook-tape-
backed tab

Gusset
with zipper*

Hook tape
sewn to tab

Loop tape
sewn to
sleeve

*The moss-green ski parka
in the photo on p. 4 has this cuff.

Consider This

Use colorful webbing for interesting closures. Here, the hook-and-loop tape has been sewn to the back of webbing pieces, then attached to the flap and cuff. (See also the photo on p. 173 for a closeup view.)

sound elementary, keep it in mind while making the cuffs. It may help to place the cuff pieces side by side while working on them to make sure they face in opposite directions. I emphasize this point because I've made two of the same side cuff more than once!

The pattern uses $1\frac{1}{4}$-in. elastic in the casing but three rows of $\frac{3}{8}$-in. elastic can be substituted if the casing lines are stitched slightly wider than the elastic. As an alternative to elastic, a separate pattern is provided for a stretch panel that can be made from a heavy stretch (nylon) fabric or ribbing. On the renewed jacket and Will's Gore-Tex® parka (p. 116), I used a remnant of stretch black Gore-Tex®.

The main cuff piece and tab can be interfaced or interlined if using an insulation. The seam allowances are $\frac{5}{8}$ in.

You will need:

- Shell fabric from the garment

- Interlining or interfacing for the cuff and tab

- Optional—matching or contrasting stretch insert fabric for variation

- For the cuffs, either 7 in. of $1\frac{1}{2}$-in. loop tape *or* 14 in. of $\frac{3}{4}$-in. loop tape that is placed side by side. Each patch of tape will be $3\frac{1}{2}$ in. by $1\frac{1}{2}$ in. in the placement box.

- For the tab, either 4 in. of $1\frac{1}{2}$-in. hook tape *or* 8 in. of $\frac{3}{4}$-in. hook tape that is placed side by side. Each patch of tape will be 2 in. by $1\frac{1}{2}$ in. in the placement box.

- $\frac{1}{2}$ yd. of $1\frac{1}{4}$-in. elastic or $1\frac{1}{2}$ yd. of $\frac{3}{8}$-in. elastic as noted above.

Cut from the shell fabric:

- Two cuff pieces

- Two cuff elastic casing pieces (or two stretch panel pieces to be cut from stretch fabric)

- Four tab pieces

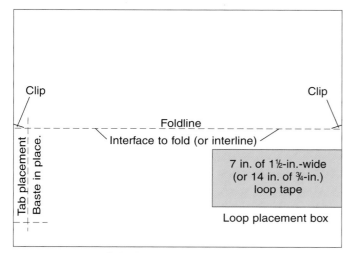

Clip

Clip

Foldline

Interface to fold (or interline)

Tab placement

Baste in place.

7 in. of 1½-in.-wide
(or 14 in. of ¾-in.)
loop tape

Loop placement box

Cuff: Cut 2 from shell fabric.

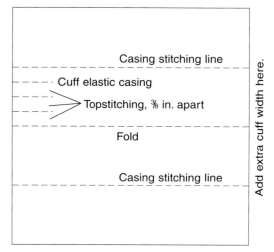

Casing stitching line

Cuff elastic casing

Topstitching, ⅜ in. apart

Fold

Casing stitching line

Add extra cuff width here.

Cuff elastic casing: Cut 2 from shell fabric.

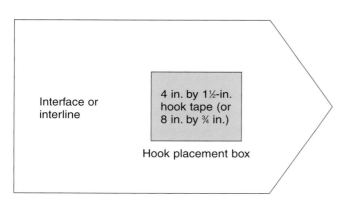

Interface or
interline

4 in. by 1½-in.
hook tape (or
8 in. by ¾ in.)

Hook placement box

Tab: Cut 4 from shell fabric.

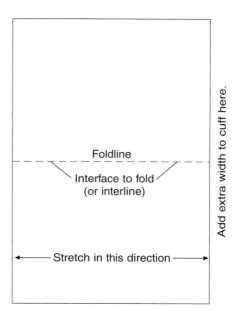

Foldline

Interface to fold
(or interline)

Add extra width to cuff here.

Stretch in this direction

Variation: Cuff stretch panel (used
instead of casing). Cut 2 from heavy
stretch nylon or bonded stretch.

1 Clip the cuff pieces at both ends of the foldline, and interface (or interline) to the fold. Interface two tab pieces.

2 Stitch hook tape to two tab pieces at the placement box as shown in the top photo at right. If using two strips of ³/₄-in. tape, overlap the inside edges so that one row of stitching will go through the two layers.

3 Place tab pieces right sides together and stitch. When stitching corners, shorten the stitch length ¼ in. before reaching the point of the corner, then stitch with the small stitch to ¼ in. past the point. Trim seam allowances, clip across corners, and turn to right side (center).

4 Topstitch from the right side of the tab, using an edgestitching foot, and, if desired, make a second row of stitching ¼ in. away or whatever distance matches the rest of the garment (bottom).

5 Stitch loop tape to the cuff on the placement area. Match the tab to the placement line on the cuff. The tab hook tape should overlap the cuff loop tape so it is held in place even when the cuff is at its loosest. (See the top left photo on the facing page.) Baste the cut end of the tab at the placement area on the cuff.

6 Prepare the 1¼-in. elastic piece by placing it along the foldline on the elastic casing piece, with 1 in. extending beyond the casing ends; then baste through the elastic at the seamline. Mark the elastic 4½ in. from the basting line (center left). Stretch the elastic until the mark reaches the opposite edge of the casing next to the fold. Baste the elastic in place.

Stitch the hook tape to the right side of tab piece.

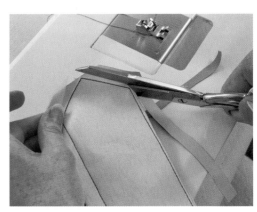

After stitching with right sides together, trim the tab seam allowances and clip across corners.

Topstitch the finished edges of the tab with one row of edgestitching and a second row as desired.

Stitch loop tape to the placement area on the cuff piece. Baste the unfinished end of the tab to the placement area of the cuff (upper right in photo).

Wrap one end of cuff around the unfinished end of the casing with right sides together.

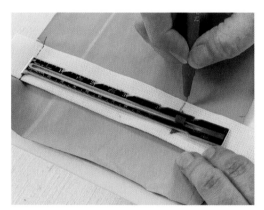

Measure the elastic 4½ in. from the basting line and pin it to the other end of the casing.

Stitch through all layers at the stitching line. Repeat for other end of casing/cuff.

Topstitch through all layers at ⅜ in. or preferred intervals while stretching the elastic extensions so that the casing lies flat.

Topstitch as desired. Note the position of the cuff for topstitching: The presser foot rides on the right side of the cuff, though the cuff is inside side out.

The finished adjustable cuff, ready to be sewn in.

7 Fold the casing, wrong sides together, over the elastic at the foldline so that the casing ends line up evenly. Stitch across the ends and through elastic.

8 To topstitch, pull the ends of the elastic so the casing lies flat (bottom left photo on p. 141). Pull the layers evenly across the throat plate to avoid breaking the needle. Topstitch at ³⁄₈ in. intervals across the casing. Trim the excess elastic beyond seam allowances.

9 If you are using the stretch panel instead of the elastic casing, fold the panel wrong sides together at the foldline. Baste the ends and continue as with the elastic casing.

10 Wrap one end of the cuff around the prepared casing (or folded stretch panel) right sides together (top right on p. 141) and stitch (center right on p. 141). Repeat for the other end of the cuff and casing (or stretch panel).

11 Trim seam allowances as necessary, turn to the right side, and topstitch on the inside (bottom right on p. 141).

The sleeve length may need to be adjusted to accommodate the cuff. The finished length of the cuff as shown in the photo at left is 2½ in., but the sleeve should have some blousing above the cuff (as shown in the ease chart on p. 58). Subtract the length of the cuff from the sleeve measurement with a bent elbow, add the desired amount for blousing (the longer the arm, the more that can be added for blousing), and adjust the sleeve pattern to this finished length (not including seam allowances).

The finished cuff will be approximately 12⅞ in. in circumference at the largest. The end of the sleeve may need to be adjusted to accommodate that size (or the size to which you have altered it). Most likely the sleeve will be too wide at the cuff edge and require a tuck or two. The tuck(s) in the sleeve edge should be made so that the fabric lies over the top of the sleeve and the tuck folds under at the outside of the wrist (at about the location of a back-sleeve seam on a curved sleeve).

Mark the right and left sides of the cut edge of the sleeve so the cuff will be situated the same on both sides, with the tab folded over the top of the cuff and pointing toward the back of the sleeve and with the elastic casing under the sleeve. To stitch the cuff to the sleeve shell, place cuff and sleeve right sides together and turn the sleeve inside out to stitch in place. Use the instructions on p. 122 for finishing with a lining. For an unlined garment, fold the seam allowances toward the sleeve and topstitch in place. Trim the seam allowance.

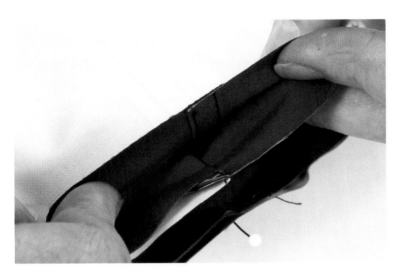

Align the cuff to the sleeve edge. Double-check the right versus the left cuff; the tab goes over the top of the wrist, toward the outside of the sleeve.

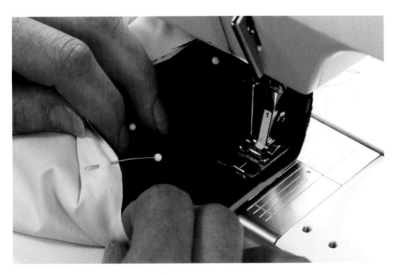

Stitch the cuff to the sleeve edge, working inside the circular opening.

Consider This
Pulling drawcord through an eyelet or grommet and a casing is much easier with a latch-hook tube turner. Thread the tool completely through the casing, hook the cording braid, and close the latch before pulling it back through the casing.

Detachable Hoods

When it's wet, nothing can beat having a hood, but when it's not raining it can be less than desirable to have it following you around. That's why I prefer a detachable hood. You can find them attached in many ways: snaps, buttons, hook-and-loop tape, and with a separating zipper.

Finding a well-fitting pattern for a hood is sometimes a chore. They are often more decorative than functional, and if they function well, they can be ugly. Try Resources on p. 182 for a better selection of patterns that function and have some style. There are patterns with detachable hoods that can be "borrowed" for another pattern body or borrow from ready-to-wear (see p. 118).

A shaped bill at the front of the hood will minimize rain blur. Patterns can easily be redrawn for a more pronounced bill shape or an added bill. A hood that has really good shaping usually has either a center panel (from back neck to front) or a curving seam across the top (from ear to ear) to fit the head shape better.

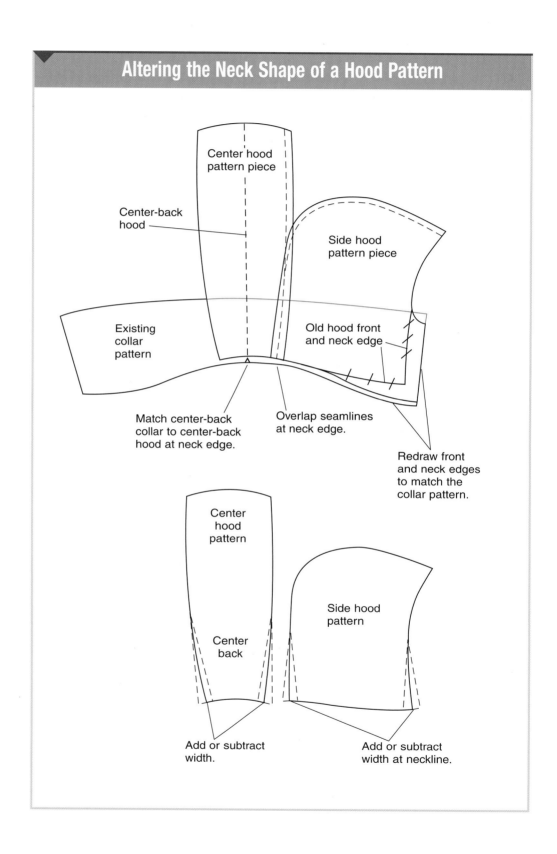

Altering the Neck Shape of a Hood Pattern

Center hood pattern piece

Center-back hood

Side hood pattern piece

Existing collar pattern

Old hood front and neck edge

Match center-back collar to center-back hood at neck edge.

Overlap seamlines at neck edge.

Redraw front and neck edges to match the collar pattern.

Center hood pattern

Side hood pattern

Center back

Add or subtract width.

Add or subtract width at neckline.

Matching the neck edge When you borrow a hood pattern from one pattern for another, compare the shape and measurement at the hood's neck edge with the neck edge of the existing collar. By overlapping the seamlines of the hood and collar along the neckline, you can compare length and shape. This will show changes that are needed to adapt the pattern. If the hood front edges are designed to meet or overlap at the front, be sure to include that in your comparison by matching center fronts on the hood and collar. If the hood is too long or too short at the neck edge, width can be added or removed at seams or at the front edges. The shape of the neckline is also important to match. Use the neck edge of the collar pattern to adjust the shape.

Notions To make a hood detachable with snaps or hook-and-loop tape, the hood can be entirely constructed before the snaps or hook tape is attached. Either can be applied to the lining of the hood along the neck edge before or after the lining and shell pieces are stitched together, but if they're applied afterward, the stitching will show on the right side. The same is true of the corresponding collar pattern pieces. Snaps or loop tape can be applied through all layers, or the outer shell only, before the collar has been lined, which allows the stitching lines to be seam-sealed on w/p/b fabrics.

> ## T I P
>
> Buttons on the collar and buttonholes in the lower edge of the hood make a special decorative (yet functional) detail for some outerwear.

Reinforcement with a mid- to heavy-weight interfacing or stable fabric under the snap area is important when applying to single layers or knits (like fleece).

Making a zip-on hood A short separating zipper at the back neck in the collar seamline and inside the base of the hood is an easy detaching feature. The zipper should not extend past the shoulder seams because the curve becomes too severe for the zipper to function well. If you can't find a short enough separating zipper, shorten a longer one (see p. 84).

1 After you have the shoulder seams stitched, staystitch just to the inside of the seamline. Place the right side of the side of the zipper without the pull to the right side of the back piece (the bottom of the zipper will be on the left when looking from the back), and baste in place. Clip the curve on the neck edge to match the zipper more easily.

Place one side of the separating zipper to the neck edge of the back, right sides together. Baste in place.

Place the collar to the neck edge, right sides together, and stitch with the neck edge up, using the basting line as a stitching guide.

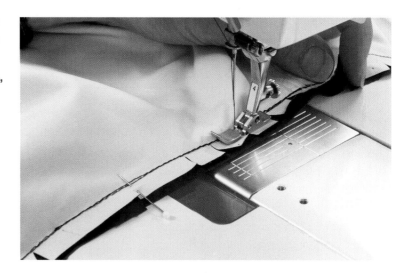

Position the hood lining over the zipper. Pin the lining to the upper zipper tape to find the appropriate placement.

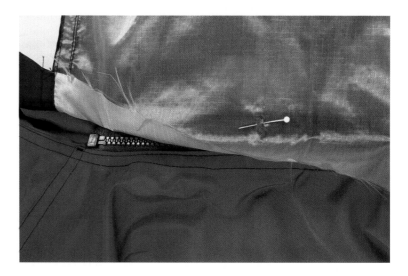

2 Stitch the zipper into the collar seam. A zipper foot may be needed to get close enough to the zipper teeth (or offset the needle to the far left). To prevent leakage and seam-sealing problems on the back collar, stitch the zipper in before the lining is attached, then seam-seal.

3 Zip the remaining side of the zipper to the zipper in the collar seam, then place the assembled hood lining over it in the correct placement (matching center back). Pin the upper zipper edge to the hood lining, leaving enough room for the seam allowance.

4 Separate the zipper and stitch the remaining zipper side to the lining.

5 After the zipper is in place, the hood can be finished. Place right sides of the hood and hood lining together and stitch around the outside edge, leaving a 4-in. to 6-in. portion unstitched at the back lower edge. Trim seam allowances and clip the corners.

The zippered opening (shown in the upper left photo on p. 156) on this collar opens to pull out a hood that is attached to the lower inside edge of the zipper tape.

6 Turn to the right side and topstitch around the edge, catching the seam allowances of the opening in the stitching line. Topstitch the upper edge of the zipper tape through all layers (optional).

For a hood that hides in the collar, an in-fabric or in-seam zippered opening (as shown for pockets on p. 155) can be sewn into the outer collar. The center portion of the finished hood can then be stitched to the inside of the zippered opening at the lower edge of the zipper seam allowance. Leave the hood edge that will be stitched to the zipper tape unfinished for a seam allowance.

A finished hood can also be snapped in place. The snaps can be applied to the collar and hood after the two pieces are complete.

Hopefully, the information in this chapter has given you the freedom to adapt your

A snap-on hood can be added when the jacket/shell and hood are completed separately. The collar and hood should be carefully aligned and marked for snap locations.

outerwear so it's more comfortable and better suited to your specific needs. In the next chapter you'll find my suggestions on the best methods for installing pockets, flaps, and zippers.

Chapter 7

Design-As-You-Go: Pockets and Flaps

I've found that I am most successful when I reduce a project—including the designing and making of outerwear—down into smaller units during the planning and construction stages. After I complete these smaller parts, I can then more easily bring them together for finishing. Pockets and flaps are design features that can be viewed in smaller units and then constructed individually on the unassembled (or partially assembled) major garment pieces. They are also great design-as-you-go features that can dramatically improve a coat's warmth and weather protection, can be added wherever you need them, and are simple to make.

Pockets

A very common complaint about outerwear design is that the pockets don't work well or there simply aren't enough of them. I've found that there are simple variations of a few pocket styles that offer easy solutions to pocket problems. In this chapter you'll find instructions on making them and placing them so they work best for you.

Most of the pocket types useful in outerwear designs originate from two general groups of pockets: patch pockets and in-fabric pockets (in a seam or not and with or without zippers). Patch pockets, like over-lays, are stitched to the right side of the base fabric. They may or may not have a flap to cover the opening to prevent moisture from collecting inside the pocket. An in-fabric pocket is stitched and cut into the fabric with the pocket bag—the pocket back— on the wrong side or inside of the base fabric. There are many variations and combinations of these two types of pockets.

TIP

For a pocket that will warm your hands the fastest, use a microfleece, single-faced fleece, or even a firm mesh knit for the pocket bag/back or as a lining to a patch pocket. The soft texture of the fabric provides quick warmth for the hands when it is desperately needed.

When designing any pocket, but especially a cargo pocket, determine how big it needs to be. To ensure that the pocket will be big enough, lay some of the objects that you might carry in that pocket together on a flat surface (water bottle, fishing reel, gloves, sunglasses, whatever) and measure over the height and length of that group of objects. These measurements can be used to deter-

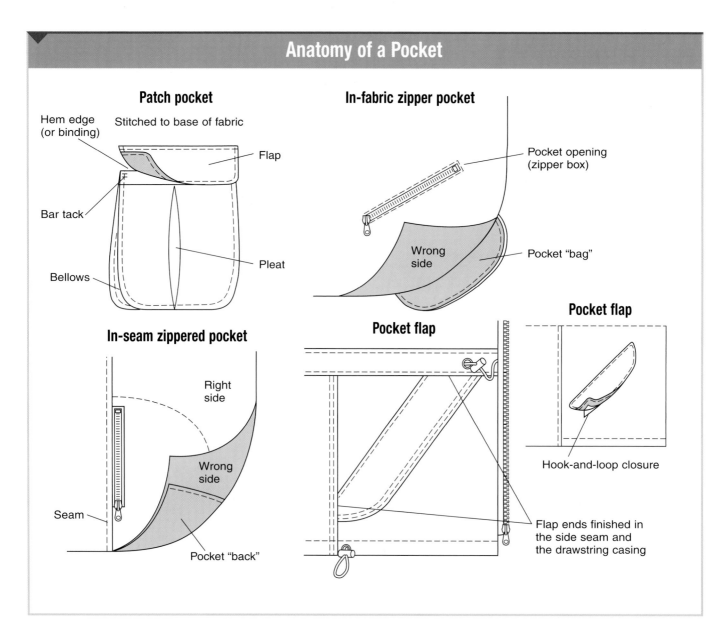

Patch pocket

Hem edge (or binding)

Stitched to base of fabric

Flap

Bar tack

Pleat

Bellows

In-fabric zipper pocket

Pocket opening (zipper box)

Wrong side

Pocket "bag"

Pocket flap

Hook-and-loop closure

In-seam zippered pocket

Right side

Wrong side

Seam

Pocket "back"

Pocket flap

Flap ends finished in the side seam and the drawstring casing

mine a size for the pocket. The pocket opening should also be large enough to get the biggest object through.

Design any shape of patch pocket by drawing the finished size and shape first, then adding seam allowances. Cut it out from the desired fabric. Turn under the seam allowances and pin (or use temporary spray adhesive) to secure the pocket to the

placement area and topstitch in place, using one or more rows of topstitching. Straight edges are the easiest to stitch, but curves can often be prepressed, using a low-temp iron before stitching in place. Chapter 5 provides more information about creating any shape of pocket you want, using overlay techniques with seared nylons.

Pocket Placement

In order for a pocket to be comfortable and practical, the height and angle of the pocket should be matched to your body. In general, hand pockets on jackets should be placed slightly below the ribs and elbow and have a vertical opening so the hand can slide in easily. The lower the pocket placement, the more the opening should be slanted to the horizontal. Avoid placing the pocket too low, though, which causes the shoulders to be drawn forward when the hands are in the pockets. A good way to place a pocket is to take measurements from a jacket that has well-placed pockets. Measure the pocket's height and width from the shoulder and center front, and transfer the measurements to the new jacket.

Patch pockets

The great thing about making a patch pocket is that what you see is what you get. It's nothing more than a shape, hemmed at the top and attached to the base fabric on the remaining sides: a functional pocket. By adding a flap and a hook-and-loop tape closure, it becomes more waterproof. By adding a pleat or bellows to the front (as seen in the photos on p. 154) it will hold more. Design interest may be added by piping the outer edge, giving the flap an unusual shape, or using a contrasting fabric at the back of the pleat. Either side of the opening of a patch pocket should be bar-tacked or box-stitched to prevent the stitching lines from being pulled out.

A patch pocket can go anywhere it will fit, but use the information above to help decide the best placement for comfort as a hand warmer.

For a hand warmer, a patch pocket might serve better with a side opening. The opening should start a few inches above the bottom to prevent losing things out of the pocket.

In-Fabric Pockets

A pocket that goes through the garment to the wrong side is an in-fabric pocket. Sometimes you'll see it in a seam and sometimes in the field of the fabric. Both of these options are discussed here. As a single-layer application, like in a fleece jacket, both types can be made using a single pocket back. In an insulated/lined garment like a parka, it's usually necessary to have a pocket bag that can be either a single piece that is folded or two pieces (front and back) that are stitched together.

In outerwear, in-seam pockets often have a zipper and flap to prevent the pocket contents from falling out and moisture from getting in; the instructions below cover both of those features. Inner layers don't necessarily need a zipper and flap, but I usually use a lightweight zipper anyway to prevent knit linings from sagging at the pocket. Many variations of these pocket styles can

Adding a Box Pleat and Bellows Pleat to a Patch Pocket

Add more carrying capacity to a patch pocket by adding a box pleat, which expands the pocket panel at the front, and a bellows, which gives the pocket more depth at the sides. These alterations can be done separately as well as together, and the bellows can be designed to extend around all the topstitched edges of the pocket.

Box Pleat

1. To make a pleat on the face of the pocket, first cut the pattern apart where you want the pleat. Decide on the width (e.g., 2 in.) for the back of the pleat, including the width on each side of the inside of the pleat (e.g., 1 in. each side). Draw the desired total width (e.g., 4 in.) on paper and cut out. Tape to the pocket pattern pieces as shown in the photo below. Instead of taping, you can add seam allowances to the sides of the pocket pleat back and to the two pocket front

halves, then stitch them together. This provides the opportunity to have another color inside the pleat.

2. For a sharp, neat edge, fold the front pleat at the foldline (the original cutting line) and edgestitch each side of the pleat.

3. Bring the edges of the pleats together at the center of the pleat and staystitch the top and bottom of the pleat.

4. Hem the top of the pocket. If using hook-and-loop tape for a closure, stitch it in place now before stitching the pocket to the garment. Turn under the seam allowances and topstitch the pocket to the base garment or add bellows, as below.

Bellows

1. For a bellows pattern, measure the seamline of the pocket where the bellows is to be placed (the example shown in the illustration on the facing page doesn't extend all the way around the pocket). The bellows should have a hem allowance at the end that matches to the top of the pocket and at the other end of the example. A seam allowance of ½ in. extends under the closed end of the bellows, so the finished length is 1 in. + 17 in. + ½ in. = 18½ in. The width can be any width but is probably best kept under 2 in. plus seam allowances. The

For a pleat that has a sharper edge, edgestitch the inside edge of the fold.

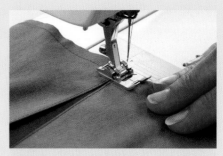

Bring the pleats together and staystitch the top and bottom edges.

Hem the top edge of the pocket.

example here is 1¼ in. depth (width of the bellows pattern) plus two seam allowances of ½ in. for a total of 2¼ in. The ends of the bellows pattern can be cut square or

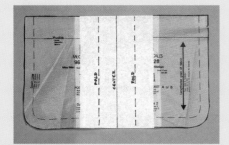

A simple pattern alteration turns a patch pocket into a box-pleated pocket.

Making a Bellows Pattern Piece

Top of bellows with hem allowance

Example: 1-in. hem + 17-in. length + ½-in. seam allowance at end = 18½ in. long

Right-side pocket

Bellow ends here

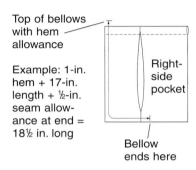

Hemmed upper edge

Corner clips

Right-side bellows

Bellows piece ⟋ 2¼ in.

Optional dart at corner

Shaped end (or square)

1. Measure pocket at the seamline to determine the length of the bellows piece. Add seam and hem allowances.

2. Cut the bellows the desired length and width. Hem upper edge. Clip through seam allowance at corners.

To help the bellows lie flat on the garment, stitch a miter (a flat V shape) from seamline to seamline at the corner with right sides together. Clip to the center of the V.

Topstitch the remaining bellows edge to the garment at the pocket placement area. Notice the shaping from the miter at the corner.

Clip the seam allowance of the bellows where it will be matched to the curve area. Stitch that edge of the bellows to the pocket.

shaped with a curve as shown so as to reduce bulk at the ends. Hem the end of the top end of the bellows piece before matching to pocket edge.

Edgestitch the bellows/pocket seam.

2. Match and stitch bellows piece to pocket and clip seam allowances at corners so that edge will lie flat when turned.

3. Finger-press the bellows under the pocket edge at the seamline and edgestitch the length of the bellows.

4. For an optional corner dart, fold the corner of the bellows piece, right sides together, at the corner/curve and stitch a small V-shaped pleat between the seam allowances to help the pocket lie flat.

5. The pocket placement lines should be the same size and shape as the

(continued on p. 154)

original pocket. As the pocket bellows is topstitched to the base garment, the folded edge of the bellows (where the seam allowances are turned under) should be placed on these lines to topstitch in place.

6. Topstitch any remaining pocket edges, as shown in the top left photo, up to the end of the bellows.

7. Bar-tack the upper hem edge and at the meeting point of the pocket and bellows edge in step 5.

8. A shaped flap (see p. 169) finishes this pocket design. It should be placed an inch above the pocket opening, stitched, and then topstitched in place. The snap closure application is shown on p. 87.

Topstitch the remaining pocket edge to the garment.

Stitch and topstitch the flap in place.

Bar-tack the hem edge to the top of the bellow.

The finished pocket.

be used for outerwear and may be found in some of the publications listed in Resources on p. 182.

A true pocket zipper has a stop at both ends and a pull tab that dangles rather than lies parallel to the teeth, like a jacket zipper does. Zippers with small coil teeth are good for pockets because they are less abrasive than large-tooth styles, but all different sizes and styles of zipper chain can be used. A lightweight coil dress zipper can be used for lighter fabrics such as in next-to-skin layers. Zippers can be altered for size and to function as a pocket zipper by changing the stops and adding tabs. Chapter 4 provides more information about zipper styles and using zipper stops.

Installing a zipper into a pocket is much easier than it might appear. Stitch a zipper box through either a single layer of the fabric, through a facing and the fabric, or through one side of the pocket bag and the fabric. The zipper box should be stitched using a smaller stitch than you would normally use for the particular fabric, especially when stitching the corners. The size of the box is variable but I prefer to make it ⅛ in. wider than the zipper teeth and as long as the measurement of the zipper just beyond the stops.

The instructions below may not always indicate switching to a zipper foot when needed. Assume that if the stitching is too close to the zipper stops, pulls, or zipper area, switch to a zipper foot. Another option is to adjust the needle position on a regular zigzag foot if it allows the stitching line to be as close as needed.

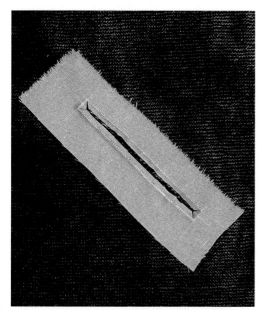

For a zippered in-fabric pocket, first stitch the zipper box, then slash through the box and clip into the corners.

Zippered in-fabric pocket not in a seam A zipper box can be sewn into some fabrics without a facing piece as in the case of mid- to heavyweight fleece fabrics or lighter weight knits that have been prefused as mentioned above. With lighter fabrics make a small facing of a woven, stable complementary fabric and cut it a few inches wider and longer than the zipper box, pinning right sides together at the box placement area.

1 Stitch the zipper box with the facing on top. Beginning and ending the stitching line on the sides of the box instead of the corners will prevent stitches from being pulled out.

2 Slash the box through the center, stopping ½ in. short of the end of the box, then clip into the corners as shown in the photo at left.

3 Turn the facing through to the wrong side and finger-press or low-temp press the sides and corners of the box flat.

4 Place the zipper under the opening and pin in place. Check the location of the pull to make sure it is at the end of the pocket you prefer. This is a personal preference—I prefer the pull to be at the bottom when closed. Just be consistent in the garment.

Consider This

Contrast piping is perfect when you don't want to make a big splash with the garment design but would like some nice colorful detail. It is easy to add using straight-grain ripped strips on straight edges and bias strips on curves. Stretch piping on stretch pants can be made with elastic cord and swim-weight nylon/Lycra.

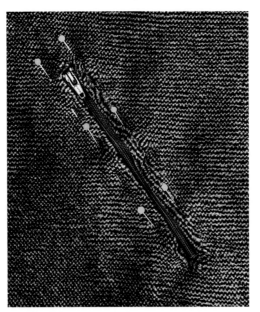

Turn the facing to the wrong side and pin the zipper under the opening.

Stitch around the zipper box on the right side and stitch the optional flap.

5 Sew in the zipper. Stitch around the zipper box, using a zipper foot through all the layers, back-tacking at the beginning and end of the stitching.

6 Optional flap (see the assembly instructions on p. 169): Stitch the flap right sides together with the garment, with the stitching line above and parallel to the zippered opening, securing the ends of the stitching line with back tacks. Trim the excess seam allowance of the flap and fold over the stitching line. Topstitch inside the previously sewn flap edge.

7 Place the pocket back under the garment piece and stitch in place. The pocket back can be the same size and shape as the lower garment piece. It is placed right side to the wrong side of the lower part of the garment and basted on all edges except where the stitching is exposed at the waist, which can be top-

Turn down and topstitch the flap, then baste the pocket back to the front at the edges and waist-line, through all layers.

stitched or secured in a drawstring casing. Any shape pocket back can be used because it is stitched through all layers.

If the weight of the flap causes the front piece to sag, stitch through all the layers at the flap topstitching line.

This process may also be used to apply a pocket bag by stitching the pocket bag piece(s) right sides together with the facing piece and finishing like the bags below.

In-fabric zippered pocket using pocket bags for lined and interlined applications An insulated or lined garment needs a full pocket bag (front and back). The process is very similar to above, but the zipper box is sewn through the bag piece. The bag can be cut as two separate pieces or as one that is folded at either the opening end or the bottom end.

Choose from three types of pocket bags. Cut two of the one on the upper right.

When making a hand-warmer pocket on the front of a jacket, the pocket bag can be made long enough to secure into the front stitching line (where the front zipper is attached) so that the bag stays in place when pulling your hand out. Cut the pocket bag to reach the full width of the front piece and baste through all layers of the seam allowances.

Piping adds color and definition to a zipper and makes it easier to center under the pocket opening. The thickness of the cord also prevents fabric from getting stuck in the zipper pull.

Piping in a contrasting color was used in the bottom left photo on p. 158 as a decorative finish of an in-fabric pocket. A center-front opening zipper can also be piped before being stitched to the garment for a nice detail. Though piping is often made with bias strips to turn corners and follow curves better, another option is to cut or rip crossgrain woven synthetic shell fabric for piping straight edges, seams, or zipper edges. Make

piping ahead or wrap piping fabric around cording and stitch while applying to the edge of the zipper. When using a piped zipper, adjust the width of the zipper box to accommodate the width of the piping. A piped zipper can also be used with a faced opening.

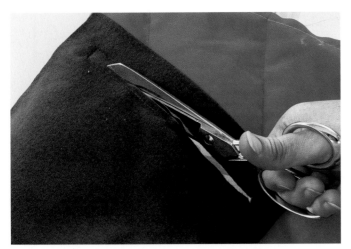

For an in-fabric zippered pocket, place the pocket bag over the zipper box area, right sides together, and stitch the zipper box. Slash open the box through all layers and clip into the corners.

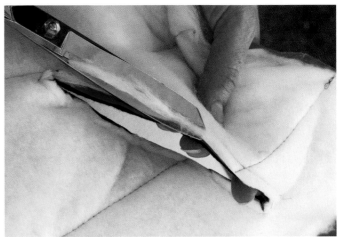

When working with insulations or fleece, trim excess batting or fleece from the seam allowance where possible.

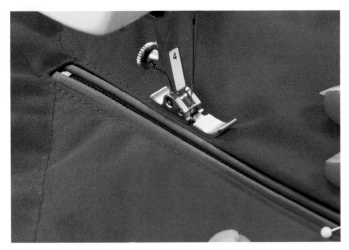

Place the zipper under the box opening and topstitch through all layers. Keep the layers underneath flat to prevent unwanted pieces from being caught in the stitching line.

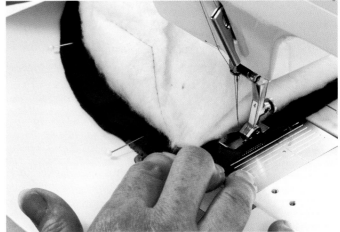

Place the remaining pocket bag right sides together with the one already in place. Holding the outer layer away from the stitching, stitch around the perimeter of the pocket bag. Stitch twice around the curve.

1 Place the pocket bag on the garment, right sides together, matching the zipper box placement lines, and stitch the box as shown on p. 155. When placing the two pieces right sides together, the bag should look as it will lie when inside the garment, with the large part of the bag to the correct side.

2 Slash the box and clip to the corners. Clip close to the corner, which will help the box lie flat when turned.

3 If the fabric is thick, like fleece or inter-lining, trim the excess bulk from the seam allowance in the zipper box.

Stitch a zipper box at the side seam the width of the zipper's teeth and glide area, plus seam allowance and the length of the measurement outside the zipper stops.

Align the zipper right sides together with the inside edge of the zipper box, as shown. Stitch from corner to corner, starting and stopping at the corners of the box.

4 Turn the pocket bag to the wrong side of the garment. Finger-press the edges of the zipper box. Place piped (or not) zipper under the box, pin, and stitch in place using a zipper foot.

5 To finish, place the remaining pocket bag piece (or fold the bag to itself for single-piece pocket bags) and stitch around the cut edges. This may require using a zipper foot for areas near the zipper box.

6 Finish with a flap if desired as shown on p. 169.

In-seam zippered pocket An in-seam zipper can be used in a variety of ways. The zipper installation shown above for pockets (single-layer garment and lined garment) can also be used for underarm vents (see p. 164), yoke vents, wrist zips (as in the jacket in the photo on p. 165), and side-leg zippers or in a collar seam for a hideaway hood. As with the in-fabric pocket above, pockets in a seam have a pocket back for a single layer garment and pocket bags for a lined/interlined garment. It is unusual to see a flap in the single layer application of this pocket because of the configuration with the seamline.

To make a single layer in-seam pocket:

1 Determine the depth and length of the zipper box from the cut edge. Measure the width of the zipper that you want exposed plus seam allowance and the desired length of the zipper. Here, the zippered pocket is in single-face (100-weight) fleece using a ⅜-in. seam allowance. With ⅜ in. of the zipper teeth and tape revealed, the box is stitched ¾ in. wide by 7 in. long (outside the zipper stops).

2 Place the zipper right sides together with the garment at the zipper box stitching line so that the excess zipper tape is in the zipper box as shown in the photo above right. The stitching line for the zipper should be lined up with the

Clip through the fabric only to the corner of the box.

Fold the zipper to line up with the cut edge. Turn the end triangles to face the ends of the zipper and stitch from the edge to the corner of the zipper box through both layers.

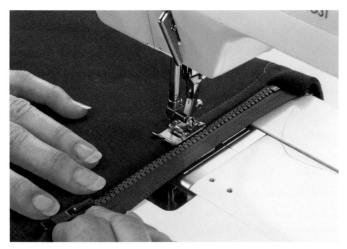

Turn to the right side and topstitch the inside edge of the zipper opening.

Place the pocket back on the wrong side of the pocket opening and pin in place.

stitching of the zipper box. Begin and end the stitching at the zipper box corner with a back tack.

3 Clip through the seam allowance of the fabric only at an angle to the corner of the box.

4 Fold the zipper back in line with the cut edge. Fold fabric down at the end of the zipper and pull the angled end (at the clip) across the end of the zipper to stitch the end of the zipper box. To make sure that the corner is square, the stitching line should create a continuous line with the folded fabric, as shown in left end of the photo.

5 With the right side of the garment up, topstitch the long edge of the zipper box.

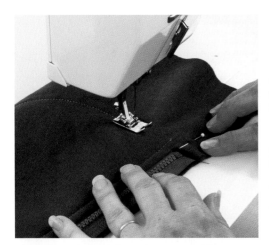

Working from the right or the wrong side, top-stitch or stitch through both layers to secure the pocket bag edge.

Baste zipper tape to pocket back. Pocket assembly finished and ready for stitching into seam.

6 Place the precut pocket back to the wrong side of the zipper area, matching at the cut edge of the garment. The pocket back should be slightly longer than the outside zipper box length at the seamline and large enough to accommodate hand width comfortably.

7 Pin through both layers—garment and pocket bag—and stitch around the pocket bag. I prefer to stitch from the right side so I can see what it will look like when finished, but you can also stitch from the wrong side. The ends of the zipper box are stitched in this pass.

8 Using the zipper foot, baste the outside zipper edge to the pocket back for easier stitching of the seamline. (If a flap is to be inserted in the seam, it should be done now.) The basting line can be used as a width guide for stitching the seam by keeping the pocket side up and following the basting line.

This pocket and zipper application were used in the black Thermal (Aqua) fleece jacket and skirt shown in the photo on p. 165.

In-seam zippered pocket with bags for lined/interlined applications

1 Place the pocket bag right sides together with the interlined (insulated) garment piece. As with a single-layer application, measure the width of the zipper to be revealed (e.g., $\frac{3}{8}$ in.) and add seam allowance for the side seam (e.g., $\frac{5}{8}$ in.), for the width of the zipper box (e.g., 1 in.), and from outside the zipper stops for the length of the box (e.g., 7 in.) Stitch the box this width and length.

2 Place one side of the pocket bag at the cut edge of the seamline at the pocket area so it extends above and below the zipper box area. Mark the zipper box on the edge of the pocket bag and stitch through all layers (keeping interlinings on the bed of the machine). Clip into

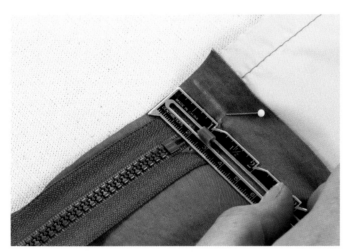

Measure the seam allowance and add the desired width of the zipper to be exposed (teeth plus glide area).

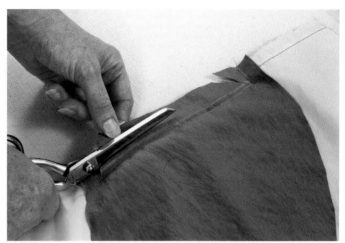

Clip into the corners and trim excess seam allowance from the box. Leave ½-in. allowance for high-fraying fabrics.

Finger-press the zipper box with the pocket bag to the wrong side of the garment. Place the zipper under the edge of the box and topstitch around the edge of the box through the zipper.

Place the remaining pocket bag to the pocket bag that is attached to the zipper, right sides together, and stitch.

> ### T I P
>
> *Don't* use a heated iron on synthetic interlinings. Finger-press instead!

the corner of the zipper box and trim some of the seam allowance on the long edge of the box, especially on bulky layers. Turn the pocket bag to the wrong side and finger-press the edges of the box.

3 Place the zipper under the prepared opening and pin though the layers in

the seamline. If the fabric has a membrane, pin in the stitching line rather than perpendicular to it. Topstitch the zipper in place.

4 Match the remaining pocket bag right sides together with the one already stitched to the zipper box. Holding the outside layers away, baste through the

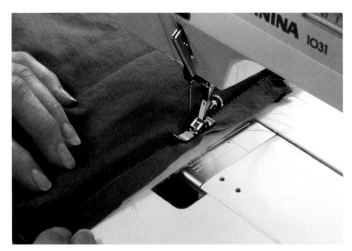

Use the basting line joining the zipper tape and pockets as a guide for stitching the seam.

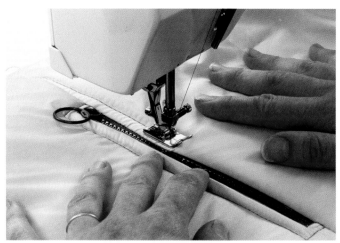

Topstitch seam allowances away from the zipper box. Hold the fabric flat away from the stitching line to prevent drag.

exposed edge of the zipper tape and the under pocket bag at the seamline.

5 With cut edges matching, stitch around the edge of the two pocket bags, keeping the outer fabric free of the stitching line.

6 When stitching the seam with the pocket, keep the piece with the pocket on top so that the basting line can be used as a guide for stitching the zipper area. It may be necessary to switch to a zipper foot when stitching through the pocket area.

7 Turn the garment to the right side. Keep the seam allowances folded away from the zipper and topstitch the seam through all layers.

An example of this in-seam zippered pocket is shown on the front of the iridescent moss-green parka in the photo on p. 4. The zippers at the wrist were also finished with this zipper application.

Pit Vents

The most important area for isolated vapor transmission is the underarm area, for obvious reasons. A lot of excess heat and vapor is released from this area.

Quick vents through all layers can be accomplished by putting two or three eyelets or grommets to the side of the seamline—one grommet won't accomplish much exchange of air for cooling. This type of venting doesn't require a pattern change. Grommets and eyelets can be applied through all layers, but the area may need reinforcing with interfacing if the fabric is lightweight.

The zippered pocket applications shown in the photo on p. 165 work well for a pit zip. For a greater degree of venting options, a double-pull, center-opening zipper can be used, such as is used in backpacks. This type of continuous zipper chain with zipper pulls applied at both ends is available from some retailers listed in Resources on p. 182. (See the illustration on p. 83.) Zippered vents can be left open to the inside or backed with a

When open, pit vents release a lot of excess body vapor.

Here's how to make a covered underarm vent with a single- or double-flap and with hook-and-loop tape closures:

1 Install an in-seam zipper (usually longer than a pocket zipper—8 in. to 10 in.) to the back piece at the side-seam edge, centered around the armscye seam as shown in the photo on the facing page.

2 Measure to determine the size of the flap. The finished length and width of the flaps should be larger than the zipper area, with a little extra width for hook-and-loop tape and manipulating the zipper pulls. Finished double flaps are about 1 in. to 1½ in. wider than the zipper area. A single flap should be cut a little wider, 1½ in. to 2 in. wider than the zipper area to match up with the loop tape that is stitched to the garment. Cut out the flap, and remember to add seam allowances to the cut edges.

3 Add hook-and-loop tape where needed on the flaps. (See p. 167.)

> ## T I P
>
> For ease of opening the zippered vents, the outermost (or a single) flap should face toward the front of the garment.

mesh gusset, which is especially appropriate for underlayers.

For a covered vent that is used frequently in w/p/b shells, construct flaps in the same manner as for a pocket or front/storm flap. The armscye of the sleeve must be attached before this type of vent can be sewn. The vent should be installed before the lining is installed.

4 To finish the outer edges of the flap, fold the flap right sides together and stitch the short ends. Clip the corners and trim the seams, then turn to the right side. Topstitch near the foldline on the long edge.

5 Draw flap placement lines with chalk or other marker on the shell at the zipper

This surprising jacket and skirt combination is made from Aqua Fleece, also used for dive suits. The flexibility and comfort of the fabric makes it very wearable. A rolling presser foot was helpful when topstitching. All in all, a quick outfit to make!

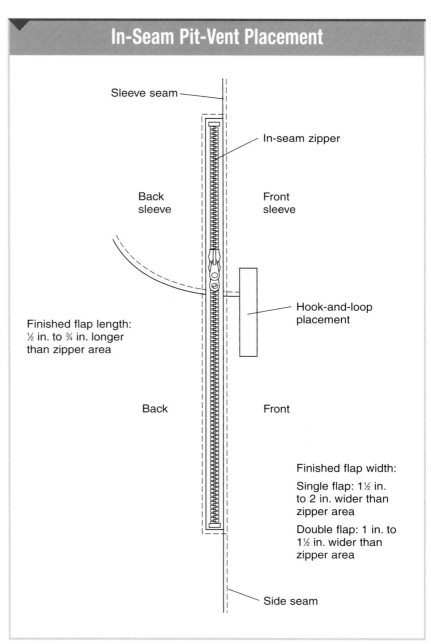

In-Seam Pit-Vent Placement

Sleeve seam

In-seam zipper

Back sleeve

Front sleeve

Hook-and-loop placement

Finished flap length: ½ in. to ¾ in. longer than zipper area

Back

Front

Finished flap width:

Single flap: 1½ in. to 2 in. wider than zipper area

Double flap: 1 in. to 1½ in. wider than zipper area

Side seam

location that is half the finished width of the flaps from the center of the zipper on either side (or on the back only for single flap placement). The placement line should be parallel to the zippered opening and the line indicating the length of the flap extending above and below the zipper evenly. Place the under-flap (or only flap) right sides together with the garment with the seamline of the flap overlapping the placement line (the flap should be lying away from the zipper). Stitch at the seamline and trim the seam allowance.

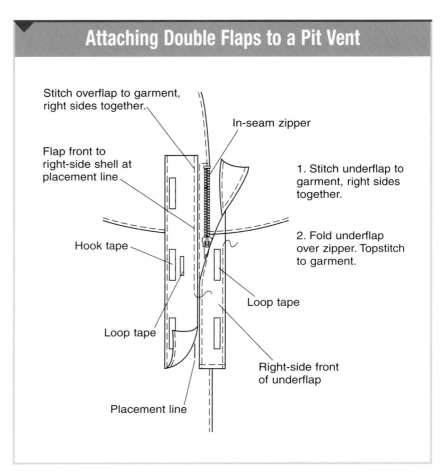

Attaching a Single Flap to a Pit Vent

- Sleeve back
- Sleeve front
- Topstitch
- Front of flap
- Hook-and-loop tape
- Open at flap center-fold edge
- Jacket back
- Jacket front

Attaching Double Flaps to a Pit Vent

- Stitch overflap to garment, right sides together.
- In-seam zipper
- Flap front to right-side shell at placement line
- 1. Stitch underflap to garment, right sides together.
- Hook tape
- 2. Fold underflap over zipper. Topstitch to garment.
- Loop tape
- Loop tape
- Right-side front of underflap
- Placement line

6 Fold the flap over the zippered opening and topstitch near the previous stitching line. Repeat for the outer flap, holding the inner flap out of the stitching area.

7 With the underflap lying over the zipper and the front flap over that, topstitch the flap ends through all layers to finish.

8 Shells that are lined may need to have the vent zipper area of the lining cut the same as the vent zipper box or left stitched close. The seam allowances can be folded under and hand-stitched to the wrong side of the zipper tape after seam-sealing the stitching lines of the flaps.

Pocket Flaps, Storm/Wind/Gutter Flaps, Chin Guards, and Tabs

There is one thing that the individual designer often finds intimidating about sewing the shell layer of outerwear, and that's all the flaps, chin guards, and tabs that are needed for keeping water out of the cracks and crevices of a shell. Fortunately, these are some of the easiest pieces to sew and definitely are design-as-you-go features.

Pocket Flaps and Basics of Flap Design and Placement

As you design the flap, make sure the pocket zipper and topstitching are covered com-

Keeping Flaps Out of the Way

To keep the flap(s) from flipping out under the arm, place loop-tape sections at the armscye seam area, and the corresponding hook tape is sewn to the back of the flap as in the illustration. Place hook-and-loop strips on double flaps with the underflap having loop tape on the top and the overflap having hook tape on the back. The strips can be attached before or after the ends of the flaps have been stitched and turned to the right side. The illustrations show the application before edge finishing, so that the hook-and-loop-tape stitching lines are not seen from the right side.

A trick for keeping a single or outer flap folded out of the way, which allows for better ventilation, is to sew both a strip of hook tape (for the main closure) near the fold- or seamline of the flap back, and also a narrow strip of loop tape just inside of that. When overheating occurs, the zipper can be opened and the flap folded against itself and kept out of the way.

Adding Hook-and-Loop Tape to a Pit-Vent Flap, Single Flap

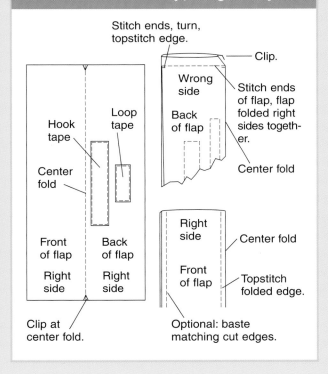

Adding Hook-and-Loop Tape to a Double Flap Vent

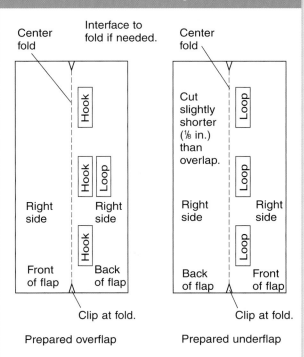

Consider This

Covering a problem area or adding a detail can be as easy as sewing on a patch. These colorful patches were inexpensive and required only a single line of stitching to attach. Use a zipper foot and stitch just inside the rolled edge. If the fabric underneath is coated, seam-seal to prevent leakage.

pletely. If there is any closure attached to the flap, an extra ½ in. to ¾ in. in depth beyond the closure is advised to be able to grasp the edge more easily when opening and closing, otherwise the flap can be made with only ¾ in. or so beyond the edge of the pocket opening. It's also a good idea to angle pockets and flaps away from the body because this will help move moisture away. After the flap shape is finalized, add seam allowances as you cut out the flap pieces from the pattern. Many patch pockets and flaps can be premade and positioned around the garment pieces to see how the parts look in different locations.

TIP

With sewn-on pocket flap designs, I find it helpful to cut a piece of paper or fabric to represent the finished flap as I'm working out the design. This flap design can be placed on the paper pattern or cut garment piece and moved around to see how it looks and to mark the flap placement.

Hook-and-loop tape or snaps can be added as a closure to a pocket flap. It's easier to stitch the tape down before the flap is stitched in place. Snaps can usually be applied afterward.

Decide before sewing the flap if you want to add an invisible closure. This can be made by sewing one or more sections of hook-and-loop tape to the right side of the flap lining. When the flap is assembled, the stitching line for the tape will be hidden. Then sew corresponding sections of hook-and-loop tape to the garment body. This is easiest to do with pocket designs that have a bag that can be moved out of the way when stitching the tape in place. This clo-

sure can also be used for front flaps over a separating zipper.

Flap options A straight-sided, rectangular flap can be made two ways. One way is to cut a single piece of fabric on a fold with seam allowances on the cut edges for attaching to the garment and seam allowances for finishing the ends. Fold the flap, right sides together, and stitch the flap ends that will not be enclosed in a seam. Corners should be clipped and seam allowances trimmed before turning the flap to the right side. Stitched edges should be finished with a row or two of topstitching and a basting line along the remaining cut edges to hold the edges in place.

More variation of shape can be accomplished with a two-piece flap. Cut two pieces of the flap—front and facing—with seam allowances for all cut edges. Stitch, right sides together, all edges that will be exposed. Clip and trim seam allowances and corners, then turn to the right side and topstitch. With either type of flap, the short ends can be left unfinished when they are enclosed in a seam.

Three stitched-on pocket flaps A flap can be independent of a seamline by finishing three sides. Place the flap right sides together with the garment at the pocket placement, stitch, trim excess seam allowance, then fold over the pocket (see the top right photo on p. 156). A topstitching line close to the original stitching line will help the pocket lie flat, and an optional stitching line at the upper end of the pocket will protect against moisture trickling under the flap (see the bottom photo on p. 156).

Flaps can be inserted in a seam. The patch pocket shown in the illustration on the facing page is placed just below the

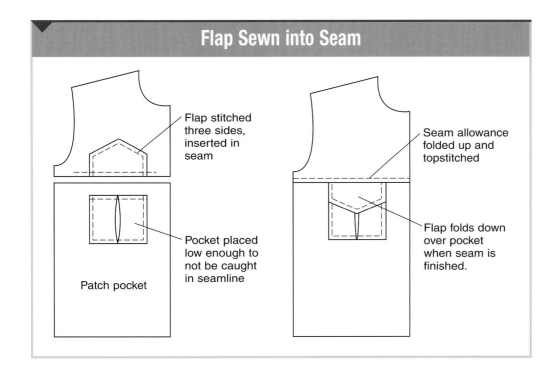

Flap Sewn into Seam

Flap stitched three sides, inserted in seam

Pocket placed low enough to not be caught in seamline

Patch pocket

Seam allowance folded up and topstitched

Flap folds down over pocket when seam is finished.

seamline so that as the seam is sewn, the flap will be secured in the seamline directly over it. The seam allowances are folded up so that the topstitching will go through all layers.

The third method, as shown in the illustration on p. 170, is a combination of the two above. The long edge is stitched right sides together, trimmed, folded over, and topstitched. The two ends can be stitched into seams or under overlays. Make this type of flap extra long and cut off the excess after it is stitched in place. This is the way that the flaps on the remade jacket were sewn in place (see the photo on p. 121).

Front Zipper Flaps by Any Name

Flaps that cover the front zipper opening are called different names: front flap, zipper flap, wind flap, and storm flap, to name a few. The function of this type of flap is to keep moisture from going through the zipper. This flap may also be used on the side of a pant leg.

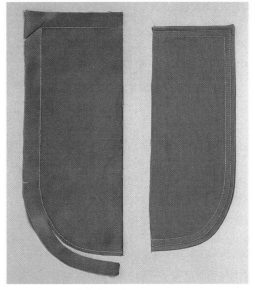

A two-piece, shaped pocket flap.

The outermost front flap is most often referred to as a storm flap, but may also be referred to as a front flap, rain flap, or wind flap. The gutter flap refers to a second flap, which lies under the outermost flap to pro-

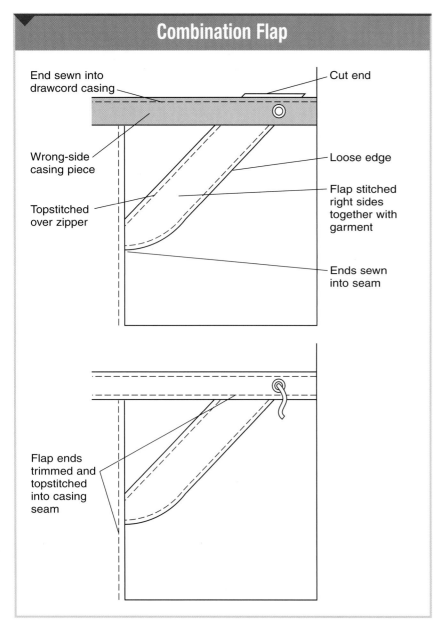

Combination Flap

End sewn into
drawcord casing

Cut end

Wrong-side
casing piece

Loose edge

Topstitched
over zipper

Flap stitched
right sides
together with
garment

Ends sewn
into seam

Flap ends
trimmed and
topstitched
into casing
seam

For outer flaps I like the ease of adding flaps to the left and right of the center front of the jacket. This allows for easier assembly and seam-sealing, in addition to giving room to maneuver the zipper pull when complete. They are sewn in place while the jacket is still unlined, in the same way that the pocket flaps are sewn: Stitch, right sides together, on the placement line (the flap extending away from the zipper that it will cover), trim seam allowances, then fold the flap over the zipper to topstitch in place (see above).

You can also cut a front flap as part of the jacket front or insert a flap into the seamline when installing the zipper, but I find that adding flaps using the method below produces far better results. For a quick and easy zipper-flap combination, see the sidebar on p. 176.

Front flap size and placement When making a front flap, first decide what kind of closure you want (hook-and-loop tape, snap) so you can make the flap the correct width. Front flaps also should be given enough width to be easily sewn to the shell just outside the center-front zipper area, cover the zipper and closures, and still have a little bit of gripping area for manipulating the closure. The length of the flap is usually the length of the center front or at least long enough to cover both ends of the zipper. If you have an inside flap, a shorter outer flap from the collar seam to the bottom of the jacket is still functional. As mentioned above, using a piece of paper or fabric to represent the design of the flap will make it easier to make decisions on design.

Before you stitch on a zipper flap, decide if you want it to open on the right or left. Traditionally, jackets open on the right for men and the left for women. Zippers in a

tect the wearer from driving rain that gets forced under the outer flap. A flap that is under the zipper and inside the garment may be referred to as a zipper flap or wind flap, but we'll refer to it as an inner flap here. Manufacturers differ in their names for different kinds of flaps but are usually clear in advertising literature as to what their functions are and where they are located.

Front Flap Placement and Stitching Lines

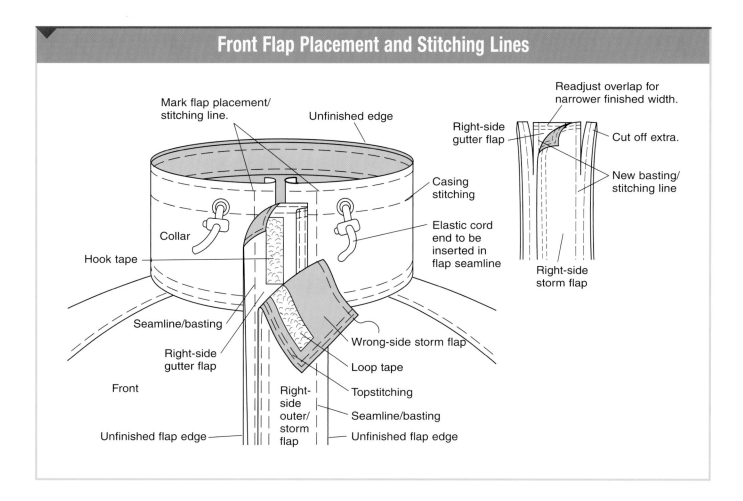

Mark flap placement/stitching line.

Unfinished edge

Readjust overlap for narrower finished width.

Right-side gutter flap

Cut off extra.

Casing stitching

New basting/stitching line

Collar

Elastic cord end to be inserted in flap seamline

Right-side storm flap

Hook tape

Seamline/basting

Right-side gutter flap

Wrong-side storm flap

Front

Loop tape

Right-side outer/storm flap

Topstitching

Seamline/basting

Unfinished flap edge

Unfinished flap edge

pants fly follow the same rule. If you want to be traditional, make sure the outermost flap is facing the correct way. I prefer a right opening on my gear because I'm right handed and it's easier to manipulate the snap or hook-and-loop tape. I don't think people really notice which way my parka opens. When sewing for men, though, I think it's safer to stay with a right-handed opening. I can almost guarantee you they will notice the difference right away! For a right-handed opening, the outermost storm flap is sewn to the left front and closes to the right. If there is an outer gutter flap under the storm flap, it is sewn to the right front and closes to the left under the storm flap.

When making two outer flaps—a gutter and a storm flap—make them the same size. They will overlap and match exactly when centered over the zipper.

1 Baste the unfinished edges of the flap at the stitching line (on the flap only, where the flap will be sewn to the garment). Then you can match up the flaps so that only the seam allowance extends beyond on either side.

2 Center the flap combination over the zipper to double-check the coverage. Making straight flaps wider than needed (except if hook-and-loop tape is pre-placed and stitched) helps in the assembly when you aren't sure how wide you

Integrating Front Flaps with Other Design Features

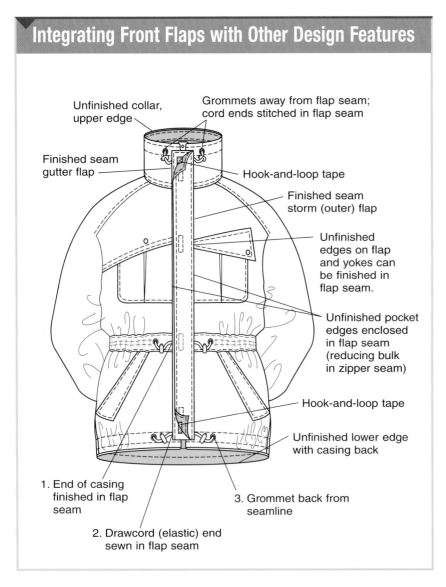

Unfinished collar, upper edge

Grommets away from flap seam; cord ends stitched in flap seam

Finished seam gutter flap

Hook-and-loop tape

Finished seam storm (outer) flap

Unfinished edges on flap and yokes can be finished in flap seam.

Unfinished pocket edges enclosed in flap seam (reducing bulk in zipper seam)

Hook-and-loop tape

Unfinished lower edge with casing back

1. End of casing finished in flap seam

2. Drawcord (elastic) end sewn in flap seam

3. Grommet back from seamline

want the flaps to be. The finished width of the dual flaps can be adjusted after comparing with the assembled (unlined) shell to decide on the right width for the flap combination.

3 Once the right width has been determined, baste the new adjusted stitching line on the flap (to be matched with the stitching placement line on the shell, below in step 4). (See the illustration on p. 171.)

4 Mark the stitching placement line on the shell with chalk or other sewing marker. The placement lines should be equidistant from and parallel to the zipper all the way down. To double-check the width, divide the *finished* flap width in two (e.g., one-half of 3 in. is 1½ in.). The placement line should be that distance (e.g., 1½ in.) from the center of the closed zipper on either side.

5 After the size and positioning of the flaps are finalized, closures can be applied before the flaps are stitched to the garment. Closures should be placed in specific locations on front flaps: near the top, at the neckline seam, at the waist, and at the bottom. These are areas that tend to pull and, without a closure, may gap. Between the closure at the neckline seam and the waist there is usually space for one or more evenly spaced closures, and sometimes between the waist and the bottom.

6 With the flaps connected by the closures, stitch one side of the flaps in place along the stitching line on the wrong side of the flap, keeping the finished edge of the other flap out of the stitching line (and the zipper seam allowance flat and out of the way). This allows double-checking to see if the unit is stitched in straight and lying flat.

7 After one side is stitched in place, fold the unit flat over the closed zipper, and turn under the remaining flap seam allowance. You should be able to see the other placement line. If not, readjust the placement line or the flaps. (With hook-and-loop tape, there is some crosswise leeway for repositioning.)

This chin-guard style wraps over the top of the zipper to protect from abrasion by the zipper pull and from wind through the zipper.

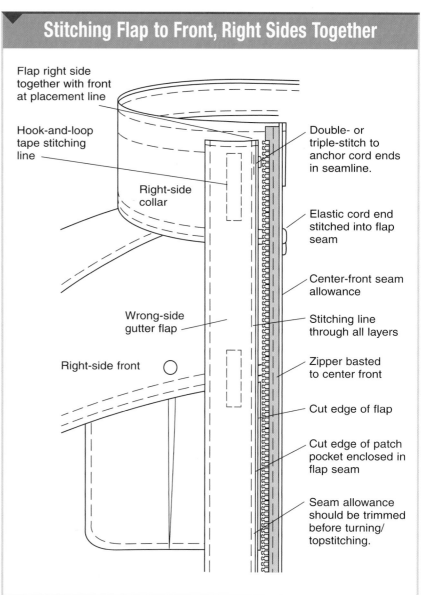

Stitching Flap to Front, Right Sides Together

Flap right side together with front at placement line

Hook-and-loop tape stitching line

Right-side collar

Wrong-side gutter flap

Right-side front

Double- or triple-stitch to anchor cord ends in seamline.

Elastic cord end stitched into flap seam

Center-front seam allowance

Stitching line through all layers

Zipper basted to center front

Cut edge of flap

Cut edge of patch pocket enclosed in flap seam

Seam allowance should be trimmed before turning/ topstitching.

There are times you may want only one flap on the outside. Follow the placement process above and be sure that enough of the flap extends over the zipper to apply closures without interfering with the zipper.

For a better-functioning gutter flap, fold a narrow section (about ½ in.) of the inside finished edge of the flap to the outside, with right sides together. Edgestitch close to the fold. The extra "gutter" edge will provide additional protection from torrential rain and wind. See the photo above and the bottom photo on p. 132.

Inner flap or chin guard An inner flap is used as an extra defense against moisture when no flap or only one flap is used on the outside of a garment. A chin guard is an essential feature for most shells or any gar-

ment that has a zipper that comes in front of the face. A cold zipper pull and teeth can be very irritating on the skin.

A full-length inner flap should be as long as the zipper (the flap pattern should be cut the length of the zipper with seam allowances added, so that the flap covers the back of the zipper completely). The length of a chin guard is variable, but to keep it from popping out through the zipper, make

Chin Guard Variation

The chin guard shown in the photos on pp. 173 and at left (and in the photo on p. 116) is a modification of the chin guard described above, which provides complete coverage of the zipper pull. This chin guard is longer than the one above and has a curved shape at the top and bottom. The front (right) side of the chin guard is placed to the wrong side of the zipper before it is stitched in place, with the curved portion at the top wrapped to the right side of the zipper. Fold out the excess zipper tape so that the top stop of the zipper is right under the fold. Baste the prepared zipper in place, right sides together with the center front of the garment.

With the extra length on this chin guard wrapped over the closed zipper, it provides more protection for the face from abrasion by the zipper pull.

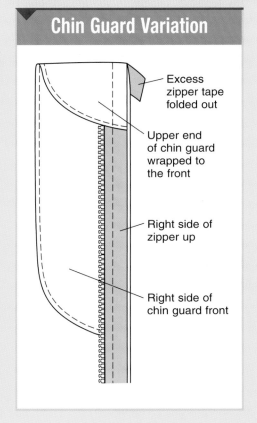

Chin Guard Variation

Excess zipper tape folded out

Upper end of chin guard wrapped to the front

Right side of zipper up

Right side of chin guard front

it long enough to end a few inches below the neckline. An inner flap can be placed on either side of the front, but if there is an outer flap, it's easier to manipulate the bottom of the zipper if the inner flap is placed on the opposite side of the front as the outer flap. A chin guard, on the other hand, is usually on the same side as the outermost flap, especially if there are two outer flaps. It is common to have two outer flaps in combination with either a chin guard or inner flap but not both. An inner flap can func-

tion as a chin guard and the two, together, would get in the way of each other.

Chin guards and full length inner flaps are cut and assembled in the same way as a pocket flap or outer flap. One difference is that a chin guard is curved at the bottom, which helps keep it out of the zipper.

Both of these inner flaps are sewn into the garment behind the front zipper after it has been basted in place. The piece is placed over the back of one side of the zipper, with the right side of the flap to the wrong side of the zipper. These flaps can be sewn to the garment before or after the outer flaps have been stitched in place but before the lining is attached.

Finishing touches on flaps Extra rows of topstitching add definition to the shape of a flap. For easier topstitching, use an edgestitching foot for the first row of top-stitching; then switch to a zigzag foot and offset the machine needle as needed so that the presser foot rides flat on the fabric and the edge of the foot follows the previous stitching line as the next row is stitched.

Piping in a contrasting color is a dynamic detail for flaps. Cut bias strips of a comple-mentary synthetic fabric to make the piping. Stitch the piping around the front-flap piece at the seamline before the flap back is stitched in place. When stitching piping around a corner, drop the needle at the exact corner of the seamline, raise the press-er foot or zipper foot, and clip through the seam allowance of the piping all the way to the needle. This allows the piping to turn the corner easily as you pivot the flap around the corner.

A subtle way to add color is to make the flap back/lining from a contrasting color. It is a visual surprise when used on the back of pocket flaps, front flaps, as bellows, or as the collar or hood lining. I added purple to my spruce green parka to give the color a little more liveliness, but a yoke or patch pocket would be too much contrast; using purple on the back of the flaps was just right (see the bottom photo on p. 31).

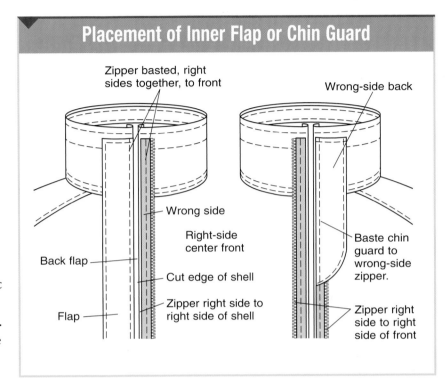

Placement of Inner Flap or Chin Guard

Zipper basted, right sides together, to front

Wrong-side back

Wrong side

Right-side center front

Back flap

Cut edge of shell

Flap

Zipper right side to right side of shell

Baste chin guard to wrong-side zipper.

Zipper right side to right side of front

By working with smaller units of pockets and flaps as well as other design features, you will gain confidence and broaden your perspective of what you can accomplish. Manufactured garments that are highly engineered will not seem beyond your skills when broken down into parts.

That's it! I hope you found specifics that you might have been looking for and ideas that will motivate you to try new things. Outerwear is a great area for sewing and it's become a fascinating world of new fabric innovations that make our life spent in the elements easier.

Go forth and make warm, dry things to wear outdoors!

Combination Front Zipper and Flap Unit

When you design-as-you-go, the more design elements that you can use as individual units, the simpler they are to use. Wouldn't it be great if you could simplify the front zipper and flaps? The combination shown in the illustration below combines the double front flap and front zipper, and can have the chin guard as shown on the photo on p. 173. This unit can easily be sewn into the front of a jacket after assembling ahead of time. There may also be times where this combination can be used as a comprehensive repair, like when a center-front zipper is broken and/or the closures not workable.

The combination of flap and zipper panel will result in having to remove width at the center front of the garment, so it is better to make the zipper combo before applying details that might come to the center front of the garment, like drawstring casings with grommets or pockets that

Designing a Front Zipper/Flap Combination

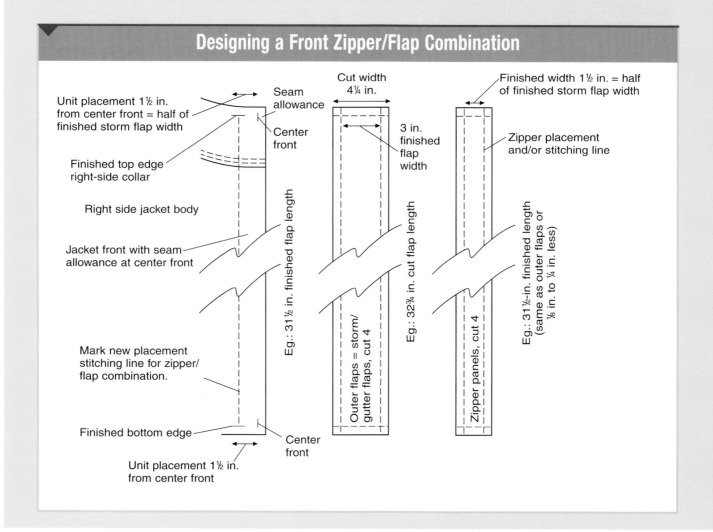

Unit placement 1½ in. from center front = half of finished storm flap width

Seam allowance

Center front

Finished top edge right-side collar

Right side jacket body

Jacket front with seam allowance at center front

Mark new placement stitching line for zipper/flap combination.

Finished bottom edge

Center front

Unit placement 1½ in. from center front

Eg.: 31½ in. finished flap length

Cut width 4¼ in.

3 in. finished flap width

Outer flaps = storm/ gutter flaps, cut 4

Eg.: 32¾ in. cut flap length

Finished width 1½ in. = half of finished storm flap width

Zipper placement and/or stitching line

Zipper panels, cut 4

Eg.: 31½-in. finished length (same as outer flaps or ⅛ in. to ¼ in. less)

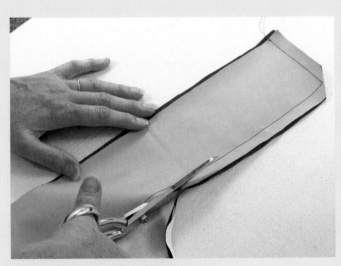

Trim the seam allowances and clip corners.

Turn the front flap to the right side to edge/topstitch as desired.

would lose width. After the zipper/flap unit is complete, it can be set aside while the other pieces are sewn in place.

For a full-length panel, measure the center-front edge, half the finished flap width in from the center-front cut edge, from hemline to the upper-collar seamline. If the flap is 3 in. wide, measure 1½ in. in from the center front at the seamline. This will also become the placement line. The zipper panel and flap can be shorter than the center front if desired. The finished zipper panel will be slightly wider than 3 in. because of the width of the exposed zipper (about ½ in.), but it can be cut off in the final placement of the flaps.

To make the zipper panel, we'll use a particular width and length for example only. The panel can be made wider or narrower, longer or shorter to accommodate a particular garment.

1. To make a finished center zipper/flap combination panel that will be the full length of the center front of the jacket and 3 in. wide, measure the center-front edge, 1½ in. from the center front seamline between the top and bottom seamlines. Mark the measurement line with chalk or other appropriate marker to use as a stitching line when the combination is complete. There is no need to trim off

the excess fabric at center front until after the flaps have been stitched in place. The front of this jacket measured 31½ in., so the finished outer flaps will measure 31½ in. by 3 in. Four flap pieces (two outer and two lining) are cut 4¼ in. wide (the desired width plus two seam allowances of ⅝ in.) by 32¾ in. long (the desired length plus seam allowances). These flaps may also be cut on a fold, which would make two pieces cut 7¼ in. wide by 32¾ in.

2. Interface or interline the wrong side of flap fronts (if needed) and apply hidden hook-and-loop tape closures if desired. Trim excess interfacing from the seam allowance. Place the front and lining pieces of the storm flap (outer flap) right sides together and stitch three sides (top, long side, bottom) as shown in the left photo above. Trim the seam allowances and clip corners.

3. Turn the flap to the right side and topstitch. Repeat for the gutter flap (inner flap). For a stitched gutter (be sure you are stitching the inner gutter flap according to which direction the garment will open), see above on p. 171.

(continued on p. 178)

Combination Front Zipper and Flap Unit (continued)

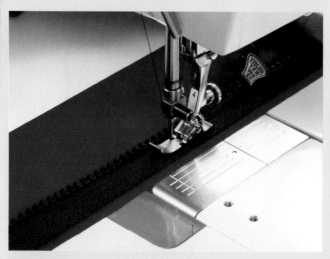

Baste one side of the zipper to the zipper panel at the seamline, with right sides together.

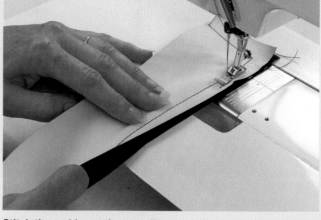

Stitch three sides at the seamline, top, zipper side, and bottom. Use the basting line as a stitching guide.

4. Place the storm flap over the gutter flap so that only the seam allowances of the flaps extend on either side. Apply snaps to both layers or sew loop tape sections to the gutter flap at the desired spacing.

5. Cut four zipper panels the same length (32¾ in.) as the outer flaps or ⅛ in. to ¼ in. shorter so that the ends of the zipper are more thoroughly covered by the outer flaps. The zipper panels are cut 2½ in. wide (1½ in. on each side of the zipper plus two seam allowances). Interline or interface the outer pieces if necessary.

6. Separate the zipper and place one side right sides together with the cut edge of a zipper panel. Shorten the zipper if needed (see p. 84). If using the chin guard variation shown in the illustration on p. 174, position it now. Pin zipper in place along the seamline.

7. Baste one side of the zipper to the zipper panel at the seamline with right sides together.

8. Repeat for the other side of the zipper.

9. Zip the two zipper halves together to make sure the placement of the zipper halves matches on each side. If a regular chin guard or inner flap is used, it can be placed over the wrong side of one of the zipper backs and basted in place.

10. Place the back of the zipper panel over the basted pieces, right sides together with the basted piece (zipper and chin guard) in between. Pin in the seam allowances and stitch around three sides (top, zipper, and lower edge), following the previous stitching line on the zipper edge.

11. Trim the seam allowance across corners and turn to the right side. Zip panels together and double-check the matching edges at top and bottom before topstitching.

Topstitch as desired. As shown here, a regular foot with the needle offset to the right provides more control for topstitching than using the zipper foot.

Completed combination zipper and front flap, ready to be stitched to garment.

12. Center the prepared flaps over the prepared zipper panel so that they lie flat together and the zipper panels are covered at the top and bottom. If the zipper panel or flap cut edges are wider than needed on either side (from the width of the stitched-in zipper), the excess can be trimmed off after the flap and zipper panels are basted together.

13. Place the finished flap/zipper combination on the previously marked seam/placement line (it's also the original measuring point from step 1.), right sides together. Stitch, using the basting line of the zipper/flap combo as a guide. The excess width at center front can be left in place until after the panels have been stitched in place or be trimmed away, leaving a seam allowance to the inside of the placement line if it is easier to stitch.

14. When attaching a lining or facing, fold the flap/zipper back against the front when stitching the lining, right sides together with the outer layer and stitch.

If you are seam-sealing and then adding a lining, stitch the lining in place with a narrower seam allowance than the first stitching pass. Don't topstitch until you have seam-sealed the center-front seamline from the wrong side of the front. Review the information for sealing the front edge on p. 76. In a single-layer shell, the seam is topstitched and the seam allowance trimmed and seam-sealed. Three-layer seam tape can be used, but I found using Heat'n'Bond to make matching seam-sealing tape from the w/p/b shell fabric resulted in an attractive seam-sealed surface between the combination flap unit and the body of the garment. It bonded to both shell and lining fabric over the exposed stitching line easily.

The flap/zipper combination in the jacket on p. 173 is assembled as shown here but differs in that the storm/gutter flaps are shorter to expose the collar portion of the zipper, with the chin guard functioning as secondary flap protection.

Glossary

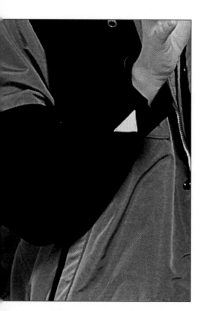

anatomic shaping - A shape that conforms closely to the body shape, especially at flexing points.

armscye - The arm-opening shape on pattern pieces; synonymous with armhole.

bar-tack - Stitching back and forth to create a wide stitch, made to reinforce an area.

batting - A sheet (or bat) form of fillers used as interlining and insulation, usually comes on a linear roll, by the yard.

bearding - Insulation micro fibers that have come through an exterior shell or other fabric, causing it to look as if it has a white beard.

bias binding - An edge finish made from the true bias (45-degree angle from grain and crossgrain) of a woven fabric. It is constructed by cutting bias strips four times the desired finished width of the edge finish (e.g., 4 x ⅜ in. = 1½ in.). The binding is then placed right side to the wrong side of the garment edge and stitched at the seamline (the width of the finished binding from the edge, e.g., ⅜ in.). Binding is wrapped around the seam allowance and stitched to the right side, folding the seam allowance of the binding under while topstitching. The right-side binding edge should just cover the previous stitching line. The topstitched binding method can also be used with strips of crossgrain knit and Lycra knit fabrics. To counteract some bias twisting problems, try stitching with the bias on the bed of the machine on the first pass so that both stitching lines are sewn in the same direction.

bonded fabric - Fabric that has been adhered to another fabric or laminate (such as Windbloc fleece) to provide a certain function or appearance.

bonding - The process of joining two or more layers of fabric or laminate together with an adhesive.

box-stitch - Stitching a box shape or rectangle to reinforce an area.

CLO - Units for measuring relative warmth. Factors included in calculation are body coverage, thermal retention of insulation and fabrics, breathability, activity level of individual, and so forth. For means of comparison, an active skier may require protection of 4.3 CLO. Thinsulate 100 provides about 1.3 CLO, and Polartec® Thermal Stretch has about 1 CLO unit.

coated/uncoated fabrics - Liquid coatings applied during fabric production (to the right or wrong side) to inhibit water transmission in the finished fabric (or to perform some other function, such as wind blocking).

color blocking - The process of creating smaller sections (or blocks) of color from a large pattern piece by cutting the pattern, adding seam allowances, and sewing the pieces together.

component layering - Dressing for weather in separate units—using individual pieces for warmth, water repellency, and wicking moisture—that can easily be added or removed as weather and needs dictate.

cord lock - A piece of hardware that clamps a drawcord and is used to adjust cord length.

denier - The size of a filament yarn.

double bias binding - Double bias strips are cut six times the desired finished width (e.g., 6 x ⅜ in. = 2¼ in.), then folded lengthwise so that the cut edges are matching. Place the cut edges of the bias to the wrong side of the garment edge and stitch at the seamline (one finished width measurement, e.g., ⅜ in.). Wrap the folded binding around the seam allowance to slightly cover the previous stitching line, then topstitch in place. *See* "bias binding" for a description of cutting bias strips and other tips.

drawcord/shockcord - Cord used for adjusting fit and air flow. Often used at the waist, the lower hem, and the top of the collar. Shockcord is elastic, often used in climbing and hiking equipment, and in smaller diameters is easily used for drawcord purposes.

D-ring tabs - A small length of finished fabric or webbing used to hold a D-ring in a garment seam.

dwr - An abbreviation for a "durable and water-repellent" treatment (finish) applied to fabric for increased performance.

ease - The extra "room" built into a garment for flexibility and comfort.

fabric treatment - A chemical finish added to a fabric to enhance or encourage a specific function. There are water-repellent treatments, heat-exchanging treatments (versions of Outlasts!), hydrophilic (water-loving) treatments, and antimicrobial treatments.

face fabric - The right side of a fabric, which faces the outside.

fiber - The smallest basic unit for creating fabric.

gutter - A ditch stitched into a garment where water can be directed away from the interior of the garment.

hand - The hand of a fabric is the way a fabric feels and drapes when handled.

high-loft soft insulations - Lofty microfiber insulations made to give the appearance of down.

hydrophilic - Having an affinity to water. They are fabric treatments used to transport moisture. See also "hydrophobic."

hydrophobic - Having little or no affinity to water. Synthetic hydrophobic fibers are treated with hydrophilic chemicals to enhance moisture transport in wicking fabrics.

interlining - A functional inner layer (or underlining) that is not seen; used in the construction of a garment (utilized in this book for insulative layers).

lamination - In this context, lamination unites a piece of fabric to a sheet of membrane, such as PTFE Teflon or some other sheet material by a bonding process. See "membrane laminate."

loft - The thickness of a fabric or insulation.

membrane laminate - A thin monolithic sheet bonded (laminated) to the right or wrong side of fabric in order to enhance certain qualities such as water repellency or wind blocking. Gore-Tex® (PTFE: polytetrafloroethylene) is an example of a laminate.

microfiber - Tiny man-made fibers measured in microns.

microfleece - Soft, lightweight fleece constructed with microfibers; has a short-napped velour hand.

negative ease - The amount a garment's pattern is made smaller than the body measurement when fitting superstretchy fabrics.

overlay - A layer of fabric or trim that is laid over (and subsequently stitched to) a base fabric/garment layer.

piping - A folded-over trim containing cording that is usually sewn in seams.

ply - A strand of yarn that can be twisted or combined with others to make multiple yarns (often 2- or 3-ply in outerwear fabrics) or thread (for sewing purposes).

scrim/remay - A thin interfacing-type fabric bonded or loosely attached to an insulative fabric. Used to keep microfibers from "bearding" through fabrics.

seam profile - In this context, the slight fold made by the seam allowances and the topstitching lines.

shell - Refers to an outer layer garment, with wind- and water-resisting capabilities.

shockcord - See "drawcord."

single-faced fleece - A fleece fabric that is napped or meant to be used with a particular side as the right side.

skin suit - A stretchy, close fitting, thin, lightweight, single layer, full bodysuit. It is used in downhill racing, cross-country skiing/racing, and ice skating/racing to obtain streamlined aerodynamics.

snow cuff - A protective cuff, usually attached to the inside of a snowpants' hem, that prevents snow from getting up the pant leg.

surface density - An indicator of how tightly woven a fabric may be for natural water repellency when using synthetic fibers.

tensile strength - The resistance of a material to lengthwise stress.

thermal value - The amount of warmth provided from a garment or fabric (in this context).

thread count - The number of threads per inch, weft and warp. For example, 160 x 90 nylon taffeta has 160 threads in the weft per inch and 90 in the warp.

tricot knit - A flexible knitted fabric that may be used for linings and as a protective backing for laminates (e.g., Gore-Tex®) when made from lightweight synthetics. When made with Lycra in heavier weights, the fabric is used for swim and cycling garments, and for stretch bindings.

weave - A pattern or method in which a fabric has been woven (interlaced).

webbing - Woven or braided, narrow, flat, or tubular trims, very durable and most often used with hardware.

w/p/b - An abbreviation for "waterproof and breathable," the capacity of a fabric or coating/lamination to be both waterproof and breathable at the same time. Must meet government guidelines for waterproofness while maintaining the ability to transmit vapor.

yarn - Multiple fibers gathered into a strand and sometimes twisted.

Resources

Beacon Fabric and Notions
(800) 713-8157
www.beaconfabric.com
Fabric and notions

Boulder Mountain Repair
607 S. Broadway, Unit E
Boulder, CO 80303
(303) 499-3634
www.bouldermountainrepair.com
Recycling and refurbishing outdoor equipment
(except for footwear)

Cascade Layers
P.O. Box 86453
Portland, OR 97286-6453
(503) 235-0747
cascadelayers.com
Rochelle Harper's business: mail-order brochure $2;
ideas, information, and outerwear-sewing related
products

The Green Pepper
1285 River Rd.
Eugene, OR 97404
(541) 689-3292
Fax (800) 767-5684, (541) 689-3591
www.thegreenpepper.com
info@the greenpepper.com
Free catalog; outerwear patterns

Oregon Tailor Supply
2123 S.E. Division St.
Portland, OR 97202
(800) 678-2457, (503) 232-6191
Fax (877) 233-9621
www.oregontailor.com
Free catalog; notions: snaps, zippers

Outdoor Wilderness Fabrics
16415 N. Midland Blvd.
Nampa, ID 83687
(800) 693-7467 (orders only), (208) 466-1602
Fax (800) 333-6930, (208) 463-4622
www.owfinc.com
owfinc@owfinc.com
Free catalog; outdoor fabrics and supplies

Quest Outfitters
4919 Hubner Circle
Sarasota, FL 34241
(800) 359-6931
www.questoutfitters.com
questoutfitters@home.com
Free catalog; retail store

Ragged Mountain Equipment
P.O. Box 130
Route 16-302
Intervale, NH 03845
(603) 356-3042
Fax (603) 356-8815
  and
Albany, NY
(518) 453-6120
www.RaggedMountain.com
email@RaggedMountain.com
Fabrics and supplies

The Rain Shed
707 N.W. 11th St.
Corvallis, OR 97330
(541) 753-8900
Fax (541) 757-1887
www.therainshed.com
Outdoor fabric and supplies; catalog and retail store

Rose City Textiles
2515 N.W. Nicolai
Portland, OR 97210-1814
(800) 482-4990, (503) 229-0395
Fax (503) 224-7472
www.rosecitytextiles.com
retail@rosecitytextiles.com
Outerwear fabrics; wholesale pricing and retail
store; swatches

Seattle Fabrics
8702 Aurora Ave. N
Seattle, WA 98103
(206) 525-0670
www.seattlefabrics.com
seattlefabrics@msn.com
Catalog $3 (refundable); fabrics and supplies

Wy'East Fabrics
P.O. Box 7328
2895 Valpak Rd. NE
Salem, OR 97303
(503) 364-8419
Fax (503) 391-8057
www.wyeastfabrics.com
info@wyeastfabrics.com
Catalog online; outdoor fabrics; equipment and
gear; supplies and repair

Canadian Resources

Evelyn's Sewing Centre
17817 Leslie St., #40
Newmarket, ON L3Y 8C6
Canada
(905) 853-7001
Fax (905) 853-6253
www.evelynssewingcentre.com
helpme@evelynssewingcentre.com
Retail store, outerwear fabrics, and supplies

Fabrics for the Great Outdoors
4560 Dixie Rd.
Mississauga, ON L4W 1N2
Canada
(800) 798-5885, (905) 629-4694
Fax (905) 629-4714
www.fabrics-outdoors.ca
fabrics-outdoors@sympatico.ca
Free Catalog; outdoor fabrics and supplies

Jalie Patterns
2478 Rue Martel
St.-Romould, PQ G6W 6L2
Canada
(418) 839-7214
Fax (418) 839-9599
www.Jalie.com
Outerwear patterns

MacPhee Workshop
Box 10, Site 16
R.R. 8
Edmonton, AB T5L 4H8
Canada
(888) 622-7433, (780) 973-3516
Fax (780) 973-6216
www.macpheeworkshop.com
hmacphee@macpheeworkshop.com
Catalog $4 (U.S.); outerwear fabrics and supplies

Pitter Patterns/Elements
358 Danforth Ave.
P.O. Box 65100
Toronto, ON M4K 3Z2
Canada
(800) 458-5185, (416) 604-7111
Fax (416) 604-8814
pitter_patterns@hotmail.com
Outerwear patterns for children and adults

Sundrop Outerwear Textiles
#310 – 2071 Kingsway Ave.
Port Coquitlam, BC V3C 6N2
Canada
(604) 464-5236
Fax (604) 464-5237
www.sundroptextiles.com
sundrop@sundroptextiles.com
Outdoor fabrics, patterns, and supplies

Textile Outfitters
735 10th Ave. SW
Calgary, AB T2R 0B3
Canada
(403) 543-7676
Fax (403) 543-7677
www.justmakeit.com, www.textileoutfitters.com
moreinfo@justmakeit.com
Catalog free in Canada, $2.50 in U.S.

Retail Stores
Check telephone yellow pages under "Sporting Goods, Retail" for used gear and repair products.

Denver Fabrics
2777 W. Belleview Ave.
Littleton, CO 80123
(800) 996-6902, (303) 730-2777
www.denverfabrics.com

Malden Mills Retail Stores:
2401 Utah Ave. S, #150
Seattle, WA 98134
(206) 682-7037
 and
46 Stafford St.
Lawrence, MA 01841
(800) 371-3986, (978) 557-3242
www.maldenmillsstore.com

Information and Services on the Web
DuPont Performance Insulation
www.dupont.com/insulations
Information on their insulations

Sport Equipment Chain Stores on the Web
www.campmor.com and www.rei.com
Resources for gear and supporting products

Outfitter Magazine
www.outfittermag.com/articles/871feat1c.html
Comprehensive fabrics and fibers resource directory

Penny Schwynn
www.specialtyoutdoors.com
Sewing contractor providing service in modifying, sewing, and repairing of outdoor gear and clothing; web site provides free information to sewing enthusiasts

Professional Association of Custom Clothiers
P.O. Box 8071
Medford, OR 97504
(541) 772-4119
Fax (541) 770-7041
www.paccprofessionals.org
info@paccprofessionals.org
Referral to custom clothiers across the U.S. and parts of Canada

3M Insulation Products
3M.com/thinsulate
Information on its insulation products

W. L. Gore & Associates
www.gorefabrics.com
Information on their fabrics, including Gore-Tex®

Additional Reading and Information
Mail-order catalogs (such as those provided by the companies listed above) are often good sources for technical information relating to fabrics, construction techniques and tips, and the use of various types of hardware.

The Essential Outdoor Gear Manual by Annie Getchell (Ragged Mountain Press, Camden, ME, 1995). Equipment care and repair, materials resource list, reading list.

The Magnificent Book of Kites by Maxwell Eden (Sterling Publishing Co., New York, NY, 1998). Design and construction of kites; good tips on working with nylon and hot tools, and making templates and Teflon cutting wheels for hot tools.

Patterns from Finished Clothes by Tracy Doyle (Sterling/Lark, New York, NY, 1997).

Sew and Repair Your Outdoor Gear by Louise Lindgren Sumner (The Mountaineers, Seattle, WA, 1988). Basic sewing and repair—garments and gear, gridded patterns.

Sew the New Fleece by Rochelle Harper (The Taunton Press, Newtown, CT, 1997). Basic and creative alternatives for fleece and pile construction.

Index